Play and Playfulness

یادبود ناقابلی
به دوست بهتر از جانم احمد
محسن Dec. 1. 2011

Play and Playfulness

Developmental, Cultural, and Clinical Aspects

Edited by Monisha C. Akhtar, PhD

JASON ARONSON
Lanham • Boulder • New York • Toronto • Plymouth, UK

Published by Jason Aronson
An imprint of Rowman & Littlefield Publishers, Inc.
A wholly owned subsidiary of The Rowman & Littlefield Publishing Group, Inc.
4501 Forbes Boulevard, Suite 200, Lanham, Maryland 20706
http://www.rowmanlittlefield.com

Estover Road, Plymouth PL6 7PY, United Kingdom

"Self-Other Action Play: A Window into the Representational World of the Infant" by Anni Bergmann and Ilene Sackler Lefcourt is reprinted with permission from *Children at Play: Clinical and Developmental Approaches to Meaning and Representation* by A. Slade and D. Wolf © 1994 by Oxford University Press, Inc.

"The Butterfly" by Pavel Friedmann, "Homesick" by Anonymous, "The Little Mouse" by Koleba, from *I Never Saw Another Butterfly* by U.S. Holocaust Memorial Museum, edited by Hana Volavkov, © 1978, 1993 by Artia, Prague Compilation © 1993 by Schocken Books. Used by permission of Schocken Books, a division of Random House, Inc.

"Play and Very Young Children in Object Relations Family Therapy" by Jill Savege Scharff originally appeared in the *International Journal of Applied Psychoanalytic Studies*, February 2, 2006. Reprinted with permission of John Wiley and Sons.

British Library Cataloguing in Publication Information Available

Library of Congress Cataloging-in-Publication Data
Play and playfulness : developmental, cultural, and clinical aspects / edited by Monisha C. Akhtar.
p. cm.
Includes bibliographical references and index.
ISBN 978-0-7657-0760-4 (cloth : alk. paper) -- ISBN 978-0-7657-0762-8 (electronic : alk. paper)
1. Play--Psychological aspects. 2. Play--Social aspects. 3. Child development. I. Akhtar, Monisha C., 1954-
BF717.P5757 2010
155--dc22

2010028989

™ The paper used in this publication meets the minimum requirements of American National Standard for Information Sciences—Permanence of Paper for Printed Library Materials, ANSI/NISO Z39.48-1992.

Printed in the United States of America

To the loving memory of my parents

Maya Chakraborty,

who taught me how to play,

and

Nani Gopal Chakraborty,

who embodied playfulness.

Contents

Preface

Listening to my mother's musical renditions of poetry and observing my father's delight in the unfolding of each day, I grew up in India in a household that was filled with laughter and love. These are firmly etched in my memory, as is the sound of playing in the puddles that appeared after a monsoon rainfall, and the sound of birds chirping as they shook off the dust of a hot summer morning. Such fond memories of my childhood constitute the emotional foundation for this book on play and playfulness although later life experiences, especially those involving my children, have also informed me about matters of play. However, it was my serious yet playful work in my training analysis that provided the intellectual momentum for this undertaking. To both, my childhood and my analysis, I owe my deepest gratitude.

Play is an inevitable part of human nature, occurring in young children, adolescents and adults and across all cultures. Johan Huizinga (1955), in his seminal work on play, defines it as follows:

> Summing up the formal characteristic of play, we might call it a free activity standing quite consciously outside "ordinary" life as being "not serious" but at the same time absorbing the player intensely and utterly. It is an activity connected with no material interest, and no profit can be gained by it. It proceeds within its own proper boundaries of time and space according to fixed rules and in an orderly manner. It promotes the formation of social groupings that tend to surround themselves with secrecy and to stress the difference from the common world by disguise or other means. (p. 13)

While this definition of play has largely withstood the test of time, in the psychoanalytic realm it takes on a greater dynamic texture and different affective hues. As the preferred currency of interactional transactions used by children, all child analysts (and adult analysts as well) have encountered it sometime or the other during the course of their professional work. Despite this, play has often been relegated to a marginal status in the psychoanalytic armamentarium, remaining obscure and unavailable for technical consideration in larger realms of analytic praxis.

This book attempts to rectify this situation. It is aimed at broadening and deepening our understanding of play and is divided into four main sections. The first section examines the developmental context of play. The second section explores the psychopathology of play. The third section ventures into the elucidation of play outside the clinical setting. The book ends with a final section on play and psychoanalytic technique. In its entirety, it provides a rich review of the historical context of play, from the earliest commentaries with their classical theoretical underpinnings to contemporary approaches emphasizing the integration of self, object relations and relational trends in analytic thinking.

The first section has three chapters that examine the evolution of normal play within the developmental context of a child's relationship with the maternal and paternal figures and explore the dynamics between parental figures and the child as they play together. This section concludes with a chapter that deals with the period of adolescence during which major developmental and adaptive tasks are conducted in the form of play; even the adolescent rebellion has a quality of playfulness.

The book begins with a chapter by Anni Bergman and Ilene Sackler Lefcourt on mother-child play. They focus on the development of self-other action play, which occurs within the context of an affectively attuned mother-child relationship. Using separation-individuation theory as a conceptual framework to understand the emergence of this play, they describe how babies are preprogrammed to elicit playfulness in others. Self-other action play facilitates the development of significant psychological processes and the later development of symbolic capacities.

In the second chapter, James Herzog addresses a frequently ignored subject in the psychoanalytic literature: how fathers play with their children. He focuses on two aspects of such play. One is between fathers and their children and the second is how father and mother, together, play with their children. Herzog highlights the fathers' role in helping a child create and develop a play space by modulating and sublimating their own aggression and sexuality. This can only happen if the fathers themselves have worked through these aspects of their own psyche and have an ongoing alliance with their partners in life. Herzog examines and emphasizes the fundamental necessity of a parental alliance for optimal development of the child especially in the area of differentiated self-other representations.

In the final chapter of this section, Christine Kieffer explores the relationship between adolescence and the capacity to play. This developmental phase propels the adolescent to seek out new identities, individuate from the family of origin, and emerge with mature ties, ready to assume more adult responsibilities and tasks. Kieffer suggests that this occurs within a matrix of peer interactions and socially sanctioned relationships; it is a form of play. While the push to individuate and become more autonomous characterizes much of the adolescent literature, more contemporary (and more culturally attuned) literature is also presented which emphasize a more interdependent aspect to human nature.

Having covered some developmental aspects of play and playfulness, we now turn to the elucidation of derailment of play. The section which follows has three chapters that expand upon the pathological developments in play emerging from unmetabolized anxieties and fears, the developmental origins of normal and pathological playfulness (the latter leading to perversion and character pathologies), and the impact of traumatic experiences on a child's capacity to play.

This section begins with a chapter by Hossein Etezady, who explores the developmental nature of play and places it within a historical context of the child analytic literature. He recognizes its use as a diagnostic and assessment tool and examines the inhibition of the capacity to play, especially in neurotic compromise formations. The child's use of play to communicate internal psychic imbalance is elaborated and technical interventions, helpful in working with the neurotic inhibitions of play are described.

Etezady's chapter is followed by a contribution by Salman Akhtar. His review of normal and pathological expressions of playfulness highlights the ontogenetic origins of these configurations and the underlying dynamics. He also delineates the clinical relevance of these ideas. The connection between playfulness and pathological character organization is also explored with a handy documentation of the possible types of pathological playfulness. This serves as a useful conceptual framework for diagnostic and clinical purposes. In keeping with the topic, Akhtar's paper is filled with lighthearted humor that is likely to draw a chuckle from the reader, from time to time.

My own chapter on trauma and play is next. It traces the evolving perspectives on play, with a focus on the deleterious impact of trauma on how children play. Highlighting the repetitious yet dynamically communicative nature of play in traumatized children, the chapter references contemporary technical approaches in working with them. Privileging play as a natural developmental phase, the chapter attempts to provide a more nuanced understanding of the analytic relationship, wherein play chronicles the assimilation and accommodation of traumatic memories during the course of clinical work.

The third section departs from the clinical context and considers the role of play in the larger sociocultural and political context. It consists of four chapters covering a wide range of topics including the relationship between culture and play, manifestation of play activity during times of societal trauma, the widely recognized connection between play and creativity, and finally the unfolding "application" of play in geopolitical situations and political arenas. This section begins with a chapter by Danny Freeman who focuses on a broader, global, sociocultural aspect of play. His unique contribution weaves in mythological tales and folklore into patterns of play, in a cross-cultural context. The author explores how these myths serve as culturally sanctioned props that children use and manipulate in the service of their psychological development. Furthermore, he explores how myths facilitate the consolidation of one's personal identity. This unique and universal function of myths, when examined within an anthropological context, provides valuable insight into how individuals navigate life's inevitable anxieties and fears. The author provides rich examples of myths to highlight his propositions on this subject matter.

In the next chapter, Ira Brenner introduces us to how children during the Holocaust used play to survive and cope with the horrors of their daily life. The intimate connection between playing and creativity is explicated further as the author draws us into how children in concentration camps used commonly found objects—for example, pieces of wood—to create melodies of music. This orchestrated "aktion" provided temporary relief to lives that had already been condemned to nonexistence. In this context, the definition of play, goes beyond current formulations and the author explores the theoretical implications of this further in his paper.

Lucy Daniels contribution in the following chapter captures the connection between playing and creativity. She underscores both the similarities and the differences between these two activities. Furthermore, she underscores the additional dimension of using dreams as potential space in which to examine the rudiments of creative thinking and action.

The final chapter in this section addresses a new and intriguing dimension in the application of play and playfulness. Vamik Volkan illustrates how global diplomatic relations, once under the purview of a codified and rigid set of rules, have undergone change. As what is commonly referred to as "globalization" of the world continues, alarming levels of ethnic strife, political warfare and conflicts between nations have emerged. Volkan informs us how playing and playful behavior have now become integrally associated with diplomacy. He provides a rich array of examples to illustrate his creative and novel approach to international relations.

The last section of the book returns to the clinical realm and its three chapters elaborate on technical considerations in using play in one's work with aggressive children, within the family context and finally in adult analytic work. These are written by Mali Mann, Jill Scharff, and Melvin Bornstein.

Mali Mann's crisp elucidation of working through aggression within the crucible of play in a therapy setting provides practical clinical knowledge for child analysts working with behaviorally challenging children. She examines how children's sense of agency, their ability to think about their behavior and their ability to self-regulate their feelings are essential to their psychological development. Symbolic play is an integral to this process and so is the therapists' role in facilitating this form of play.

Jill Scharff explores how unconscious communication in play occurs in family interactions. With a theoretical orientation grounded in an object relations family therapy framework, Scharff helps family members explore their underlying defensive structures, basic assumptions, and underlying anxieties. Her lucid paper is rich in clinical detail. It outlines how a therapist can help family members build skills to deal not only with their presenting problems but also address anticipated future developmental challenges.

The book closes with a chapter from Mel Bornstein, who elucidates the place of playfulness within the adult analytic relationship. This often repudiated aspect of clinical work is highlighted in its palliative ability especially as the evolving analytic relationship grows in intimacy and depth. Playfulness, according to Bornstein, takes us into the heart of a human relationship, where feelings of shame, love, humiliation, rage, anger, and anxiety co-mingle and appear as transference and countertransference reactions. But Bornstein takes us beyond this conundrum of analytic discourse. The analyst's task, he says, is to make sense of this internal chaos and to do just that; the whole being of the analyst must be present. It is in a playful yet meaningful exchange with the analyst does the patient eventually reclaim fragmented parts of him or herself to heal and bring some order to an internal chaotic world.

My summary of this compendium of multifaceted discourse on play is but a brief introduction to the vast topic of play activity. Play is a nuanced and subtly textured activity that is multiply determined. The contributions in this book are exquisitely attuned to this fact. They are rich in theory and clinical material and represent diverse ways of thinking about play and its manifestation and uses in our work. It is my hope that "Play and Playfulness" will enhance knowledge and empathy in this realm, encourage further discussion on this subject matter, and prove to be a clinically and theoretically relevant contribution not only to the child analytic field but to psychotherapy and psychoanalysis in general.

Acknowledgments

This book has emerged gradually from my years of training in clinical psychology as well as psychoanalysis. After obtaining a graduate degree in clinical psychology at Wayne State University, Detroit, Michigan, I developed a clinical practice working with children and their families. Though my graduate training had provided me with the necessary skills to begin my practice, I decided to pursue analytic training to further strengthen both theoretical knowledge and clinical expertise. I completed my adult, child, and adolescent analytic training at the Michigan Psychoanalytic Center. Over the subsequent years, my clinical work with my patients has contributed extensively to my development as a therapist. Their contributions to me and to my professional development ultimately formed the foundation for this project.

This is a collaborative enterprise, as the depth and vastness of topics covered required the contribution of those who are known for their expertise in various specific areas pertaining to play. I am deeply grateful to my group of contributors for their willingness to believe in the idea, to take time to think and write, and to entrust me with their words and wisdom. This project could not have been actualized without the support and goodwill of each and every one of them.

I am indebted to my child supervisors at the Michigan Psychoanalytic Center. Dr. Jack Novick and Ms. Kerry Novick guided me in my development as a child analyst, providing valuable input on my cases and helping me to know how to "play" in the clinical situation. They have become the beacons of hope in my life as a child analyst. Dr. Peter Blos, Jr., who also oversaw my clinical work, was instrumental to my growth in yet another way. His seminal writing on the topic of adolescence fostered my own creativity in my work with this population.

I am also grateful to the Child Psychoanalytic Faculty in Michigan who livened our Wednesday night discussions and maintained an atmosphere of safety for my learning and growth. Drs. Michael Coleman, Ivan Sherick, Nancy Blieden, Jonathan Sugar, and Carol Austad provided collegial input and immensely valuable professional support. In addition, I was fortunate to find friends like Kehendi Ayeni, Marcy Broder, Diana Constance, Paula Kliger, Carol Levin, and Sue Orbach, who ultimately became a sort of family in which I could develop and blossom.

I am also grateful to my analytic colleagues at the Psychoanalytic Center of Philadelphia, my more recent analytic home, Drs. Susan Adelman, Jennifer Bonovitz, Ira and Roberta Brenner, Hossein Etezady, Theodore Fallon, Ruth Fischer, Ralph and Lana Fishkin, John Frank, Rao Gogeneni, Henri Parens, and Ann Smolen. They provided a holding environment in which I could flourish.

To Melanie Wright, who typed and prepared my manuscript, I express gratitude for the care and thoughtfulness she has shown throughout the unfolding and completion of this project.

I am profoundly grateful to my husband Salman Akhtar, whose editorial skill, experience, and expertise as an author, as well as loving encouragement helped me bring this project to fruition. His trust in me and my ideas, devotion to my development as an author and editor, and playful participation in this venture cannot be easily described in words. Suffice it to say, he helped me transform an elusive apparition in my mind into a tangible reality.

Part I

Development

Chapter One

Self-Other Action Play: A Window into the Representational World of the Infant

Anni Bergman and Ilene Sackler Lefcourt

"It is the mother, the primary source of satisfactions in early infancy, who represents 'the world' and it is through the attachment to mother that the child discovers himself and the world outside." —Selma Fraiberg, *The Magic Years*

From the beginning, babies, by virtue of their babyness, elicit playfulness in others. Smiles special for baby, unique tempos of speech and body movement, and games passed down through the generations comprise the first mother-infant play.[1] The mother of a two-year-old baby recently asked us, "Would you like to see our first game?" She and her infant, gazing into each other's eyes and smiling, became engaged in a dialogue. She lifted her baby from her lap, raised him slightly above her head and said, "bouncy, bouncy!" She then returned him to her lap. The baby moved his body upward and looked at her expectantly. This provided the signal for her to lift him again. After several repetitions, he stopped signaling; she was immediately sensitive to the change in his behavior and the game was ended.

The first play experiences, between mother and baby, promote the baby's most rudimentary sense of self and other within the context of an intimate, affectively attuned relationship. The games of early infancy create a mutually regulated action dialogue between mother and infant. The earliest mutually regulated dialogues provide the foundation for what will become self-other action play. Self-other action play is play in which themes of self, other, and self with other predominate, and the formation, transformation, and interrelatedness of self and object representations takes place. Self-other action play is one of the baby's ways of integrating a variety of experiences of self and other and reveals the formation and integration of self and object representations. Self-other action play leads to the capacity to role play, which requires the ability to take the perspective of the other. Role play becomes a new interactional language, and also a way to master all kinds of experiences, including those which are frightening or traumatic. The capacity to role play indicates that interactions with others have been internalized, i.e., they have become part of the child's representational world.

Our understanding of the representational world of the infant before symbolic capacity is established has been enriched by researchers who have studied in detail how infants internally organize their experience (Stern, 1985; Beebe and Lachmann, 1988). In addition to the formation of progressively organized images of self and other, several theoretical constructs of the infant's intrapsychic organization of lived experience have been proposed: "scripts" by Nelson (1981), "generalized episodes" by Bretherton (1984), "working models" by Main (1985), and "representations of interactions that have been generalized (RIGS)" by Stern (1985). These formulations refer to the infant's intrapsychic organization of lived experience and include actions, interactions, and the likely course of events based on average experiences. Recent mother-infant interaction research indicates that interaction structures are represented in a presymbolic form and lay the foundation for symbolic forms of self and object representations (Beebe and Lachmann, 1988).

Separation-individuation theory, which is based on detailed observational study of the developing mother-infant relationship, enriches our understanding of play during the preverbal and earliest verbal period of development. We will use the subphases of separation-individuation theory to designate the major developmental shifts during the first three years (Mahler, Pine, and Bergman, 1975). We will attempt to show that self-other action play serves different representational functions at different ages and promotes the linking and integrating of existing simple representations to form new, more complex representations. Beginning with Freud (1908), psychoanalysts have explored the significance of children's play: "Might we not say that every child at play behaves like a creative writer in that he creates a world of his own or rather reassembles things of his world in a new way which pleases him. . . . It would be wrong to think he does not take the world seriously; on the contrary, he takes his play very seriously and expends large amounts of emotion on it. The opposite of play is not what is serious but what is real" (pp. 143–44).

Play is the way in which the child attempts to allay anxiety by overcoming and mastering those situations that have caused it (Waelder, 1933). In the life of a child, the anxiety-provoking situations of today become the subject of tomorrow's play, as do the physical, emotional, social, and cognitive problems as well as pleasures. A framework for interpreting play was initially provided by libido theory (Peller, 1954). Winnicott's (1953) notion of the "intermediate area of experience" captures the aspect of play we wish to address: "The intermediate area of experience unchallenged in respect of its belonging to inner or external (shared) reality constitutes the greater part of the infant experience. . . . It is an area which is not challenged, because no claim is made on its behalf except that it shall exist as a resting place for the individual engaged in the perpetual human task of keeping inner and outer reality separate yet inter-related" (p. 90).

Our understanding of Winnicott's "intermediate area of experience" and of separation-individuation theory have enabled us to conceptualize self-other action play and the way in which it promotes the formation of representations.

PLAY WITH OBJECTS CONNECTED TO MOTHER: LINKING REPRESENTATIONS

A baby at five months is clearly attentive to the outside world. This marks the beginning of the differentiation subphase, the first subphase of separation-individuation which takes place from about five to nine months. We will describe two kinds of play during the differentiation subphase which we relate to the formation and integration of self and object representations and thus describe as self-other action play.

The first of these types of play is with objects that belong to mother, such as her jewelry, keys, eyeglasses, etc. Originally initiated by baby, this play is quickly responded to and elaborated by mother. These objects are of interest to infants at this age because of certain physical attributes that appeal to babies: for example, they are shiny or make special sounds. However, we assume that they are of special value to the baby because of their connection to mother's body. They belong to mother; they are part of mother; yet they can be taken by baby and thus become baby's. Playing with these objects in mother's presence promotes the mental processes that create a relationship between an inanimate object and the specific person with whom it is associated. It is the relationship, created by the infant between mother and the objects that belong to her combined with the intrinsic pleasure derived from the manipulation of these objects that gives the object special meaning. Mental processes imbue the objects that belong to mother with "momminess." This is play in Winnicott's (1953) "intermediate area":

> The intermediate area to which I am referring is the area that is allowed to the infant between primary creativity and objective perception based on reality-testing. The transitional phenomena represent the early stages of the use of illusion, without

> which there is no meaning for the human being in the idea of a relationship with an object that is perceived by others as external to that being. (p. 90)

Play with inanimate objects that belong to mother reveals the emergence of the mental capacity to invest an object with feelings one has toward another and transfer attributes of one object to another. This capacity to link and integrate representations represents the first step in the developmental pathway to symbolic functioning.

SEPARATION AND REUNION PLAY: LINKING REPRESENTATIONS OF INTERACTIONS

The second kind of self-other action play that begins during the differentiation subphase is more clearly interactional. We refer here to games of peek-a-boo and what we call "I give it to you—you give it to me" and "I drop it—you pick it up." "I give it to you—you give it to me" is the game in which baby hands an inanimate object to mother and mother hands it back to baby. This self-other interaction is repeated several times and is usually accompanied by a sing-song phrase. This mother-infant play activity seems to provide the baby with an experience of separateness and connectedness. "I drop it—you pick it up" is the familiar, endlessly repeated activity, initiated by babies, in which the baby drops, and eventually throws, an object and mother retrieves it. We believe that repetition of the sequence: holding onto an inanimate object, letting go of the object and having the object returned promotes the formation of representations of expected sequences.

Games of "I give it to you—you give it to me," and "I drop it—you pick it up" deal with issues of letting go and repossessing of inanimate objects which we think are related to issues of separation and reunion with loved ones. When the baby's actions are responded to with playfulness, these activities become a pleasurable game of mastery.

The classic game of peek-a-boo is typically introduced by mother into the mother-baby play repertoire at this time (Bruner, 1976). Mothers, while pulling a sweater over baby's head, may elaborate the activity of dressing into a game of peek-a-boo. In another form of peek-a-boo, mother covers baby's face with a diaper and baby learns to pull it off, or mother covers her own face. The external, self-other action often changes in games of peek-a-boo as mother and baby interchange roles of hiding and finding. The specific games of peek-a-boo, played by each mother and baby, including the roles played by each, will have their own personal signatures and reveal aspects of their relationship.

One special characteristic of these games that deal directly with appearance and disappearance is that they typically are accompanied by crescendos and decrescendos of excitement. The increase and decrease of arousal is mutually regulated and results in a experience of fluctuating, moment to moment state sharing (Stern, 1985). The reappearance after brief disappearance evokes the joy of re-finding, i.e., rediscovering mother. Furthermore, the experience of "making" mother retrieve the lost object enhances feelings of the self as agent. At a time when babies are increasingly confronted with feelings of loss and separateness, and just on the brink of becoming capable of more independent activities, in particular locomotion, we believe that the emergent experience of self as agent and highlighted experiences of state sharing, i.e., attunement (Stern, 1985), may be particularly exciting. We are reminded of Pine's (1985) concept of moments, which he believes to be structure-building.

At about eight months, there is a marked change in baby's reaction to mother's absence for even brief periods. Momentary losses of mother elicit a variety of distress reactions (Mahler, Pine, Bergman, 1975). In his presentation entitled "The Origin of Conflict during the Separation-Individuation Process," McDevitt (1988) traces the development of anxiety and conflict throughout the separation-individuation period and notes that play becomes an important part of active coping behavior in response to separation toward the end of the first year.

Games of peek-a-boo and "I drop it—you pick it up" after the onset of separation anxiety can provide the baby with experiences of control over loss and retrieval, and separation and reunion. While in the presence of mother, these games promote the formation of representations related to separation and help transform painful experiences into pleasurable play.

A representation of mother as permanent (i.e., a sense that mother exists even when she is out of perceptual awareness) is promoted by experiences of separation followed by reunion, and contributes to the baby's ability to tolerate separations from the mother. The expectation during separation that mother will return is the result of repeated experiences of separation and reunion. We surmise than an integration of the representation of mother, the representation of separation from mother and the representation of reunion with mother are taking place and are helped by the issues of separation and reunion.

TRANSITIONAL PHENOMENA: EVOKING A REPRESENTATION OF MOTHER IN HER ABSENCE

Gradually, the baby's mental representation of the mother may be evoked in her absence. For example, upon awakening, a baby may coo or babble, possibly evoking the mother's presence. Or, the baby begins to be able to soothe himself as he has been soothed by mother. Sucking his fingers or making tongue and lip motions and sounds might evoke the feeling of sucking the breast; the blanket or cuddly toy has aspects of the mother's soft body. A dramatic and poignant example of the capacity for self-soothing and the way in which transitional phenomena promote self-soothing occurred when Jessica McClure, an eighteen-month-old girl, was trapped at the bottom of a well for fifty-eight hours (Shapiro, *Time*, 1987). After moments of crying for her mother, she began to sing to herself the songs that her mother sang to her, thus evoking a representation of mother which helped her to endure the traumatic separation. The process of attaching aspects of the mental representation formed from knowledge of the actual mother to the representation of an inanimate object (or in the case of Jessica, a song) contributes to the capacity to evoke the representation of mother during her absence. We are describing a pre-symbolic process by which not only lived experience determines the formation of representations, but also the linking of already-existing simple representations forms new, more complex representations. The new representations formed by the linking of already existing representations of mother to representations of a related inanimate object have special developmental significance in that the representation phenomenon, regardless of its content, becomes emotionally invested.

Stern (1985) states: "Each process of relating diverse events may constitute a different and characteristic emergent experience. . . . I am suggesting that the infant can experience the process of emerging organization, as well as the result and it is this experience of emerging organization that I call the emergent sense of self" (p. 45). We are suggesting that emergent experiences result in the emotional investment of the internal world. Self-other action play constitutes a kind of emergent experience and may shape the predetermined, uniquely human capacity to form symbols.

It is not simple that the representation symbolizes the actual object, but also that the emotional investment in the inner sense or feel of mother eventually enables that inner experience or representation to substitute for the actual mother. In a similar way, an emotional investment in representations is necessary for the creation of a transitional object. "It is true that the piece of blanket (or whatever it is) is symbolical of some part-object, such as the breast. Nevertheless, the point of it is not its symbolic value so much as its actuality. It's not being the breast (or the mother) is as important as the fact that it stands for breast (or mother)" (Winnicott, 1953, p. 91–92). The attachment to the transitional object results not only from the fact that it symbolizes the love object, but also that it is an external manifestation of the emotional investment in the developing representational world.

PLAY AWAY FROM MOTHER AND THE INTERNAL SENSE OF BEING WITH MOTHER

The next subphase of separation-individuation is practicing (ten to fifteen months). During the practicing subphase, there are dramatic increases in physical ability and a great upsurge of pleasure in locomotion and functional play. Infants this age practice, with great interest and compelling motivation, their quickly emerging capacities to crawl, climb and walk, and their rapidly increasing manipulative skills. Enthralled with their play activities, infants vigorously begin to explore the other-than-mother world and at times appear oblivious to mother. During this subphase, physical distance between mother and infant can be initiated by baby. The infant no longer has to endure passively being left, but can actively begin to leave, and in this way practices separations and reunions. As long as the mother is not too far away, the infant's practicing subphase behavior continues with exuberance. If the distance is too great or mother is away for too long, the joy in practicing wanes and the infant becomes low-keyed (Mahler, Pines, and Berman, 1975).

Babies this age crawl and then walk away from mother, returning often, not with the intent to play with her but rather to facilitate their own play. At these times, babies may use mother's body as if it were an inanimate object to climb on, step on, push and pull—a stepping stone to the world to further baby's activities and to extend baby's reach. The infant's external obliviousness to the actual mother is accompanied by an intrapsychic way of being with mother, and it is this internal sense of being with mother that enables the infant to separate from her.

This internal way of being with mother is related directly to actual experiences with mother. The memories of actual experiences of being with mother are retrievable, when separated from her, when an attribute of the memory is present (Stern, 1985). Perhaps the bodily pleasures and elation that accompany play activities during this subphase are the attributes that evoke the internal sense of being with mother. But it is also the other way around: the inner sense of being with mother increases the pleasure in play activities and the mood of elation characteristic of this subphase. Optimal amounts of the actual mother's presence and emotional availability are required in order for the baby to pursue these play activities and to derive pleasure from them. Although exceedingly interested in the other-than-mother world, the infant needs to reestablish frequent eye or physical contact with mother. Furer called this touching base with mother "emotional re-fueling" (Mahler, Pine, Bergman, 1975). There is an ongoing interplay with actual experiences of being with mother, the internal sense of being with mother, play in the other-than-mother world, and the pleasure and mood of elation. The interrelatedness of these experiences suggests the integration of inner and outer reality and of self and object representations.

It is central to our thinking that the spontaneous, inner sense of being with mother that enables the baby to separate physically from her is itself an important intrapsychic phenomenon that promotes development. This inner sense of being with mother during the practicing subphase permits the continuous developing mental capacity to create or evoke the inner sense of being with mother. (This was seen in the previously noted case of Jessica McClure).

During the practicing subphase, intense pleasure in independent locomotion and newly acquired motor capacities propel the toddler to embrace a new separation and reunion game. Chase-and-reunion games are a new form of the earlier peek-a-boo game and serve a similar function. They are initiated by both mother and baby, and often involve a rapid alternation of roles of chasing and being chased (Kleeman). Peek-a-boo, a self-other action game of separation and reunion, becomes infused with the functional pleasure derived from motor capacities.

PLAY RECREATING ESSENTIAL WAYS OF BEING WITH MOTHER: FLUIDITY OF REPRESENTATIONS

A commonly observed game during the practicing subphase that further suggests the integration of self and object representations is baby feeding mother playfully. This self-other action play suggests an experience of self-other ambiguity. How does one play? "I, baby, do to you, mommy, as you have done to me"; or "I am now mommy and you are baby, therefore I feed you as you have fed me"? This game and similar ones provide an actual experience of being with mother while evoking representations of mother, of self and of self with mother. The ambiguity inherent in this play of who represents whom suggests the fluidity which is inherent in the process of integrating representations.

The pull-toy, another favorite play activity during the practicing subphase, raises similar questions (Shopper, 1978). Baby walks proudly with his pull-toy behind and looks back at the toy frequently. How do we understand the meaning of this play? "I am mommy with a pull-toy baby who goes everywhere with me," or "I am baby and have a mommy pull-toy who will go wherever I go"? One might ask similar questions about riding on kiddie-cars which begins to be a favorite activity. Riding on his own car, does the child feel strong and powerful like his mother? Or does the child now have a pretend parent always available on whom to ride? We believe it is the ambiguity about self-other symbolic meaning that gives these games special power and makes certain possessions coveted in special ways. Once again, the very uncertainty of who represents whom reveals an essential fluidity and simultaneity of representations, and the process of linking and integrating representations, form new representations.

GAMES OF SHARING: INTEGRATING REPRESENTATIONS OF SELF AND MOTHER

During the rapprochement subphase (around fifteen to twenty-four months), another important change occurs. The child's wish to share objects and activities directly with mother and to engage mother in play becomes striking. As the toddler becomes increasingly aware of his vulnerability, helplessness, and smallness, his relative obliviousness to mother demonstrated during the practicing subphase begins to wane. In an attempt to bridge the separation between self and other, children of this age bring many things to be touched and held by mother. During the early rapprochement subphase, a child literally fills his mother's lap with the other-than-mother world. A common playground activity is to wander from mother and return with "treasures" that the child demands to be held and kept by mother. These things range enormously in size and can include everything from favorite toys to objects such as pieces of wood, scraps of paper, metal, bottle tops, etc. "Each time the toddler finds her, he brings along a new piece of the world outside, and each time he leaves her, he takes with him a part of her. Increasing this part is an image" (Bergman, 1978, p. 158).

In this way, the child creates a physical bridge between mother, self, and the other-than-mother world and facilitates the formation of a psychological bridge. The psychological bridge we refer to is constructed of representations of mother, self, and self in relationship to mother, as well as of representations of inanimate objects. This self-other action play adds to the stability and integration of developing representations.

During the rapprochement subphase the toddler's newly acquired and valued skills are repeatedly demonstrated for mother in order to receive her admiration and approval. Mother and toddler coming together in this mutually pleasurable and gratifying way helps the child to tolerate his feelings of vulnerability, helplessness, and ineptness by having his competence mirrored and admired. These shared moments also help bridge the gap of separateness. While observing a toddler jump up and down with mastery and delight, his mother looking on with admiration, one gets the feeling that the child becomes "filled" with mother's admiration and love. This is reminiscent of the way in which inanimate objects touched by mother seem to be transformed—transformed by "somminess." It is not uncommon during the rapprochement subphase for a child to refuse a cookie unless first touched by mother or to have a hurt healed by mother's magical kiss.

The child's conflicting wish for autonomy on the one hand and for mother to be ever-present on the other hand culminate in the rapprochement crises. Attempts at omnipotent control of both self and other is the way in which the toddler tries to solve this inherently insoluble problem. A great need for mother's emotional availability (Mahler, 1963; Emde, 1980), combined with frequent outbursts of anger often make even brief separations stressful. We will attempt to show how self-other action play helps the child to deal with the conflicts that arise during the rapprochement crisis.

BEGINNING ROLE PLAY BETWEEN MOTHER AND BABY: REPRESENTATIONS OF EMPATHIC EXCHANGES

During the rapprochement subphase, a maturational leap in symbolic functioning and important developments in play occur. Although we believe that precursors to symbolic functioning or more rudimentary forms of symbolic functioning are evidence in earlier play, the symbolic meaning of a child's play gradually becomes clearer. The unfolding of this process is revealed during the rapprochement subphase.

Beginning role play with mother is initiated by the rapprochement toddler. Mother often takes a fairly passive role as the child tells her what to do. She allows herself to be used to meet the needs of the toddler's inner life. A common script enacted by children of this age requires mother to cry when baby leaves, or to cry when she has been hurt. For example, toddler leaves the room and says, "Mommy cry." Toddler then returns and says, "Here I am. Mommy, stop crying." They hug. This role play is less ambiguous in terms of role designation than the play described during the practicing subphase. Baby plays mommy, and mommy is supposed to play baby. Typically, this kind of game is repeated over and over and represents active pleasurable mastery in play of the painful situation of being left. In a slightly more complex scenario, the mother of a twenty-month-old boy reports that he bites her playfully but sometimes quite hard. She pretends to cry. He runs and brings her his blanket, the beloved transitional object, to comfort her. He shifts from being the playful biting baby, or the aggressive hurtful baby, to being the comforting caretaker. This game is repeated over and over. Early role play typically involves the exchange of roles between mother and child addressing issues of vulnerability, separation, and aggression, and experiences of empathy, reparation, and love. The ability to play these games, i.e., to put oneself in the role of another, requires the beginning ability to objectify the self (Piaget, 1954; Stern, 1985) and the capacity to perform link and integrate representations. The representations integrated include representations of mother, self with and without mother, actions of mother, and self performing the actions of mother. This kind of role play reveals early identifications with mother and the working through of issues and conflicts related to separation and reunion and aggression and reparation. Role play further promotes the integration and elaboration of self and object representations. The integration of self and object representations will eventually result in a self that can be both like and different from mother, both comply with and oppose mother, and both love and hate mother. Role play with its expansion and elaboration of representations promotes identification which will be instrumental in the resolution of the rapprochement crisis.

FURTHER DEVELOPMENT OF ROLE PLAY: THE CONSOLIDATION AND EXPANSION OF REPRESENTATIONS

As rapprochement conflicts begin to be resolved (around twenty-four to thirty months, the "on the way to object constancy" subphase begins. With self and object representations now more firmly established, the child is further able to enact needs, impulses, and conflicts through role play. Therefore, during this phase, our ability to learn about the representational world of children through their play is dramatically increased. Now role play begins to include characters from the outside world. It is no longer limited to role exchange between mother and child as it begins to include the child's everyday experiences with people such as: mail carrier, bus driver, fix-it man, police officer, doctor, etc.

We wish to emphasize that role play which includes characters from the other-than-mother world begins when the self is firmly enough established to be able to put itself in the place of the other; this is the hallmark of the "on the way to self and object constancy" subphase. This expanded role play enables the child to elaborate and consolidate aspects of development that were first established during earlier developmental phases when issues and conflicts were negotiated within the parent-child context. Now the child is able to extend characteristics of self and other and the relationship between himself and significant others to the widening world. The roles that are enacted express the child's knowledge of the people who surround him, help the child expand that knowledge, and furthermore, represent important aspects of the now more consolidated and ever expanding inner representational world. Such role play reinforces both connections with and separations from emotionally significant others because each role enactment embodies a crucial aspect of the self and the other. We wish to suggest that this kind of role play is directly related to self-other action play that occurred earlier and continues to deal with the basic themes of self-other interaction.

We believe that the internal experience during role play can be best understood in terms of Winnicott's intermediate area of experience (Winnicott, 1953). Both a certain fluidity and constancy of self and object representations remain characteristic of role play, and a particular kind of integration of self and object representations and of inner and outer reality occurs. Role play serves the child's simultaneous needs to both express and disguise his impulses, anxieties, and conflicts (Bornstein, 1945).

Mail carrier is a favorite game of children on the way to object constancy. This role play allows children to continue the pleasure of bringing "treasures" to mother, a pleasure that began during the early rapprochement subphase. Mail carrier role play, a game that has anal phase components, puts giving and receiving of valued things into a context that assures the child that his gifts will be received with approval and delight. Children this age have observed that adults are often excited about getting mail and that it connects them with people who are somewhere else. Thus the child not only reinforces the bridge between self and mother, but also acknowledges the relationship between mother and others.

Doctor, a popular game throughout childhood, begins at this age. Doctor play usually originates as a reenactment of the child's visits to the doctor and gradually is elaborated. Many children alternate between the role of doctor and patient while others consistently choose one role or the other. Doctor play provides the opportunity for exploration of the body, a self-other action play activity that began during the differentiation subphase, and to address concerns about the integrity of the body and the genital difference which become of concern during the second year. Both passive wishes and sexual and aggressive impulses are expressed. Doctor play is self-other action play that often involves direct and intimate body contact between self and other.

Playing doctor also enables many children to reconstruct and work through traumatic experiences of illness and injury. A twenty-two-month-old girl who suffered a severe injury to a finger which resulted in a great deal of blood, an emergency visit to the hospital, injections to her finger and buttock, and a huge bandage that covered her hand completely, frequently played doctor in the following weeks. She alternated between playing the role of the frightened crying patient, the angry defiant patient, the detached hurtful doctor, the concerned healing doctor, the frightened guilty mother, and the comforting loving mother. The enactment of self and other roles related to the accident facilitated the integration of representations and the resolution of the impact of the traumatic experience.

Sometimes role play can serve the interpretive consolidation of both masculine and feminine identifications with an appropriate gender role. For example, a two-and-a-half-year-old little boy whose father was in the construction business chose the role of fix-it man. He loved tools and was not satisfied with toy imitations. The boy was clearly identifying with his father as he walked around the house with his little tool box, talking to his mother about all the things he was fixing. In his collection of favorite tools he also included the vacuum cleaner, which was regularly used by his mother. Thus the role of fix-it man included both male and female identification within a male role. The incorporation of a female identification into a male gender role supported this little boy's growing masculine identity without relinquishing the identification with his mother. In addition, role play of fix-it man probably helped him cope with the discovery of anatomical difference, an important developmental issue of children his age as well as with the still present issue of vulnerability of the rapprochement subphase.

Bus driver and elevator operator are favorite games of separation and reunion. Issues and conflicts of earlier subphases of separation-individuation as well as oral and anal phase development are addressed. The child controls the make-believe mechanical door that enables passengers to leave and enter the bus; passengers are dropped off and must wait (and often pay) to be picked up. In this way, the child may be dealing with issues of what goes in and out of the body, as well as issues of separation and reunion with love objects. Perhaps this game of separation and reunion is a new edition of the earlier games of peek-a-boo. The small toddler feels powerful as he pretends to drive the huge bus and in this way continues to work on rapprochement subphase issues of feeling relatively small and helpless.

"Police," "cops and robbers," "superhero and villain" and variations thereof include the enactment of aggressive impulses and reveal beginning superego structure formation. Many children alternate between the police and criminal roles, while others exclusively play one role or the other. The good-bad split in roles is a significant aspect of this play and promotes the integration of good and bad self and object representations. In addition, the police in pursuit of the criminal may be an elaborated version of the earlier game of chase and reunion. Within the child's life experience, the authority of the police is understood to be more powerful than that of his mother and is to be respected by him as well as by his mother. This aspect of police play enables aggression mobilized toward mother in response to her limit-setting to be modulated, thereby facilitating object constancy.

Many of the issues and conflicts addressed in role play during the "on the way to self and object constancy" subphase originate in earlier developmental phases and continue to be issues for life. Many role play games appear to be elaborated versions of earlier self-other action play. The roles enacted have been observed by the child in his ever-widening world and in some way capture not only internal conflicts seeking resolution or developmental issues to be negotiated, but also significant aspects of the adult that the child is aspiring to be and is already becoming, as well as elements of the external world within which he lives. Role play moves this process beyond the parent-child relationship while simultaneously incorporating it. Resolution of issues and conflicts which first emerged in infancy need no longer be exclusively bound to the parent-child relationship. In this way role play serves a unique function in development.

SUMMARY

During the separation-individuation process, self-other action play promotes the child's formation and integration of self and object representations and his adaptation to those conflicts and losses that are part of normal development. The capacity to role play, that is, the capacity to reenact one's own lived experience or one's own experience of another, is the culmination of a process that is rooted in earlier forms of self-other action play, and further promotes the integration of self and object representations. In addition, role play games seem to share action themes in common with earlier play.

The ability to create relationships between objects, between representations and objects, and between representations is a mental capacity that is required in order to role play. We believe that this occurs for the first time in play during the differentiation subphase when a relationship is being created between mother and those objects that belong to her, i.e., her jewelry, clothes, etc. This developing mental capacity, the capacity to link and integrate representations, is next revealed during the rapprochement subphase during play that creates a bridge between mother and self and mother and the rest of the world. The second mental capacity essential to role play is the ability to evoke a representation when desired. This capacity is first revealed during the practicing subphase and was described as an inner sense of being with mother that enables the infant to separate from mother.

We have suggested that linking and integrating of representations occurs in self-other action play throughout separation-individuation. During the differentiation subphase, play with mother's possessions facilitates the linking of representations of mother with things that belong to her. During the practicing subphase, the fluidity of representations of self and other inherent in certain play activities and the ongoing mutual regulation of and reciprocity between actual experiences of being with mother, the internal sense of being with mother, participation in play activities in the other-than-mother world and the pleasure and elation that is derived from those activities suggest the integration of self and object representations. During the rapprochement subphase, play activities in which the child fills mother's lap with inanimate objects, thereby filling mommy with the world and the world with "mommi-ness," and play in which the child performs skills for mother, thereby filling the self with mother's loving admiration, promote the integration of representations of mother and inanimate objects, and mother and self. These play activities create a psychological bridge through representations that can connect the separate mother and self.

During the fourth subphase, "on the way to self and object constancy," play that includes roles from the outside world begins. This occurs when the self is firmly and flexibly enough established that the child can not only put itself in the place of emotionally significant others, but also to extend this capacity to include those beyond parents and other family members. This kind of role play is related to self-other action play that occurred during earlier phases and continues to deal with the basic themes of self-other interaction. It enables the child to elaborate and consolidate aspects of development that were first established during earlier developmental phases when developmental issues and conflicts were negotiated almost exclusively within the parent-child relationship. During this phase of development, because of more advanced representational and symbolic capacities, those same issues and conflicts can be addressed in more derivative form allowing for the further elaboration and consolidation of development. Resolution of issues and conflicts that first emerged in infancy need no longer be exclusively bound to the parent-child relationship.

NOTE

1. Throughout this contribution, "mother" is used to refer to the caretaking other regardless of gender, and masculine pronouns are used to refer to the child. This has been done to distinguish clearly references to mother and references to baby. The unique aspects of the father's role in the processes discussed will not be addressed here.

Chapter Two

Fathers and Play

James Herzog

> "Fathers tend to excite their children. They throw them up in the air. They poke at them. They demand attention. They do not sit quietly waiting for the child to seek them out. In this way, the father draws the child out of the symbiosis and becomes a bridge to the external world." —Ruth Fischer, "Fathers, History and Psychoanalysis"

This chapter addresses the complex topic of the ways in which fathers play with their children from a clinical psychoanalytic perspective. As such, the idiographic will be highlighted. It will juxtapose these observations with earlier work in which normative paternal play modes were addressed. The relationship between father-child play and father and mother together with child play will be a constant focus. I shall present two rather extensive excerpts from two analyses. The first is the analysis of a child who brought his father to his treatment. The second is the analysis of a father who brought his child to his. In each of these analyses, play between father and child had been derailed and deformed. Through the prism of the pathological, aspects of the physiological will be revealed.

EZRA

Ezra at seventeen returns to analysis because of troubles galore. He has called 911 in a panic, telling the confused operator that his name is Paul Lorenz. When she asks for his address, he gives Bergasse 17 and then states that he is the Rat Man. It helps him when she counsels that he would be better served by calling his psychiatrist. He has postponed his admission to university because it has become impossible for him to read and if this were not enough, he is deeply troubled about his sexual life. He tells me that he is only turned on by sadomasochistic fantasy and that it has now crossed over into action. He chokes his girlfriends and whips them with his belt. "The girls seem to like it, I have to do it and you and I know what this is about," he tells me. "And that is not all: I have started to use my father's paddle on my ass. For the longest time, I just paddled my own hand with it."

We do both know quite a bit about what this is about. What a triumph, I think that Ezra has returned. Has his earlier psychosis returned or has our quite grueling but seemingly successful analytic work enlarged his observing ego to the point where we can examine his concerns in a helpful fashion? I am very happy to see Ezra again. He seems to feel the same way saying: "It's good to be back and I also think that it was a good thing that we interrupted for several years." Ezra speaks easily with many references to our earlier analytic work. Almost seamlessly, he takes up where we had left off. Now for the back story.

Is child analysis the treatment of choice for severe psychopathologies? Many points of view might be mustered in response to this question. It is not uncommon for a child to enter analysis after multiple other modalities have been tried and have failed. In this manner, child analysis sometimes becomes the treatment of choice by the process of elimination.

Ezra came to see me at the age of nine. His parents Fritz and Marissa worried about him from the moment of his birth on, I am told. "The labor was prolonged and difficult. His head looked crunched after the nineteen hours of labor," his father, a neurologist says. "I did my best to deliver him," his mother, a physicist, continues. "He was my first. It was so much easier with Penelope and Lukas." Both parents go on to tell me that their family is totally dominated by Ezra's difficulties. It is a sad family they maintain. I am told that the parents are no longer very friendly with one another and that mother particularly deplores the sternness which Fritz displays toward his first born son. "It is the only thing that gets through to him," the forty-five-year-old father states. "Before Ezra, I did not believe in spanking. Now I say thank God that it exists." Marissa visibly shuddered as he spoke.

Ezra was difficult from early on. His sleep patterns were erratic, but most disturbing was what the parents called his "touchiness." He seemed to be disturbed by everything. Beginning at about the age of two, he would routinely hit each parent, although his mother was the most frequent target. When he was three, a behavioral pediatrician was consulted and he proposed that Fritz try to exert his authority. Fritz began to raise his voice which seemed to only disorganize the boy further. At about this time Penelope was born and real trouble ensued. Ezra seemed committed to her elimination. At every opportunity, he would strike her. Marissa developed the hypothesis that he particularly had it in for females.

When the boy was four, he entered school. This was an unmitigated disaster. He was pugilistic, did not follow directions, and shouted out during games. He did seem to quiet somewhat with a male teacher who held him and in effect "specialed" him. The school insisted on a psychiatric evaluation and the parents were readily agreeable. The child psychiatrist diagnosed bipolar disorder and started the boy on Resperidol. He became sullen and withdrawn. He was more manageable at school but still had eruptions at home. When he was five, his father started to spank him when he would hit his mother. Ezra developed a kind of mantra. He would say again and again: "No hitting or hitting." This was understood by the family to mean that Fritz's discipline had been effective, but it was the final straw between the parents. Marissa felt that her husband had become a barbarian. "I would rather be battered black and blue than have Fritz spank Ezra," she declared.

Lukas was born the next year. Meanwhile the school had asked Ezra to depart and had suggested a residential placement. At the age of six, this was effected. Ezra boarded five days a week and spent the weekends at home. He now bore the diagnosis of both bipolar disorder and "other psychotic processes." He also was found to have visual-spatial processing difficulties. At the school, he mastered reading and quickly achieved grade level in all subjects. Testing revealed him to have a superior IQ and projectives were surprisingly normal. An intensive regimen of cognitive behavioral therapy was conducted. As with the pharmacotherapy, the results were not impressive. What was impressive was Ezra's relationship with one male teacher. This seemed to repeat his earlier school experience.

The consulting child psychiatrist at the school, in conjunction with the faculty, approached the family about trying an analytic approach. Both parents were quite enthusiastic. Mother herself knew quite a bit about analysis and father, a skeptic, was fully behind the recommendation. His reason was the following: "spanking works with Ezra," he said, "but I can see that I will have to up the ante to really get through to him, use a belt or paddle or something and that I am conflicted about initiating. Let's try analysis so that I do not have to beat him."

Ezra came to my office looking quite flushed. He was a tall boy, blond like his father. He looked uneasy. I invited him to sit down. He remained standing. I wondered what he would like to do. He walked toward the bookshelf at one end of my office. Wordlessly, he moved his arm in such a way as to push all of the books on one shelf onto the floor. I felt somewhat startled, but as if something important were transpiring. Still silently, Ezra stared at me. I composed myself and said, "I have been told that you are a reader." The redness of Ezra's face grew more intense. I moved toward the books thinking that I would pick them up. As I approached, Ezra slunk toward the other end of the room. "Will you help me?" I now inquired. "Aren't you going to spank me?" the clearly both frightened and interested boy responded. So we had begun. What was this dance? I already knew something about it from the history, but there was clearly so much more to learn.

I checked in with my own feelings. I felt no urge to spank Ezra. He seemed terrified even as the book assault felt purposive and somewhat experimental. Rather than feeling punitive, I felt curious. I said, "No, I shall not spank you, although I am interested in your question. I shall ask mine again. Will you help me pick up the books?" "No, never, fuck you," was Ezra's response. Oddly, I thought that we were off to a good beginning. Both spanking and fucking had entered our discourse.

The first several months of the analysis were something of a stand off. Ezra was very wary of me. He kept his distance both physically and emotionally. The bookcase continued to be the scene of the action. Every four or five days he would knock some books down. I noticed that each of these "eruptions" featured a smaller number of overturned books. I commented on this diminishing casualty number. At first there was silence. Each eruption was followed by Ezra's pantomiming his fleeing from me. After, perhaps, the fifteenth iteration which featured only one book being upended, he said: "You are right, quite an astute quantitative observation." I felt thrilled.

About six months into our work together, Ezra stopped overturning the books and instead began reading one of them. I now understood that we were in a library—the library of his mind. As he read silently, I asked him if he would like to read aloud to me. "No," was his response. Emboldened, I asked if he would like me to read aloud to him. "Yes," he replied. I wondered if he had a choice as to what I might read. I was both astonished by his response and completely unsurprised. He asked me to read Foucault's *Discipline and Punish: Birth of the Prison* in French. I said, "I did not know that you understood French." Ezra responded: "There is a lot about me that you do not know." I said, "That is clearly the case and I would like to learn as much about you as you will share with me." "We shall see," Ezra now responded. There was a gentler tone in his voice.

"Cherchez la Femme! Naturlich, spreche ich franzoesich," Ezra now stated. "Auch Sie, nicht wahr?" This was getting stranger and stranger, or, more accurately, more and more interesting, I thought. Ezra was now saying "Find the woman" and it was clear that he spoke in French and in German. I conjectured that he was speaking the mother tongues of each of his parents and that he seemed to be directing me toward his mother. I also considered that who the woman was might not be so clear cut and that it would be wise to keep an open mind about each of these multilingual utterances.

I decided to respond in English as this was the language that we had spoken, or at least the language that I had been speaking in our work up till now. "What is it about *Discipline and Punish* that you think would be interesting?" Ezra stared at me intently. Again he seemed to flush. He did not answer my verbal question in any of the three languages which I now knew he could employ.

Ezra's father, Fritz, came to see me. He opened his briefcase and took out a small paddle. He handed it to me. "I think that you should use this to spank Ezra," he stated. "I have begun to use it at home. It is quite effective, I can assure you. I bought a second one so that we can both use the same technique and the same implement on Ezra. Much less confusing for him that way."

I tried to maintain my equanimity, but I found it more difficult to do so with Ezra's father than I had with him. Even so, there was a way in which he, like his son, seemed more gentle than his actions, more latent than manifest in their meaning. As I was composing myself and trying to figure out what I might say, Fritz continued, "You might want to call me Paul Lorenz," he now stated. "I know that you and I are on the same page, Captain Novack." Although still discombobulated, I now had regained my orientation. Fritz was addressing me as the Rat Man had addressed Freud in a deeply conflicted moment when he conflated his analyst and the cruel Czech captain who had originally described the rat torture. I thought that Fritz was communicating to me about his fragile psychological state, speaking of trauma, his own and his son's and in his confused way trying to be helpful. I responded by thanking him and I said that I thought that Ezra and I were figuring out his psychology and by so doing that spanking had become unnecessary in the office and I hoped that this would be true at home too. "That would be such a welcome development," Fritz now stated. "I shall leave the paddle here for you, however, as a sort of insurance policy."

I was somewhat shaken by Fritz's visit but I also thought that I understood something new. Ezra was dealing with his father's mental status as well as with his paddle. Father's threats were real as well as symbolic. It was no wonder that it had taken us many months to enter the library of his mind. We had first to negotiate the question of his safety symbolically and on far more literal levels. Yet, this too, was far from clear and still there was the directive from Ezra to find the woman, whoever she might be. Very briefly, in considering my changing reactions to Fritz, I found myself wondering about his sexuality, could he be conflating fucking and spanking, was he telling me much more than I could understand even with his reference to a landmark case of Freud's? I assumed that this was, of course, true even though it all remained quite elusive for me, more of a whiff than a distinct and identifiable scent.

Ezra seemed both more skittish and strangely more serene on his next visit. "Where is it?" were his first words. "Right here," I responded, removing the paddle from my desk drawer. "I just wanted to see it," Ezra now said. "My father never pretends. He only does things. Mommy knows how to pretend. He doesn't." "I wonder why that is?" I asked.

Calmly, Ezra now states: "It runs in his family. His father whipped him and now he whips me. Mommy's father did not whip her. But he did whip her brother. I used to think that men only hit boys. It seemed unfair and so I started to hit girls. Bad idea. A lot of trouble." "Is that why you thought we should read the Foucault? To learn more about all of this hitting?" I now asked. "Good idea, don't you think?" Was Ezra's response. "But what if you cannot tell who is a boy and who is a girl," Ezra now blurted out. He looked genuinely distressed. "Then you would not know whom to beat?" I inquired. "Yes," responded Ezra. "I can see how that could be a problem," I stated. I then asked, surely emanating in part from my countertransference, "but does one have to beat?" "About that there can be no question," was Ezra's response. I felt that my questions about beating and sexuality were gaining admission to our play space in a way which Ezra was titrating and orchestrating according to his play mode preferences.

So we began our reading and the text we evolved together occupied us for some time. Interestingly, we did not read from the book itself, although it was always present. Ezra sat next to me, actually very close to me. He smacked his hand with the paddle which his father had left in the office and he dictated a story for me to transcribe:

"Long ago," it began, "a very big man covered with yellow hair bellowed into the wind. His hair was very very long and the fierce wind whipped it around his body. Everywhere it struck him it left a red welt. He became known by his marks. He was called Red Welt and everyone was afraid of him. Red Welt said that it was his own wind which had caused the yellow hair to mark his body. All force came from within him. He was the force.

One day, as he roamed the world, eating every living creature he encountered, he met the first life form that he did not want to devour. He was surprised because he wanted to cover her with his long blond hair rather than to blow wind out of his bottom and cause his hair to whip her and knock her to the ground. Her hair was dark and her skin was white. He called her "dark white" and the two of them were the father and the mother of the world. Thus begins *Punish and Discipline*, Ezra "read." The percussive accompanying of the paddle on his hand had become contrapuntal with his narrative voice.

So we were elaborating a creation myth—Ezra's. I was not surprised to learn that it reflected his processing of Fritz's story and of Marissa's. I was not surprised that it retold his father's torture and torturing and that it recounted his mother's horror and helplessness. I thought that we were reading together about the meaning of the familial psychosis which had become the text of Ezra's disorder and that this accompanied reading could only be therapeutic. Our reading together and exploring the library of Ezra's mind becomes our principal focus. My role expands. I listen and I transcribe. Ezra renames our volume. It is no longer *Punish and Discipline* but is now called the story of how all of this came about. Ezra says that we are the two authors and he calls us Pad and Dle. I think that this is a reference to the object supplied by his father. I ask about its counterpart at home. Ezra responds: "That is far less important than that we are here." I agree but state, "What happens at home matters even as we are learning about the story of how all of this came about." "I will let you know if there is a problem," Ezra now tells me.

We begin to talk about Pad and Dle. They have always liked each other. Theirs is an easy relationship because they have a common purpose. They are historians. "Studying the past is a lot easier than living the past," I am told by Pad. As Dle, I ask how one might become the other. "Studying the past helps to keep it there," Ezra now states. So in our work, we are evolving not only theories of pathogenesis but also methods of management and of models of therapeutic action.

In spite of what might have been regarded as Ezra's reassurance about life at home, I continued to feel uneasy and I asked him if it would be all right for me to talk further with his father. His response was, as always interesting. He wondered if he could be present. I agreed. Fritz was also totally amenable to this arrangement. I wondered how it would unfold. My first observation was that father and son seemed very comfortable with each other. They entered the room arm and arm. Ezra sat down next to his father. I now realized that I was, perhaps, the least comfortable member of this triad. Fritz began to speak. "Thank you for taking the paddle. Since I left it with you, it has not been necessary to use it at all at home. I do not know how that has happened, but it has." Ezra smiled. I now said, feeling less anxious, "As Ezra says, studying the past makes it less necessary to enact it." "I said live it, "Ezra corrects me. "Yes, live it," I amend. "My dad has a question for you," Ezra now continues. "And what might that be?" I wonder. "I would like the name of an analyst for myself," Fritz now says. "I need to study many things myself."

In reporting on Carlotta's analysis at the 44th IPA Congress in Rio de Janeiro (Herzog, 2005a), I remarked on the amazing power of our work to mobilize inherent strengths in her father. A similar phenomenon seemed to be occurring here. Fritz needed an analyst, so I helped him find one. As we continued our explorations in the Library of the Mind, transformations in Red Welt's Psychology and Behavior began to emerge. It seemed that he was not the threatening and sadistic farting force that he had seemed to be. Rather this was an elaborate disguise aimed to divert all from the fact that he was actually not male but a deeply conflicted woman who tried desperately to hide his wish for penetration. Amazingly, Red Welt named his vagina completely hidden by his whipping yellow hair "Cherchez la Femme." I hypothesized to myself that we were simultaneously exploring Fritz's intrapsychic confusions and conflicts, and that we had embarked on a beginning deconstruction of Ezra's bisexual identifications and conflictual dilemmas.

Pad and Dle continue their reading. They, that is we, turn to the fascinating question of the genders, the sexual preferences and the ways of being together of the readers. Not surprisingly, sadomasochism is a highly cathected representational area. It makes a body flush and it actually makes it harder to determine who is male and who is female. Hitting is like a great wind coming from inside. It is bigger than anything else. We come to understand together what it is that Ezra struggled to decipher and what it was that he needed to unravel, first as he felt it from and with his father; secondly as he experienced it from and with his mother; and thirdly as he was immersed in it between his mother and father together. No wonder that he tried action and intense verbal productions. No wonder that he was diagnosed as operating outside of the usual boundaries of reality. His realities were intense, overwhelming, irresistible, and initially un-representable. We needed to repair together to the library of his mind and we needed to find a way to read an as yet unwritten text together.

The analysis is relational, reconstructive, object related, and intensely real. For Ezra, psychoanalysis is the treatment of choice. The mysteries of his psychosis can be read in the analytic Spielraum and the reading proves highly therapeutic. Finally, I would like to suggest that Ezra shows us as do so many children in analysis the ways in which that which cannot be contained and titrated between the parental couple is delegated to the psyche of the child where it resides as a space occupying lesion. This self with mother and father together representation is often the nucleus of highly dys-regulating symptomatology in a child. An earlier formulation of this situation was presented in Porto Allegre in my paper on "triadic reality" (2005b), i.e., the self with mother and father together representation and the play space.

In the analytic work during Ezra's adolescence, he and I met four times a week. We began in earnest to read Foucault. Ezra talked to me about the trouble between his parents. They had now separated and father had a male lover. We revisited much from the childhood work, all of which Ezra remembered. There was none of the much touted repression of child analytic work. Ezra's psychosis had not returned, rather he was deeply troubled by what appeared to be a sculpting of his sexual life about which he had major conflict and many questions.

Our major focus was on the transference neurosis. What had happened between him and me then and what was happening now. Ezra wanted to know where my spanking feelings were and why I had not acted upon them. He was deeply curious about my personal life and about my sexuality. Earlier, there had been no room for such interests even as we explored the most primeval of passions within him and between him and his parents. As we deepened our exploration, he asked, "How are love and pain connected? Must this connection be physical or can it be in the realm of feeling only? Must I be exactly like my father or my mother or do I have other options, including just being me?" To his question, I appended mine: Was this newest disturbance an actual manifestation of self with mother and father together? If so, would its emerging into consciousness afford Ezra relief? I remembered the Rat Man and father's hunger to reveal his psychology. I pondered the earlier spanking and its relationship to father's homosexuality and to the unhappiness between his parents. I thought that Ezra was depicting his parents' sexual relationship in his s-and-m fixation. As our work continued, we were to learn that the answer to all of these putative formulations was a resounding "Yes."

Analysis may well be optimally conducted in segments which are developmentally dictated. This may well be true of adult work. Might one conjecture that here again, work with children and adolescents powerfully illumines why and how this might be true. And might we note that Ezra's play both directly with me as in the book disbanding and then in displacement when we wrote the book together moves what his father actually did to and with him into an observable externalized setting where we can examine it together.

RAY

Ray comes to talk with me about his father and his fathering. He is forty-four, a stay at home father and has been in a previous analysis. He is married to Margery, a highly successful vascular surgeon and they have two children, Joey and Vicky. Ray's chief complaint at the time we begin our work appears to be a negative one. "I do not want to be my father," he states. We are to learn ever more about what this statement means to Ray.

The decision for Ray to stay at home and be his children's primary caretaker is not our initial focus. Rather, Ray is concerned about his son Joe's naughtiness and his own reaction thereto. He gets very angry with Joe who he thinks is actually a normal four year old and has on several occasions spanked him quite hard. None of this sits well with Ray. As he speaks, he says thoughtfully, "I think that my chief complaint is that my paternal limit setting interferes with my being able to play—or more accurately, I get so mad that I lose the capacity to play."

Ray tells me about his first analysis. It began while he was in law school and allowed him to make the transition from continuing with his initial plan to become a trial lawyer and increasingly recognize his wish to write murder mysteries. He and his analyst were able to accomplish much of this vocational clarification while focusing primarily on Ray's deeply conflicted relationship with his own father Harry. Ray summarized this work by saying: "My issues were clearly about murderous feelings. I was conflicted about the mode I would utilize to manage these feelings. The work was very serious, deadly serious." Ray smiled as he finished his statement and then looked quizzical. "There was actually nothing playful about my analysis, I just realize. It was all about misery and I felt miserable most of the time."

To myself, I noted, that Ray felt like a playful fellow. Yet, he was proclaiming that both his relationship with his son and his relationship with his first analyst were devoid of such affect or interaction. We begin our analytic work. As Ray shifts from sitting across from me to lying on the couch, I note that his mood darkens perceptibly. He talks to me about Margery and about his lack of sexual interest in her. Simultaneously, I begin to learn that he is highly aroused by pornography which he views on the web. In fact, when his children are in preschool during the morning and it is his writing time, he almost exclusively patronizes certain web sites which he tells me will remain unnamed at the moment. I think I detect some of what I had felt to be playful in this thinly veiled tease.

Ray wonders about me. He was surprised, he tells me, that I looked so old. He had expected a younger hunk. His previous analyst had said that I was at the top of my game. When he first saw me he thought to himself that that must be in the nursing home. Yet, there was something about the way that I walked, talked, and even thought that suggested that maybe I was still functional. "Functional as what?" I inquired. "As a fucking and spanking guy," Ray responded spontaneously. "How do you feel about these capacities," I now wondered. "I want you to have them and I want to have them. I did not feel that Dr. B (his previous analyst) did."

I felt interested in my possession of these attributes as a positive. I wondered about their transferential meaning and I remembered that Ray was spanking Joe but unable to play with him. I thought about the necessary inclusion of sexuality and aggression in a man's repertoire as it pertains to work, play, and love. I realized that he had been expecting a hunk and had to deal with something different and that he was not having sex with his wife. I tried to listen.

Ray said that he thought that my wife was a doctor. Then again, perhaps, I wasn't married. His wife had said something once about knowing someone in treatment with my wife. Well maybe he had made that up. It seemed kind of fuzzy to him. I wondered if he had a preference for what the story would be. "I would like you to be beating off to the same porn sites which I use," Ray responded. I chose not to ask what sites these were. I wondered what kind of brothers in arms or hands we would then be: wifeless, gay, bereft, or happy? "Margery and I do nothing together," Ray now added. "Essentially, I have been on my own since we moved here and she began her new job. I am kind of a bachelor with children and no sex life except for my hand." I had the thought which I did not articulate that Ray's entire instinctual life was conducted with his hand. He masturbated with it (I conjectured) and he spanked Joe with it (another conjecture). He could barely write, I was told—

another hand function, this one manifested in inhibition. What was happening which led to this state of affairs which constituted his chief complaint?

Our analytic work proceeded at a lively pace. We were in a realm of touch and touchiness, which had both historical and current manifestations. Ray wanted to shake my hand at the beginning and ending of each session, but felt sure that I would consider him "touched" for having such a wish. His previous analyst felt that touching was contraindicated. Soon we were to enter a huge reservoir of feeling about the ways his father had touched and not touched him. He wept as he told me about an interaction which occurred around the time he was six or seven when he was trying to teach his father how to high-five. Whatever he did so annoyed his father that he slapped Ray in the face. We spent a long time trying to understand how this play had gone bad and traversed the spectrum from enthusiasm to transgression and then punitive sting. We were not so far removed from what happened between Joe and Ray and as my patient now stated: "We were touching on important matters." Ray wondered how I might respond to his story. Would I consider him a sissy? Would I be identified with the slapping father or the crying son? Would I be excited by the scene? We considered that he felt all of these identifications and that there might even be legitimate reason that each was cathected.

In the third year of our work together Ray brought Joe, now seven, to an hour. There had been earlier allusions to this possibility but it had never been explored in earnest. On this day, Joe had had an appointment with his pediatrician and then father and son had had an ice cream together and before he knew it, Ray said, it was time for his analytic hour. Joe looked comfortable with his father and was friendly to me. We were introduced to each other in the waiting room and then Ray came in. Instead of lying down on the couch, he sat down on it and looked directly at me. "Well," he stated, "now we have an amazing opportunity. Could I invite Joe to come in and could we talk together?" I tried to think what this might mean, but felt inclined to say yes. I said as much. Ray looked very pleased and quite excited. He got up and as he approached the door, he said, "I wanted to high-five you." I said, "We both know how loaded that was."

When Joe came in, his Dad motioned him toward the chair and sat down himself again on the couch. "I was telling Dr. Herzog what happened after the Little League game," he began. Joe looked upset. "You got so mad at me for being a poor sport," he said. He looked as though he might cry. "I think I overreacted," his father now said. "I am sorry." Joe looked surprised. "We should come here together more often," he now stated and he smiled at me. I had so far said nothing, but now said, "Sometimes, it helps to have someone listen to what is causing the disagreement." Joe now says, "Are you related to Whitey Herzog?" "I don't think so," I respond, "but I am an admirer of his." "Are you a Red Sox fan," I am now asked. "And how," I answer. "Me too,"

Joe says. "When my Dad and I go to Fenway Park, he is almost never mad at me. I wish we had season tickets." I looked over at Ray and realized that he was crying.

So we were at work on how to keep a dialogue going and it seemed to require or at least be facilitated by the presence of a third person. Joe and his Dad could converse with greater ease in my office and, it appeared, at Fenway Park. Ray felt both embarrassed about bringing Joe into the office and also as though it was the most important thing he had ever done. "I didn't plan it or at least I don't think I did. It just happened. Thank God it happened," he said. "I liked the way you just answered Joe's questions. No analytic bullshit. I realize that I am rarely that direct with him. I am always on guard or something. I know this sounds crazy, but do you remember that I said that I wanted to high-five you when I was going out to get him?" "Yes," I replied. "Well it is almost as if I am always in the high five situation with him. Do you know what I mean? Tense and uncertain whether what will evolve will be a good exchange or an assault."

Ray and I were able to reconstruct that this feeling of being on guard was what always characterized his relationship with his father. He never knew when his father would hurt him. It happened often and always, he now said, unmodified by his father's loving feelings or by the titrating presence of his mother. We had struck pay dirt, I felt. We were learning what Ray needed to guard against with Joe and we were uncovering the historical antecedents. It was really not a surprise to discover that Dr. B, his former analyst, had been experienced the same way. One never knew where his aggression lay or how it might emerge. Ray eagerly now recognized this as a powerful and inevitable transference. This was why it was so important that I was natural with Joe. "You are with me too, I think," he now said. "But when I saw how you were with Joe, I could really believe it. You neither pounced with pleasure nor had to hold yourself back." Ray, we had learned always had to hold himself back and was always managing his wish to pounce with pleasure. His paternal identification with the aggressor was unmodified by a titrating identification with mother and father together.

We began to investigate this state of affairs together. We explored his parents' relationship with each other as well as his sense of what went on and still was going on within and for his father. Ray felt that his mother, too, lived in terror of his father and did everything in her power to assuage him. He spoke with his siblings. They concurred. It was as if there were six slaves and one master in his family of origin. He recalled with grim humor that his father had been referred to as "the Cardinal" in the family, a rowdy, rapscallion, Machiavellian, prince of their church.

Our exploration of his parents' relationship led us resolutely to him and Marge. Ray began to make the link between the ending of their sexual relationship and his feeling that he was both spanking Joe too much and needed to be on guard with him all of the time. He felt as though the threesome of Joe, him, and me might actually stand for the lost threesome of Marge, Joe, and him. He began to feel hopeful. "I want you to understand something," he said. "Actually, I know that you do. Spanking is not the culprit. It is being alone with too much pouncing feeling and that not being balanced by a good sex life and an alliance with your wife." I said that I thought he had it figured out. He said, "I think you are a good guy for me to be talking to. A good Joe, I almost said. Want to high-five?"

Being called a good Joe seemed to constitute a natural segue to talking about our relationship. Did the picture of me as a hunk mean that I could spank and fuck him or did it have other connotations? Was the love that he felt for me a paternal longing, a homosexual desire, a heterosexual desire, or a wish for something else? As is almost always the case, it seemed to be all of these things. Ray's father's pouncing potential and practice felt both sexual and sadistic to him. He recognized all of these features in his relationship with Joe and he wished for them from me. "I like to talk about all of this with you," Ray said. "It feels real." Simultaneously, he told me that he had begun to woo Margery again. She was receptive to his return and told him that she had missed him. She also said that she knew that her role in what had evolved was very significant. She said that she would like to come and talk with my wife. Ray told her that that would be too weird but that he would ask me for a referral. Perhaps, most significantly, Ray said that he felt the return of his capacity to play. "It is like recovering from a fatal illness," he said.

Fathers play with their children by using their modulated and sublimated aggression and sexuality to create and to populate a play space. This can only happen when the man who is the father has mastered these aspects of his own psyche and has had developmental help there within his own childhood and has ongoing concomitant partnership at the present time. In average expectable circumstances, a man's father helps him with the latter and his wife is a crucial ally in the latter. Each of these factors was problematic for Ray. His father was unmodulated in his experience and his wife's unavailability had become institutionalized. In his sexual and aggressive bantering with me, he was able to begin to rework these issues. By so doing, he became better able to create a working and workable play space with his son.

Almost thirty years ago, Eleanor Herzog and I conducted a series of home based observations in which we documented the differences in the ways in which fathers played with young children in the presence of the mother from the ways in which mothers played with young children in the presence of the father. We observed that mothers tended to be homeostatically attuned. They matched their young children in terms of activity level, intensity and degree of organization. Fathers, on the other hand tended to be disruptively attuned. They increased the intensity and activity and decreased the level of organization. The classic illustration of this was a mother who acted as a kind of assistant in a building project and a father who initiated a dive bombing game in regard to the emerging building. Children liked both experiences; boys being more comfortable with the paternal play mode than girls. We hypothesized that these two modes provided children with two distinct types of experience; being matched and matching. We concluded that both were essential. We also suggested that repetitive cycles of the father's increasing the level of excitement and disorganization and then presiding with the help of the mother in a necessary calming process constituted the core experience in self regulation in regard to the drives for the child. A striking correlate of our initial observations was that the relationship between the parents was a crucial factor in how this all played out. Mothers had to approve of their husbands' utilization of their own drive structure in the play process in order for it to be a developmentally salutary ingredient in the child's experiential repertoire.

In later work, this necessity for a parental alliance in optimal development has given rise to the concept that self with mother and father together representations are a crucial part of self structure along side with self with mother and self with father representations. I would like to suggest that it was this very feature which Ray and I were working upon. He brought to our work, fomented and focused by his first analysis, a father hunger and a father and mother together hunger. In his own way, he was able to "play" with each of these. The analyst allowed his patient to conduct the analysis according to his own script and in so doing it was established that a child could be safe in such a setting. The self with analyst representation then became a self with father and a self with mother and father together representation which was fecund, safe and modulated. It was not just transferential but also developmentally nutritive. It encouraged the return of play and in so doing helped Ray in his espousing and in his fathering.

It is not surprising then to note that in both of the analyses reported the deformation in the play function involves the father's sexuality and his aggression. Hypertrophied by the stress in the parental relationship and by the transgenerational deprivations and excesses which each story features, these forces are applied to and exchanged with the son in a deleterious rather than a growth-promoting fashion. It is as if the paternal play-style itself is completely unmodulated and therefore no longer an ameliorative and nutritive ingredient.

Increasingly, I have come to think that this is a plausible model for therapeutic action. The analytic Spielraum, play space, is defined as a two person setting of a very specific sort, a dyadic attempt to access triadic reality. The analysand brings his history and his attempted restitutions and formulations. The analyst is asked to accompany. In so doing, the analyst evokes and allows not only the emergence of but also by the process itself a reworking of less than optimal self with mother, self with father and self with mother and father together representations. It is this reworking which transforms the analysand's mind, allowing him to look anew and in a triadically structured way at his earlier conclusions, enactments, actualizations, and impediments. The analyst is there to allow this new way of looking to emerge safely. His or her technical armamentarium essentially serves this purpose. This is the therapeutic action! It is an extraordinarily interesting question as to the multiple ways in which technique either facilitates or obviates this process. Here again, I have come to think that it is when the self with mother and father together representation and its ensuing transference is activated and malleable that optimal work is done. I mean to juxtapose this notion to more familiar concepts of paternal and or maternal transferences.

Chapter Three

Adolescence as a Time to Play

Christine Kieffer

> "Adolescence is the shedding of family dependencies, the loosening of infantile object ties in order to become a member of society at large, or simply of the adult world." —Peter Blos, "The Second Individuation Process of Adolescence"

Perhaps no other developmental phase conjures up such a wide range of intense affect and ambivalence in the observer as adolescence: excitement, envy, voyeuristic preoccupation alongside repulsion, exasperation, and, perhaps above all, sheer bewilderment—this phase of development evokes within us all of the characteristics of this age group. While one may not associate the activity of "play" as readily with this age group as compared with, say, toddlerhood or latency (and certainly many teenagers themselves might find this notion abhorrent!), if we think of play as a process of trying on new identities, mimicking admired others, and then transforming this into an individual signature, renegotiating self-other relationships through differentiated action and words—then the ferment of adolescence is an important time to play. This chapter will examine this developmental period as a time in which, simultaneously propelled forward and drawn backward, adolescents strive to individuate from their early love objects and form a new identity that enables the formation of mature ties. Several brief clinical vignettes will be offered in illustration of these concepts.

ADOLESCENCE AS DEVELOPMENTAL PHASE

Until Anna Freud's (1936) groundbreaking contributions to a psychoanalytic theory of adolescence there had been, as she herself noted, a relative lack of interest in this developmental period. However, particularly since the 1960s during the time of the development of a "youth culture" associated with the emergence of the postwar American "baby boom," there has been a burgeoning interest in understanding this time of life. This supports the notion of adolescence as, in part, a socially constructed idea. For example, in the Middle Ages when life was "nasty, short, and brutish," childhood was not carefully delineated from adulthood and adolescence meant little beyond the onset of puberty after which one soon became a parent. (The developmental phase of "mid-life" is also a relatively recent construct.) Today, however, at least in highly industrialized nations, adolescence seems to describe a period of life that is increasingly elongated, although at the same time, the demarcation between youth and adulthood seems to have become blurred, at least in the West, with parents and children dressing more and more alike and engaging in similar activities—that is, more like adolescents, whose youthfulness has become idealized.

And yet, as Anna Freud noted, adolescence seems to exist as a definable developmental phase, heralded by the onset of puberty and characterized by a renewed effort to establish compromise formation between ego and id. That is, puberty brings with it an increase of libido along with burgeoning impulses that are now concentrated on "genital feelings, aims, and ideas of objects" (1936, p. 148). The truce that was effected in latency has now given way to an intense struggle, however, unlike the prepubertal period, the ego of the early adolescent is firmly consolidated, leading to conflicts with the superego as well. While adolescent acting out of these conflicts tends to capture a greater level of attention, adolescent neurotic symptoms may also be clustered around withdrawal into excessive amounts of fantasy and inhibition.

Anna Freud (1958) has observed that adolescent upheaval is but an external indication of the internal adjustments that are in process, thus withdrawal and passivity is not to be taken as a sign of quiescence. Moreover, the "good" boys and girls actually may be in more urgent need of psychoanalytic intervention, given the salutary aspects of adolescent action, which is a form of regression in the service of increased ego development and consolidation. She notes that while the compliance of this group of adolescents might suggest insufficient drive endowment, in reality this may reflect excessive defenses against drive activities, emanating from the superego and ego. For example, some adolescents defend against increased libidinal drive with a reaction formation of "asceticism," sometimes giving rise to eating disorders such as anorexia or a preoccupation with religiosity. (It is well known that adolescents and young adults are more susceptible to the lure of religious cults in which every aspect of thought and behavior is severely restricted.) Another way in which to describe this problem might be to view it as an inhibition of the capacity for "play."

Thus, while the adolescent period recapitulates infantile strivings, Jones (1922) was among the first to note that adolescence may be a period of unusual creativity, with idealistic aims that may lead to real and significant achievement. While Bernfeld (1923) confined his theorizing to the "protracted" adolescence of males as sometimes producing heightened creativity, the ferment of adolescence, if successfully channeled, may also give rise to achievement in both sexes (Gilligan, 1983; Kieffer, 2004; Sadker and Sadker, 1995). Anna Freud, who herself is an example of this (Young-Bruehl, 1988), maintained that the "adolescence is by its nature an interruption of peaceful growth" and that "the upholding of a steady equilibrium during the adolescent process is in itself abnormal" (1958, p. 164). Thus unpredictable and inconsistent development is a hallmark of adolescence, and, I would add, a measure of creativity and the capacity for play.

Later writers have amplified the importance of adolescence as a time of reworking of infantile conflict, including Louis Kaplan (1984) who described adolescence as a "farewell" to childhood. Derek Miller (1978) and Peter Blos (1962) have emphasized the central importance of adolescence as a time of intensely renewed conflict over separation-individuation (Mahler et al., 1975). Blos (1976; 1968) described adolescence as involving a second individuation process which, if successfully resolved, will lead to firm boundaries and stability of both self and object representations, with a resistance to cathectic shifts. Blos noted that "regressive and progressive movements alternate in shorter or longer intervals" (1967, p. 164) which, while suggestive of uneven growth, lead to eventual stability and resilience. It is the mutual and ongoing influence of drive and ego development that give rise to this seemingly chaotic process, with the ego ideal eventually exerting more influence.

Blos (1967) observed that the "play-acting" and bodily presentations or "action language" of adolescence, while emblematic of regressive processes, operate in the ultimate service of development. The glorified images of entertainment idols present the adolescent with temporary role models, and the peer group as well as other groups (Woodstock and the "mosh pit" are instances of these) serve as aids in inducing "ego states of quasimerger . . . which "serve as safeguards against total merger with the infantile, internalized objects" (p. 175). He echoes Anna Freud in maintaining that signs of resistance to regression are as much a cause for concern as its excess. In other words, he supports the notion of adolescence as a time of play, in which experimentation with self and other, affect and thought, illusion and reality may lead to a creative reworking of old conflicts that lead to a more adaptive adult identity.

Winnicott (1968), who wrote so eloquently of the nature and development of play, seemed to have little comment on adolescence other than to urge enveloping them in a supportive environment until that time of turbulence ended. In writing about adolescents whose psychological disturbance resulted in hospitalization, he tended to agree with those psychoanalysts who viewed this patient population as being particularly resistant to analytic intervention.

The influence of peers upon the adolescent has been put to therapeutic use by group therapists (Aronson et al., 2002; Azima and Richmond, 1989; Slavson, 1962), who believe that, for teens, their age cohorts may have considerably more influence than that of their analysts. Psychoanalytic group therapy may be helpful in offering multiple sources of feedback and support, and patients may experience the reactions of other members as being more authentic and truthful. This is particularly true for adolescent patients, who are provided with a larger stage upon which to construct and enact various kinds of roles and identities, and are offered a sometimes more appreciative and empathic audience, at least in their immediate view. However, the therapeutic impact of group treatment could easily deteriorate into a maladaptive experience without the presence and direction of an adult psychotherapist who, while she/he may be overtly dismissed or even disdained, is nevertheless available for support and insight when tempestuous adolescent group alliances founder or turn hostile.

More recently, some psychoanalysts have challenged the importance of separation-individuation as a necessary phase of development, particularly for adolescents. Galatzer-Levy and Cohler (1993) have asserted that autonomy has been inappropriately valorized as a developmental goal and question whether such an outcome is even attainable. They maintain that the view of adolescence as a period that is automatically fraught with stress and turbulence is the mistaken result of trying to make generalizations from analysis with a patient population—that is, a sampling error. For example, they believe that Margaret Mahler incorrectly extrapolated from her own plight of separation and uprootedness to create a theory in which separation-individuation was normative. That is, while in pathological families the best solution is to seek maximum autonomy, this may not be necessary in families that are "good enough." They argue convincingly for an alternative paradigm in which the end goal of development is not autonomy but rather the maintenance and elaboration of mutual interdependence—hence the title of their book, *The Essential Other,* in which they highlight the ongoing importance of interdependence as an aspect of mature function. Psychoanalytic researchers and clinicians, notably Karlen Lyons-Ruth (1999), have stressed the normative aspects of secure attachment (as opposed to separation) in facilitating individuation. Of course, Winnicott (1958) and Kohut (1981; 1977) respectively also have stressed the ongoing influence of a facilitating environment and a responsive self-object milieu throughout life.

Wolf (1988) has expanded the range of needed self-object functions to include an Adversarial need which entails a "need to experience the self-object as a benignly opposing force who continues to be supportive and responsive while allowing or even encouraging one to be in active opposition and thus confirming an at least partial autonomy; the need for the availability of a self-object experience of assertive and adversarial confrontation *vis-à-vis* the self-object without the loss of self-sustaining responsiveness from that self-object" (p. 55). Adversarial self-object needs appear first upon the emergence of a cohesive self during the second year of life (think of the "terrible two" stage of toddlerhood), which again becomes prominent in adolescence. It is during this time that the adolescent becomes cognizant of parental defects, with a corresponding de-idealization of early self-objects replaced by a more realistic, nuanced appreciation that emerges in early adulthood, if all goes well. A gradual rather than rapid and traumatic de-idealization of parents helps to smooth the adolescent's transition into adulthood. Thus, Wolf incorporates what has been recognized as a universal adolescent striving for autonomy into the Psychology of the Self.

ADOLESCENT COGNITION AND THE DEVELOPMENT OF PLAY AND CREATIVITY

Blakemore (2008) has presented persuasive findings on adolescent brain development demonstrating that behavior related to social cognition changes dramatically during human adolescence. This is "paralleled by functional changes that occur in the social brain during this time" (p. 267), specifically in areas that highlight face recognition and mental state attribution. She notes that these findings are consistent with that of social psychological studies which indicate that adolescence is characterized by a heightened state of self-consciousness along with the increased importance of peer relationships. Over time, the adolescent develops an increased understanding of how others think and feel or "the attribution of mental states" (Steinberg and Morris, 2001), which many psychoanalysts think of as an increase in the capacity for "mentalization" (Fonagy et al., 2002) or empathy. Blakemore interprets the confluence of these findings to mean that it is not increased capacity for mentalization that is significant so much as the improvement in the modulation of mentalizing by executive functions of the brain that leads to the development of social judgment and improved interaction in adolescents. It is important to remember that the impact of physiological and psychological domains each influence the other realm, and cannot be adequately explained with reference to a linear model of development.

Piaget (Piaget and Inhelder, 1955/1958) maintained that the fundamental problem of adolescence is not puberty but rather the challenge of taking on adult roles, which vary in timing and complexity cross-culturally (and across time). However, he also maintains that the organization of formal operations, which has the capacity to develop in adolescence, must depend upon the social milieu as well. That is, while between the ages of eleven and twelve, the brain may reach a *state of readiness* to attain formal operations, its development is dependent upon formal education as well as a social environment that promotes a future-orientation as well as one that creates conditions that promote a capacity for self-reflection, both of which are components of formal operations. "Formal thinking is thinking about thought" (Piaget and Inhelder, 1958, p. 438), that is, there is the development of a capacity for abstraction both in thought and in social relationships, which comes to fruition beginning at thirteen and fifteen years. The onset of formal operations facilitates the acquisition of complex adult social roles, but part of that process also entails the integration of thought and affect, along with the capacity to differentiate between both processes.

We can see that both research paradigms have considerable convergence with respect to the development of the capacity for abstraction, and the potential for play—with thought, ideas, and others—in adolescence. One further task of adolescence, one for which play is a particularly apt medium, is the integration of affect with cognition. Blum (2005) has noted that affects have come to acquire a central importance in psychoanalysis, which have mutually determined neurophysiological as well as psychological influences throughout life, but can be particularly challenging to adolescents and their families. Blum has emphasized the transactional nature and influence of affect exchange between infant and caregiver, noting that the "modulation and taming of affects begins very early" (p. 4) and that affect co-determines motivation and inhibition. With the advent of language, communication, and regulation of affect are radically altered, with language coming to co-determine both the sociocultural context and the evolving parent-child relationship. Language is a crucial developmental achievement here because it can serve to integrate affects and ideas with emerging systems of memory and fantasy. Blum has further noted that while anxiety has been utilized in theorizing about the role of affect as a signal, it is not a central paradigm for the significance of the positive affects, which provide signals to proceed rather than to retreat.

Stern (1985) and Tomkins (1962) have provided evidence for the independent importance of the primary affect of curiosity and interest in promoting exploration of novel situations as well as aiding in the mastery of negative affect. Plaschkes's (2005) discussion of Blum's (2005) paper stressed the importance of play in relieving anxiety and promoting mastery. Given that traumatic play has the character of repetition, concreteness and potential exacerbation of anxiety, one of the critical functions of psychoanalytic work is to help the patient to re-engage curiosity and interest introducing new interactional procedures that may later gain momentum when integrated with language.

While most psychoanalytic theorizing has been firmly anchored in linear models of development, newer models of development offering explanations that are based in non-linear dynamic systems theory have become increasingly influential, and may be particularly useful in explaining the uneven and often chaotic developmental process of adolescence. There seems to be considerable agreement in both the psychoanalytic and psychotherapy literature that adolescence—of all phases—tends to be particularly likely to unfold erratically, with rapid oscillations between reflective thought and non-reflective action. Nevertheless, as the adolescent grows older there is a gradual shift toward adaptation, with a movement toward an increased capacity for self-regulation, an internalized sense of agency, and a more stable and realistic set of goals and ideals (Kieffer, 2007). Therapeutic action (with all patients) may be conceptualized as a function of the actions and moment-to-moment exchanges from which a different self-organization eventually emerges (Jaffe, 2000). That is, all biological systems (including the analyst-patient system) self-organize and self-regulate, demonstrating multiple ways to achieve a common developmental outcome, a principle that von Bertalanffy (1968) termed "equifinality." This is relevant to therapeutic action in that during times of transition when subsystems are not as strongly cohesive (as is typically true when treatment begins), small changes in the environment of the individual can create large reorganizations (Seligman, 2005; Harris, 2005).

Another systems principle of relevance to development—and to psychoanalytic intervention—is that of "emergence," which refers to a situation of synergy, one that is more than the sum of its parts a concept that can be particularly useful in accounting for therapeutic action. As Galatzer-Levy (2002) defines emergence, it accounts for two instances, "when bringing together component parts results in something that simply could not have happened, and situations where, from a human point of view, something novel and surprising appears from a situation that is not even suggestive of this novelty—something arrives 'out of the blue'" (p. 710). This theory can help to explain the often observed phenomenon in psychoanalytic work with adolescents (indeed, with all patients) in which seemingly dormant periods can oscillate with stretches of rapid change and development. While we are trained as psychoanalysts to expect that the process of change in development and treatment is both continuous and steady, this is often not the case, particularly with adolescents.

The phenomenon of emergence also can help us to understand the workings of play and creativity, the appearance and elaboration of which can be sudden and seem mysterious. One never seems to know—in art or psychoanalysis—when the muse will arrive, but when it does something is created from elements that may at first seem disjointed and even paradoxical. Creativity would seem to be an emergent phenomenon (Kieffer, 2010a; Kieffer, 2010b).

THEORIES OF PLAY AND THE ANALYTIC PROCESS

The psychoanalyst who has been associated most closely with a theory of the nature and importance of play and playfulness has, of course, been D. W. Winnicott. Winnicott (1971) locates the origin of play and the capacity for creativity in the development of the infant's usage of the "transitional space" that develops in the phase of relative dependence as he becomes aware of the primary caretaker as a separate object that is not under his omnipotent control. This is a prolonged phase that is characterized by a paradoxical awareness of separation even while the infant continues to develop through a sense of continued and secure connection to the mother. The capacity for play is thus a developmental achievement in which the infant seeks to bridge the now recognized gap while elaborating unique patterns of object relations and transformation of anxieties. Play involves an "acceptance of the paradox that some activities are neither real nor unreal" (Akhtar, 2009), a general characteristic of all forms of creativity.

Frank Summers (2005; 1999) has expanded upon Winnicott's concept of the spontaneous gesture, integrating it with the work of Hans Loewald (1960). Loewald's work, evoking Freud's image of the analyst as sculptor seeing the statue within the block of marble, emphasized the role of the analyst in holding a view of the patient's potential in mind as she interprets the patient's attempts to re-create transference configurations, guiding him toward renewed development. Therapeutic action, according to Loewald, is dependent upon the patient's identification with the analyst's vision of the patient, a theory which has considerable overlap with Winnicott's view of psychological development and therapeutic action. Relational psychoanalysts view both theorists as contributing early views of a two-person, co-constructed model of the mind, one which bases movement toward autonomy and creativity as grounded in the matrix of an ongoing embeddedness in the psychological surround (Mitchell and Aron, 1999).

Summers' work shifts the focus of clinical inquiry from maladaptive historical patterns to a more promising future, including a place for the patient's active role in therapeutic action. He grounds his theory in Winnicott's emphasis on the role of the "containing and holding functions" of the analyst during the patient's regression to dependence, as well as the analyst's response to the patient's attempt to evoke a new, needed response from the analyst—that is, to the "spontaneous gesture." In development, this gesture moves the child to new experience, exploration and mastery, and the mother's response follows the child, by meeting it with a spontaneous gesture of her own. However, he suggests that we must "consider the real possibility that the patient's experience of the future may be blocking growth as much or perhaps even more than the effects of the past," p. 34), thus he considers the analyst's co-authorship of a new sense of future possibility to be a key to therapeutic action.

Thus, Summers integrates the work of Loewald and Winnicott, also interweaving concepts from infant research, developing a model of the therapeutic encounter as a "potential space" in which the analyst helps the patient to "create the self," that is, create a new narrative of the self that contains more adaptive ways of relating and achieving. Citing the results of Bowlby and Ainsworth's (1988) studies of attachment, Summers notes that securely attached infants had mothers who "were more emotionally available and made a push toward autonomy" (p. 12). He also cites the work of Demos (1992), who found that a child's sense of agency is best promoted by the parent who, instead of providing immediate gratification, "allows the child to experience distress and helps to resolve it in a way that makes the infant feel like a co-participant in the relief of tension" (p. 12). Therefore, Summers concludes that children do not simply receive meaning from parental ministrations but rather *create meaning from the relationship*. Since the research on adult development contains overwhelming evidence of a lifelong need to grow, this provides us with cause for increased optimism about adult patients' capacity for continued development within the analytic encounter.

However, Summers' model of coauthorship does not fully take into account the potential pitfall of inducing compliance in a patient with a "false self" personality organization. Winnicott frequently waited for the patient to reflect upon his own experience and to provide spontaneous gestures first, and was careful not to "muck up a good hour" (1971, p. 62) by interrupting the patient's process. Certainly, any attempts on our part, whether conscious or unconscious, to interfere with or co-opt creative strivings would be likely to register as such, perhaps most acutely, by adolescents patients.

THE DEVELOPMENT OF PLAY IN ADOLESCENT PSYCHOANALYSIS

The relational concepts of "*co*authorship" and "*co*construction" in the analytic encounter, whether it is the coauthorship of a new narrative or the co-construction involved in creative development are particularly likely to be fraught in the treatment of adolescents. Adolescence is a time in which a quest for freedom from the constricting aspects of family opinion as well as a quest for identity comes to the forefront of development. Adolescents have a heightened need of transitional space in which to play with aspects of identity and new modes of relating, and must maintain the illusion of complete autonomy even while continuing to sense and covertly rely upon the background of a responsive, protective environmental milieu. Thus they are reminiscent of toddlers in their insistence upon letting us know, "I can do it *myself*," however, in adolescence, cognitive development can contribute to a new hypervigilance about acknowledging environmental embeddedness. They are thus quick to bridle at any hint of manipulation, let alone any overt direction.

Billow (2004) has observed that adolescents tend to be suspicious of adults'—including analysts'—motives. Billow has noted that adolescents monitor their analysts' countertransference reactions for signs of inauthenticity, observing that they may readily experience technical interventions as signs that the analyst is "playing at being an analyst rather than really being one" (p. 274). He argues for allowing a "lively, not overly interpreted relationship that lets them know their analyst" (p. 263), and thus building a potential space in which self-reflective examination may occur.

Markman (1997) has made similar observations about the adolescent patient's need to experience the analyst as authentic, describing work with a female adolescent patient in which she accused him of "playing an analyst" (p. 203). Markham, too, has observed that the adolescent is hypersensitive to any attempts at control on the part of the analyst, noting that the potential space of play will readily collapse if the analyst's activity is experienced as an attempt to seduce or manage the patient. Giovacchini (1986) has noted that the adolescent may experience the analyst as envious of his creativity, attempting to co-opt it for his own aggrandizement.

In a posthumously published essay on pathological forms of play (Winnicott, Shepherd, and Davis, 1989), Winnicott included forms of play that reflected a form of compliance with authority and domination, the latter of which may be thought of as both a rebellion against and a bid for control of authority in the psychoanalytic situation. Winnicott's description of other pathological forms, as delineated by Akhtar (2009), include a loss of capacity to play as a result of "mistrust, rigid and stereotyped play, a flight into daydreaming, a flight to strenuous exercise, and an excessive sensualization of play" (p. 212). While these other pathological forms of play undoubtedly have a significant role in adolescent psychopathology, this paper will focus upon the dimensions of adolescent "anxiety of influence" in relation to the analyst. I will now present some brief clinical examples with a particular focus upon early adolescence, when this form of anxiety may erupt with particular force.

Alicia

Alicia, aged thirteen, while initially welcoming the attention that a four-time-per-week analysis gave her, soon began to protest that she did not need to come—that she was merely the victim of a malignant environment, which was all that needed to be modified in order for her to feel content. She began to depict the analysis as a form of invasion and imprisonment, screaming, "This isn't helping—it's too much" or "You are taking over my life!" and departing the room with a thunderous slam of the door. There soon followed a lengthy period of time in which she would linger in the waiting room, noisily turning the pages of a magazine, before reluctantly coming in. Alicia admitted that she was striving mightily to make herself so unbearable that I would decide to terminate the analysis. A promising student who was often chosen for enrichment programs, she would quickly be eliminated from these programs due to various forms of misbehavior. She was alternately puzzled and suspicious about why I did not end her treatment, and further surprised that I did not "fight fire with fire" and become as enraged with her as she would become with me.

After many months of waiting in my consultation room while Alicia lingered in the waiting room, one day, feeling a bit more useless than usual, the phone rang and I impulsively answered it. Alicia darted into the room, hissing that it was *her* time and that I should not be involved with anyone else during the session. I have written about this situation at length in another paper (Kieffer, 2010c), in which I examined the role of the waiting room as boundary and bridge between dissociated self states, noting that this boundary can provide a means of titrating the intensity and duration of affect states that may be generated by immersion in the analytic process as well as by its daily disruption—for both analyst and patient. Perhaps particularly for adolescents, this boundary can serve to simultaneously express a paradoxical sense of autonomy and dependence, an attempt to carve out one's *own* space while still connected with the presence of a soothing, though perhaps depreciated other. Certainly, this dramatic incident served to make both Alicia and myself aware of the illusory nature of her complete autonomy from my influence, despite vociferous protests to the contrary, and reflected the beginnings of a new willingness to explore this apparent paradox in a more reflective way.

Bettina

With Bettina, there was also a phase in her analysis when it was of paramount importance to insist upon her autonomy from me in a particularly dramatic way, particularly during a transition into early adolescence. Bettina's analysis began when she was adopted after having been markedly neglected and abused by her original family, who had been poly-drug abusers. I have previously written about the opening phase of Bettina's treatment, beginning at age seven, when the nature of her play reflected a strong element of sadomasochism (Kieffer, 2009). The paper described a process during which I was able to make empathic contact with Bettina, through a process of engagement with play materials, which allowed us to move from rigid and stereotyped play that was reflective of dissociation of unbearable affect states to the creation of a transitional space that enabled derailed development to continue. During the entry into pre-adolescence, however, there suddenly erupted a renewed experience of me as an untrustworthy and malignant other. During this period, Bettina, in a manner not dissimilar from Alicia, frequently accused me of trying to "control her mind," emphasizing that she did not "have to tell me anything about herself" because I would be likely misuse that information. This accusation was vague, however, and she was unable to articulate more specifically how I might be hurtful to her. It soon became clear that Bettina's change in attitude was being influenced in part by a renewed engagement with her mother and grandmother through their efforts to resume contact with her, a state of affairs that was displaced onto her analysis. One day, she brought a DVD to the consultation room, which contained material that had been discovered from the first year of Bettina's life in which she still lived with her birth parents. (This had been sent by her grandmother.) For an entire month, each day, we watched a video that consisted of an adult party in which Bettina crawled around at the feet of the revelers, occasionally being held by her mother as the mother swayed in the beginnings of alcoholic intoxication. Initially, Bettina concluded from watching the video that it was "proof that her mother cared about her after all," although I had a distinctly different experience and interpretation in watching than did my patient, which I initially kept to myself. However, later in the year, Bettina revealed to me that she once more understood that her mother did not care about her, and she began to re-examine the meaning of her mother's lack of care and concern with me, as well as its connection to the development of what had been Bettina's belligerent and counter-dependent style of engagement with others. Over time, this led to a loosening of my patient's brittle defenses against attachment and connection as well as a broadening of relational capacities—both within the analytic encounter and in the larger world.

Carl

Carl began his analysis at age thirteen, arriving at each session with an enormous schoolbag (almost as large as him)—a sort of Santa's bag from which he would draw forth a seemingly endless array of gadgets, toys, and books. He would thus engage in "show and tell," handing them to me as I examined them and then gave my own associations to the various objects.

Previous attempts to encourage Carl to free associate to this material had proved fruitless, but he enjoyed my attempts to relate the various items to what I knew of his life, and as reflections of my own experience of him. That is, I understood the appearance of each new object as an association on the part of my patient. He soon joined in this new form of play, spontaneously correcting my observations and interpretations, and adding some of his own. (I have previously written about Carl in a paper that described the development of the Analytic Third, from the perspective of chaos theory [Kieffer, 2007]). One of the key aspects of forming an analytic alliance with Carl revolved around his suspicion that I would be as intrusive and infantilizing as was his mother. While this process of "show and tell" initially had a stylized and constraining quality, I was able to engage Carl in a process of thinking about the objects and their order of introduction, as well as their meaning for him, by first demonstrating my own openness to the associative process. It also was important that I allow him to influence my associative process so that we became playful collaborators. Eventually this somewhat concrete procedure was supplanted by a more traditional analytic encounter in which Carl began to talk more freely and become more self-reflective about himself. Throughout, our focus was largely upon Carl's thwarted attempts to become autonomous from his mother and develop an identity that included a sense of himself as agent—one with increasingly elaborated goals.

In summary, these brief case vignettes illustrate the eruption, in early adolescence, of an increased need for autonomy leading to a quest for a new and more nuanced identity, within the context of the analytic process. It was important for the analyst to avoid becoming mired in a power struggle and to foster an atmosphere conducive to the development of a transitional space which fostered a co-constructed playfulness. This included an authentic participation in the unfolding play without undue emphasis on interpretation for an extended period of time, as Billow and Markham have suggested.

These case examples provide support for Frankel's (1998) assertion that action is at the heart of psychoanalytic treatment. While he and Katz (1997) have argued that verbal interpretation is a form of an enacted dimension that is present throughout treatment, nonverbal action often was in the foreground as a way in to examining the adolescent's experiences which later were able to be verbally symbolized, building insight and helping to consolidate new relational experiences. Frankel and others have observed that play in child and adolescent psychoanalysis enable us to more clearly view basic processes of therapeutic action in which dissociated self-states emerge and then become subject to recognition and symbolization, leading to a renegotiation of self-other relationships.

Adolescence is a phase in which its developmental tasks are characterized by a seeming paradox: how to individuate from early caretakers while still retaining these important ties as one integrates newly forceful drive and affective states with emergent cognitive and physical capacities in ways that facilitate the creation of an adult identity and the negotiation of multiple and increasingly nuanced social roles. Early adolescence is thus a time of particular ferment and disorganization as the onset of puberty brings the paradoxical elements of these forces to the forefront of life. Adolescence allows a second opportunity for the individual to rework infantile conflicts even as it brings the unresolved conflicts of earlier years more sharply into focus. This phase, despite its opportunities for creativity, may present a particular challenge to the engagement in and use of the analytic process since the adolescent is particularly likely to struggle against the regression engendered by the beginning of treatment. Early adolescents are known to be a particularly difficult patient population to engage in a treatment process since they are neither children who gravitate to the traditional materials of play therapy nor are they well equipped to make use of the verbal associative "play" materials of adult psychoanalysis. If analysis is to be of use in adolescence it must entail an acknowledgement of these paradoxical aspects and actively permit an engagement with them toward the development of a potential space in which to work.

Billow (2004) has described the adolescent phase of development in Bionian terms as a "crisis in thinking" in which a "push in thought and action (occurs) that involves tolerating uncertainty and breaking emotional and conceptual links to a dependable, known reality" (p. 257). Billow notes that a protracted period of un-interpreted interaction needs to occur in the treatment, in which heightened projective-introjective activity predominates, however, he also argues for the importance of promoting symbolic relatedness, observing that the adolescent's need for "bonding" through action can easily come to serve as a defense against self-reflection. Thus, he points to the paradoxical aspect of therapeutic action in which action and reflection need to coexist, and inform the opposite process.

Relational psychoanalysts, including Pizer (1996) and Ghent (1992) have examined the paradoxical nature of the treatment process from the perspective of the co-constructed dimension of the analytic encounter. That is, they argue that action and reflection is an ongoing part of the *analyst's* as well as the patient's experience. The psychoanalysis of adolescents is particularly apt to bring this dimension into the foreground: those who write about their work with adolescents are particularly likely to stress their ongoing sense of confusion and sometimes keen sense of helplessness—even futility—as components of their countertransference responses with respect to bearing the paradoxical elements of the analysis.

Both Pizer and Ghent agree with Winnicott (1971) that a paradox is to be accepted as unresolvable. Ghent (1992), however, argues for an alternative in which patient and analyst can learn *together* to "tolerate the tension between the need for discovery and the need for closure; that one can live in the flux of subjectivity—one's own and the patient's—while at the same time residing in the externality that affords the perspective of distance" (p. 155). He believes that the key to the maintenance of this perspective lies in a form of mindful "surrender" rather than a reflexive "submission" in which one begins to feel helpless, all though this does not imply a relinquishment of a commitment to examining the similar processes that underlie paradoxical elements. In a similar vein, Pizer (1996) maintains that the analyst must strive to negotiate with the patient a potential space through playing with illusion and metaphor, describing paradoxical elements in the treatment through the adoption of a subjunctive mode of expression. That is, "I wish you were my father!" contains a simultaneous wish and the impossibility of that wish, permitting a playful exploration of this paradoxical experience.

While both Pizer and Ghent focused upon adult analysands in developing their theories, these modes of exploration may be readily applied—and perhaps are particularly important—in understanding adolescent development and psychoanalysis. In conclusion, adolescence is indeed a time for play.

Part II

Psychopathology

Chapter Four

Neurotic Inhibitions of Play

M. Hossein Etezady

> "Play for the child is not 'just play.' It is also work. It is not only a way of exploring and mastering the external world, but also, through expressing and working through phantasies, a means of exploring and mastering anxieties." —Hanna Segal, *Klein*

Our psycho-neurobiological makeup is hardwired to engage, attach and play. In the animal kingdom, rough-and-tumble horseplay is an essential feature of the development in the young of all mammals. To this, children's play adds the uniquely human dimensions of pretend mode and representational thinking, within a transitional space, in the intersubjective context of a secure relationship.

The "peek-a-boo" game can be viewed as a connection to omnipotent control of the object in order to guard against loss and separation and to restore threatened omnipotence (Kleeman, 1967). This restorative format is evident in later derivatives of peek-a-boo such as darting, hide and seek, and the game of IT. Peek-a-boo is the generator of laughter as an important intersubjectively shared experience and the progenitor of humor, wit, and jokes. The connection of play to creativity from this perspective is worthy of special note.

Play may be growth promoting or reparative inside or outside of the treatment setting. In treating children, play may be utilized in place of (Klein, 1923, 1926), or in addition to (A. Freud, 1927; Winnicott, 1967) free association and may be treated with techniques similar to dream analysis. Play, in form and content, may serve as an important diagnostic aid and tool of assessment. Play may serve communication, defense, resistance, or transference. It provides clues in the understanding of the source, significance and the impact of anxiety, ambivalence, depression, conflict, and their derivative symptoms. It can provide repetition, regulation, trial and error, realty testing, hypothesis testing, exploration, learning, problem solving, skill building, and mastery. Play prepares for unexpected or anticipated challenge. It provides entertainment, education, relaxation and a context for sublimation. It can be an exercise in anticipation, impulse control and testing of limits. It fosters enhancement of socialization, competition, rules and morality, group identification, compassion and integration (Erikson, 1950).

Play may well be regarded as the royal road to integration since its dynamic construct creates an amalgam containing elements of the id-ego-superego, defense-symptom, reality-fantasy, internal-external, self-other, or primary-secondary process, and many shades of primitive or complex affective tones. Integration, after all, is the bread and butter of normal development and the hoped for "treat" in psychoanalytic treatment.

In the formative beginnings of the psychoanalytic movement, love and work were considered the only two vital outlets for expenditure of life's energy. It was not until past the middle of the twentieth century that play became anointed as the third indispensable element in the metaphorical tripod of ideal balance one would aim to achieve in a fulfilling life of contentment and success. While love and work connote seriously valued domains of engagement and expenditure for time and energy, play and games, in contrast, were at one time regarded as no more than decadent self-indulgent excess, affordable only by a privileged few. Such whimsical expenditure of one's resources was regarded as wasteful and not worthy of serious attention or sober consideration. Loosely idling in the realm of play and fantasy were frowned upon as signs pointing to a weak and degenerate mind and questionable or deficient standards of morality. Indeed, an idle mind was once thought to be the workshop of the devil.

With the advent of psychoanalytic knowledge in normal development, pathology, adaptation, and routinely common vicissitudes of everyday life however, we now appreciate the vital importance of loosely idling and playfully expending valuable time and energy, aimlessly meandering from nothing to nowhere and from trivia to inconsequential, randomly and with no regard for where the spontaneous tides of indeterminate impulses and ambiguous urges may take us. The ability to submit to such unhindered expression of internal leanings and the compelling urgencies of spontaneous drives can be lost in those with developmental arrest, rigid obsessive defenses or an unforgiving superego incapable of allowing such adaptive flexibility. For others not handicapped by the loss of such capability, idling mindlessly or meandering loosely in any or no particularly deliberate direction, constitute an indispensable part of mental activity, that importantly forms a vast field of open horizons and barren expanses of uncertain possibilities, where the mind can stretch, float and transitionally dwell, and where mysteriously germinal seeds of imagination, creativity, and innovation may be cultivated. It is also in this mode of mental functioning that day dreaming, meditative contemplation, creative fantasy, and in the realm of penetrating psychoanalytic self-exploration, Freud's (1912) ingenious technique of free association, reside as constituent potentials.

Psychoanalytic treatment of children, ever since its inception, has relied on play material as a substitute for what in the psychoanalytic treatment of adults is utilized in the form of free association. Hermine Hug-Hellmuth, Melanie Klein (1923, 1926), and Anna Freud (1927), the founding pioneers of child analysis, made use of their young patients' play in the same manner as they might utilize free association in the case of analytic treatment of their adult patients. It should be noted that in cases of adults in analysis, basic technique requires nearly complete suspension and deliberate blocking of all motor channels in order to direct discharge of mental activity in the exclusive direction of verbal expression. Exclusive utilization of verbalization as the primary mode of self-expression however, is not within the capability of children whose neurological and cognitive facilities have not reached the level of maturity necessary for such undertaking. In moving freely from one to another of his objects of interest and locus of spontaneous activity the young patient in effect will *show*, rather than speak, in action and affect laden play activity, the derivatives of his mental contents and their dynamic interplay.

STAGING AN ENACTMENT

Not unlike the theatrical play, play activity in the treatment session is staged as a reenactment framed within the confines of a particular time and a specific place, populated by characters that serve to represent and deliver individual narratives which weave into a sequence of evolving complexity and conflict. The plot is introduced, then elaborated and thickened into a suspenseful peak before resolution.

In children's play the looseness of boundaries characteristic of primary process thinking shapes the experiential qualities of time and place. Events and characters can well be disguised substitutes for others charged with unwelcome affect, charged with impetus from forbidden wishes or might bear unbearable threats of superego reaction and shame. They may be displacements and condensations or might symbolically combine incompatible elements or contradicting opposites. Logical connections and dictates of reality in primary process thinking are unstable and labile. Magical thinking and omnipotent fantasies hold sway and wishes are not clearly delineated from reality, while the inner and the outer, and depending on the age and the developmental phase of the child, the self and the non-self can be represented and experienced as indistinctly mingled and relatively interchangeable.

Needless to say, the primary process quality of this nature is not the sole property of children's thinking or their play activities. Indeed, the emergence of mode of operation is routinely encountered in dreams, joke and humor, and creativity as well as states or regression in all age classes. Regression, a well known feature of pathological formations when irreversible and obligatory, may be utilized adaptively and normally, in the service of the ego and, at times, on a volitional basis. In the latter instance regression may be in the service of playful exploration, reaching back for the purpose of expanding one's consciousness and achieving new levels of awareness. Dreams, creativity, problem solving, innovation, art, humor, and psychoanalytic treatment are among the better known entities involving regression in the service of the ego. In play therapy, we encounter regression in part as the result of the child's pathology, as a phase specific aspect of the development or as regression in the service of the ego, as an inherent quality of playfulness and play itself, as a therapeutic byproduct of the analytic process or as the result of anxiety induced during the treatment.

It is easy from this description to conclude that in many respects play material can be treated technically much in the same manner as dream content. What follows a play segment, as well as what precedes it, can be thought of as association to the thematic content of the play segment. Any particular single element may be selected as a focus for eliciting additional elaborations and freely expanding associations. As Freud asserted, children's dreams are as a rule only sparsely disguised and their unconscious content is rather transparently accessible. The same applies to children's play material in that they fairly readily expose their latent content. Often the play surface presents, in fairly plain view, the child's anxiety, defensive disguises, the superego prohibitions and the forbidden wishes, all in the substitutive format of the immediate narrative. Respecting the child's defenses, when we enter the world of the child's play and join him in his imaginative elaborations, we may make assertions, suggestions, inquiries, additions, corrections, or interpretations that communicate to his unconscious what he may not be able to tolerate if placed within the reach of immediate and direct conscious access. Once the themes have been amply elaborated and within the displaced narrative of the play sufficiently clarified, we present the preconscious content, wrapped in a small, concise, and palatable verbal parcel. We then find that the child, in time and with gradual and careful dosing of our interpretations, is willing and able to recognize the forbidden wish, experience the anxiety provoking effects of his conflict, understand the significance of his defenses and the desperation of his need for his symptoms.

Play, therefore, can be utilized as a reenactment of intrapsychic conflicts and as an unconsciously determined expression of compromise formations, which in the same vein as any other mental product, contains derivatives of forbidden wishes. It is the search for such gratification that can activate inner threats of loss or punishment in the form of unconscious signal anxiety. Defensive modification such urges renders them adaptively feasible and in compliance with the demands of reality, one's aspiration or values and sense of self and identity. Intrapsychic conflicts of a normative nature are a part of the ongoing adaptive functioning in daily living. They are involved in progressive growth and ongoing integration of the native and acquired resources which underlie the foundations of psychological development and emotional growth. Sublimation and neutralization of primitive energies through this course of compromise formation fuel the psychic apparatus in pursuit of exploration, seeking novelty and gaining mastery through problem solving and relying on one's own innate resources of primary creativity. Intrapsychic conflicts of a pathogenic or neurotic nature, on the other hand produce symptomatic anxiety and disturbances of more or less disabling severity. They interfere with normal development, create points of fixation and regressive retreat into archaic and maladaptive patterns or defensive reactions that deprive the psychic organization of the neutralized energy that it needs for normal growth and structure formation. The quality and the content of a child's play reflects not only the degree and kind of intrapsychic conflicts being reenacted, it also provides concrete indications of the kind and quality of fixations, regressive patterns, personality traits, developmental level, vulnerability, or resiliency and the status of his or her object relationships and self state. We can differentially specify, with almost unwavering certainty, the clinical diagnosis of a given child, in as little time as a single session, by merely focusing on the young patient's play activity. We may be able to confidently determine not only that we are looking at retardation, organicity, psychosis, neurotic disturbance, depression, trauma, or personality disorder, but even the relative severity or pervasiveness of the particular pathology in question.

PLAY THERAPY IN A SAMPLE SESSION

David is seven years old, recently referred for evaluation and treatment of his anxiety, especially more pronounced since he observed a classmate vomiting in school. Since then he has been unable to eat except with great care, fuss, and ritualistic obsession. His sleep is poor and he needs his parents to stay with him while he tries to fall asleep. After he falls asleep, frequently he wakes up frightened and comes to his parents' bedroom asking to sleep with them. In the morning he is anxious, sad, and fearful, unable to eat or get ready to leave for school. For a while now, his parents have had to drive him to school and deliver him to the school nurse who has agreed to spend time to calm him and then walk him to his class where he can remain only with great difficulty for brief stretches of time. This has created considerable disruption in school and at home as the teacher, the nurse, the counselor, and the principal are trying to coordinate steps with each other and with the parents to accommodate to David's unrelenting anxiety and increasing inability to function at home or in school. He is most comfortable in the presence of his mother who is distraught, puzzled, and frustrated by David's increasing disability and ever widening circle of fears, worries, and anticipatory anxieties.

In our sessions David has been well behaved, compliant, and rather inhibited. He reluctantly comes to see me as his parents have told him that I can help with his worries if he spends time with me and gives me a chance to figure out with him why he is so afraid and sad nowadays. He has told me that he does not know why, but he is afraid that he will get sick and throw up, as did the boy he witnessed in school several weeks before his parents came to see me. He knows that he can use the toys in the office if he wants to, make pictures if he likes and say anything that pops to his mind during our work together. He has been quietly skeptical of all this latitude and somewhat surprised that he can do and say so much so freely, which he thinks is so different from what is allowed in school, at home, or at other doctors' offices. In previous visits he has made several pictures, has explored my games and toys, and has compared his games and toys as well as those of his friends' to what he sees in the office. He is especially attracted to the army men and soldiers as well as the figures of space men. We have had a few conversations about his family, his younger brother, parents and relatives, his friends, interests, and future hopes. His speech, actions, and reactions have been carefully measured, subdued and rather tightly contained. He watches carefully for my reactions and seems acutely aware of how he might affect me.

In today's session he is quiet and pensive. Later he looks as if he wants an indication from me as to how or where to start. I say that it looks like he has something on his mind and that he is wondering where to begin. As if driven by an internal urgency to gauge the safety of the treatment setting, he cautiously, slowly and quietly plays out the pursuit of villains who have robbed the bank and are now getting away. A police car is starting to chase after them. The robbers are speeding and the police chasing, bobbing and weaving, changing directions everywhere across the table. In contrast to the high speed and frantic content the play presentation is the curiously toned-down movements and gestures. He is noticeably restrained, his affect deliberately contained and vocalizations at a whisper level, barely audible and in brief spurts. I comment on how careful, quiet and slow all this chasing and escaping is. He says it is night time, everyone is asleep and will be mad if awakened by the noise. We chat about night time when people sleep and dangerous things he imagines happening. That bad people can do bad things and having someone who can get after them and stop them. He complains about his little brother crying at night, always wanting something, how he can't wait and how even in the middle of the night he wakes everyone up by crying and making noise. "Sometimes," he says, "I wish he was never born. I want to really let him have it, but he is such a cry baby; if I hit him I will really be in trouble, but when he hits me nobody does anything." He then adds, "I know you are supposed to love your brother and I do, but sometimes I just can't stand him." He then asks me what he should do about his little brother. I commented that just like in the cops and robbers story he showed us before, he is afraid if he does something he isn't supposed to do he will be in trouble. I added sometimes people wish they could take anything they want and do anything they please and get away with, but there is a kind of police inside them that tries to stop them and punish them for being bad. I said, "There is a part of you that wants to be in your little brother's place and have anything you want and hit or hurt or take, any time you like, but then there is another part of you that says you have to be good and not make any one mad at you. Sometimes you have such a lot of mixed feeling, they pull you to opposite directions and you are caught in the middle, it is very hard on you and you don't know what to do." He is listening. Then he returns to his game. Now the game is more free, noisy and spirited. The riders are jumping high, make wheelies, yell out, and trash talk. They are now racing, speeding around fearlessly, no longer cops and robbers, but rivals competing. He stops briefly between squeals of wheels and sputtering of engines to say, "I like coming here. I didn't used to, but now I think it's cool." I say that I am glad that he doesn't mind coming here so much anymore. Later he is calmer, leaves the toys on the table, sits on the couch and tells me about rides and trips with his parents, cars, his father's car, speeding and danger of accidents and getting tickets. I comment on the thrill and the temptation of speeding past the rules and limits against the danger of injury and punishment unless you stop yourself. When the times comes for picking up and putting away the toys before ending the session, he is having difficulty finishing up and getting ready to leave. I say it is hard to stop when we are in the middle of so much to talk about and everything we need to figure out. Still not leaving, he asks if he can bring to the next session one of his own toys.

A VIEW OF THE CONTEXT

David is a relatively healthy, intelligent, verbal, and well behaved child, raised in an intact family of affectionate and devoted parents who enjoy a stable and secure marriage. He is a nearly ideal example of a good child-patient in analytic treatment. He enjoys good object relationships, an intact ego, and a superego which is well developed and, by all accounts and considerations, entirely too severe. He is conscientious, dutiful, and somewhat of a perfectionist. Judging by the presentation of the silent, dangerous, and forbidden activity in the dark of the night (when children may wake up to noise and bewilderingly frightening commotion of the parents' bedroom), one might assume overwhelming arousal of sexual and aggressive id content, in response to a probable primal scene exposure, necessitating robust defensive superego response, resulting in severe separation and castration anxiety. Previous to the onset of his anxiety and disabling symptoms, David seemed to be thriving well. He was enthusiastically involved in sport activities and displayed natural ability and grace. He out-performed peers and cousins in his own age group and was attracting a good deal of attention and many accolades. His school work came to him easily and he had excellent grades. Since the start of his symptoms, he had completely retired from all sport activities and any competitive engagement all together. Although he was missing many classes and some days he was unable to go to school, he continued to do well academically and his grades were high as usual. He had difficulty sleeping, and could not stay in his own bedroom alone. He was eating very little, maintained a severely restricted diet and would not eat away from home. When I tried to explore his eating difficulties he could only say that he was afraid he might get sick and throw up if he was not careful. His parents reported only two episodes of vomiting in the past; once in kindergarten when he was briefly stricken with a viral infection and a second time near the end of the summer, before the start of the current school year, when the possibility of food poisoning was suspected. Everyone was relieved when he recovered soon and needed no medical attention. He had seemed frightened of the vomiting and refused solid foods for a few days. Parents reported that the sudden onset of symptoms was precipitated by his witnessing another student throwing up at mealtime in school. Shortly after this event, he seemed obsessed with the fear of becoming sick and was afraid to go to school, where he was overcome with anxiety, aggravated by a stomach upset that would relent partly, only after he was sent home in the company of his mother.

The outcome of David's treatment was good. He was seen three and later two times a week. An oscillating course of relief and relapse characterized his long term progress. By the time we had to stop his treatment as his family was moving away from the area, he was eating with far fewer restrictions, was able to attend school regularly, and had no need for his parents to stay with him at night. He was not as concerned with getting sick and his mood and anxiety had improved to the relief and delight of his parents. He had resumed many of his older hobbies and had also developed new ones. He continued to do well in school and was a conscientious worker. He was however not able to resume his athletic activities in spite of encouragement by parents and school personnel. He continued to be intolerant and easily disturbed by scenes of rowdy and unruly behavior, which might break out at different times among the students. David and his parents knew that our work was not complete and were willing to seek help in their new location, if necessary.

BEYOND THE MANIFEST CONTENT

The evenly hovering attention that Freud advocated in the process of listening to the analytic material with adults, of course is an essential element in working with children as well. As we listen we are thinking not only about the here and now, the setting, the immediate circumstances, the recent events, the material we have heard recently, but also the associations implied to the past, to the extra-analytic present, the transference and the countertransference. We endeavor to remain in tune with our own associations in response to the material and be ready to zero in more closely at the intersecting junctures where the patient's material and our evenly hovering associations appear to converge. For example, in response to David's play material many avenues of investigation are presented. What, one might wonder, is the significance of the concern about taking care not to wake up anyone? Is there a danger, or a wish, implicit in the concern about him, waking up himself via the analytic exploration? He, waking me up, as a scoptophilic transgressor-child, absorbed in the mesmerizing drama of the primal scene? Or, will I be the punitively irate father, chasing after the transgressing child who is looking to see and know what is beyond the realm of the permissible? Are we dealing with his wish-fear of David waking up his own frightening monsters and beasts of greed and sadistic mayhem, or the threat of arousing the eruptive forces of instinctual drive derivatives, or the ominous threats and condemnations of an exacting superego? And, in the same open ended, all inclusive vein, who is chasing whom? Is he the chaser-intruder or is he being chased or intruded upon? Will I be chasing and intruding or be chased and intruded upon by him? And, in any case, why and for what purpose? What is the motivation and what of the intended results? These and numerous other questions cannot be readily answered but need to hover freely within the sphere of our global attention, as the evolving analytic material gradually narrows the field and as our grasp of the pertinent meaning reaches deeper. We may wonder about the place and significance of night as well as dark, both in terms of the sinister horrors of the archaic and repressed past experience as well as in active, conscious or unconscious fantasy or the tantalizing temptation of mysteries not intended to be approached or to become known. It may serve as a welcome relief and a sweeping defensive measure to keep oneself in the dark. Overwhelming affective onslaught may be engendered by the fantasy or the actual experience of being left in the dark, excluded and traumatized by envy, murderous rage, frustrated wish, dashed hopes, and the crushed narcissism of a small, insignificant child, feeling displaced and defeated by a powerful and unpredictable rival. What happens if one is too greedy and wants everything? Does the manifest format of David's play intend to serve as denial of responsibility for active intent, as if to say it is not me but someone else, the little brother, who wants everything, not me but the father who breaks the rules, recklessly driving, unhindered by prohibitions, showing off his wears, intent on exhibiting phallic superiority?

FOUR ESSENTIAL ELEMENTS OF TECHNIQUE

By remaining equidistant from the id, the ego and the superego, neutrally but empathically attuned, we enter the play in order to meet the child where he is in fantasy, defensive displacement and affective experience and in order to make room for the development of a safe and responsive holding environment, conducive to the emergence of a therapeutic alliance and in time an observing ego, capable of self observation and self reflection. As we attend to the flow and the content of the play material we engage in a steady and focused sequence of running commentaries. Running commentary is an important element in the early part of work with the material. It serves many beneficial ends. It introduces the child to our attentiveness and our manner of receiving, valuing and utilizing what he presents. It exemplifies our mode of communication which is centered around the use of words to signify and put into a narrative order the seemingly random emergence of behavior and nonverbal expression that may not otherwise bear sufficient value or significance in the child's conscious experience. We move, gradually and in time, to clarification, by weaving our running commentary into a coherent statement of how various pieces of action and communication coalesce to present a meaningful and new view of what has transpired. The child is able to discover not only how the analytic process works but more importantly, how his mind works and how seemingly unrelated fragments of behavior and verbalization can be assembled into patterns and trends that are meaningful and lead to larger and more informative pictures. After clarifications on a particular sequence or repetitive behavioral patterns have been offered in an empathic manner so as to render our intervention palatable, the time may have come for the next order of intervention, i.e., that of confrontation. In applying the technical tool of confrontation we attempt to bring to the child's attention the fact that what we have been gathering, piecing together, and clarifying, all in the realm of displaced or disavowed play material, does indeed fall at his own door and applies to him in concrete and actual instances. Demonstrations are offered in his own statements, expressions and repeated experiences. Here we need to be particularly attuned to the child's narcissistic vulnerability and deliver the confrontational message with utmost tact, sensitivity, and exquisite regard for his capacity for tolerating the impact of the statement, lest it might be too great an insult to his age appropriate omnipotence and fragile sense of self.

The next and final element of technique to become applicable is the element of interpretation, which attempts to address the findings so far gathered and noted in running commentary, clarified in context, and eventually presented as the child's own displaced and disavowed material in the form of confrontation, and at this juncture connect them to the deeper layers of the child's emotional experience not accessible to immediate consciousness. By now what we have tried to gather in running commentary, polish in careful clarification, and finally present in tactful confrontation, is associatively so closely linked to those layers of awareness that we refer to as the preconscious, that it now takes but little effort to render the heretofore unconscious material conscious, so that where the id once was there shall the ego be. This enlightenment and deepening of the child's self-awareness and of self-reflective capability results in mastery over the conflict-producing drive derivatives, strengthening of the ego, and the expansion of the ego resources which enhance capacities in synthetic function, affect tolerance, self-regulatory capability, and superego modification. Such interpretation may connect the surface to the depth and the past to the present, both within the current realm of the emotional experience outside of the treatment setting as well as in the area of historical and psychogenetic significance, particularly as relived in the presently enlivened and affectively mobilized here and now, within the experiential domain of the transference.

PLAY AS A UBIQUITOUS DEVELOPMENTAL FEATURE

In the last quarter of the first year the infant is on the threshold of the intersubjective phase of the development of the self (Stern, 1985), self and object differentiation (Mahler et al, 1975), heralded by Spitz's (1963, 1965) "second organizer," usually arising at this juncture, in the form of stranger anxiety. While the advent of object constancy needs to await the completion of separation-individuation process at about thirty-six months of age, by nine months of age object permanence in Piaget's (1963) sense, has begun to be established. The emerging self of the neonatal period has evolved into the core self of the symbiotic phase and is by now capable of intersubjective engagement. With the establishment of object permanence the child now shows the ability to conceive of, and actively seek an object which may be lost out of sight, as for example, he follows the trajectory of a ball rolling out of sight, or a spoon falling off the table, as if to locate it, after its disappearance. Losing and relocating objects gradually become an important part of the child's cognitive and emotional repertoire. A well known and heartwarming extension of this phenomena is the universal game of peek-a-boo, which becomes a source of endless joy, delight, and consuming amusement, both for the child as well as the adults in charge of his care. Peek-a-boo remains the main staple of playful frivolity between the child and his caretakers, well into toddlerhood and beyond. Past toddlerhood, peek-a-boo maintains its fascination and anticipatory excitement as it transforms into its next morphological extension, in the form of the hide-and-seek game. An intermediate step between these two forms of play is darting. The new toddler of the practicing subphase, intoxicated by his newly acquired capability for upright locomotion and being able to more rapidly move in any direction, abruptly moves away toward a distant target of attraction, only to be interrupted by the panic stricken caretaker who runs to catch up and sweeps up the darting toddler in order to avert potential harm or to avoid impending danger. Some children soon learn to induce a less than fully attentive mother to run and sweep them up, as if by doing so they can magically transform a distant and detached mother into an engulfing and hovering caretaker.

The fascination, excitement, and energy of peek-a-boo derive from several different sources. We may begin with the evocation of the idealized symbiotic reunion and exerting magical control over the secure availability of the object. This is tentatively challenged by the pending threat of the loss of the object and the disruption of the child's illusion of omnipotent control resulting in narcissistic deflation. The suspense, ambiguity, and looming anxiety is then instantly removed by the sudden reappearance of the missing object, in the form of the familiar beaming gaze and the stimulating visage of the mother, charged with the overflowing fullness of positive affect which triggers in the infant, an explosion of laughter and delight, usually in an unending series of repetitions. We might say that this game provides the child with an opportunity to flirt, play, and benevolently experiment, with miniscule and manageable doses of loss, ambiguity, anxiety, and narcissistic deflation, before recovering and fully reconstituting at a more secure level of attachment and higher level of confidence.

Early on, the child learns to turn the passive into active by initiating the game while he covers his own eyes and then looks to find the missing object where he expects it to be. Another, later version of the game of hide and seek, is the game of IT, in which the individual designated as IT, chases and catches another member of the group who then becomes IT until he in turn, succeeds in catching still another member.

The peek-a-boo game and its nodal elements continue to influence and organize many other aspects of normative and cultural development. An example of this kind of influence is that which underlies the development of humor and the unique effect of jokes. Here we encounter higher levels of abstraction, symbolization and cognitive maturity. To appreciate this connection we may begin with the ubiquity of smile, initially as a mere reflexive motor response that early in the neonatal periods forms the "first organizer" (Spitz 1963, 1965) as a specific response to the Gestalt of the maternal visage. Laughter later is imposed upon this foundation much as speech in time overlies breathing. Laughter, in an intersubjective context, is first encountered as the central feature of peek-a-boo. It represents an organizational "click" which signifies expulsive relief, in alleviation of disturbing ambiguity, disquieting suspense of uncertainty, and anxiety, as the reassuring recovery of the lost object is accomplished and secured during the game of peek-a-boo. Having said this about laughter as a developmental acquisition we may look for the origins of humor and the capacity for use and appreciation of jokes.

Humor, as a developmental acquisition becomes available later, when the mind is capable of entertaining a pretend mode of thinking and can simultaneously hold two disparate frames and more than one version of reality in mind. Humor requires the developmental acquisition of having attained the ability to entertain and utilize a lighter, deeper, larger, and more complex perception of the apparent reality, and thereby creating a more flexible, novel and yet familiar construct that is fresh, enlightening, and liberating. Similar to the peek-a-boo game, the punch line in a joke particularly, and humor generally, serve to relieve us from the disquieting ambiguity and the disturbing suspense that is posed by a premise that has captured our attention and is in need of a liberating resolution. Like the gleaming gaze and the gleefully intruding visage of the recovered idealized maternal object in peek-a-boo, the punch line usually uncovered unexpectedly and by surprise, breaks the ambiguity, the suspense, the anxiety or the boring platitude of a challenging situation, by accessing a delightfully fresh and illusive configuration, placed instantly within our intimate grasp. It offers a closure as it opens new horizons. It is exquisitely novel yet surprisingly familiar. In this manner play, humor, and creativity share an element of surprise, innovation, and creation of novelty by taking the mundane and the routine and transforming them into a different and more meaningful configuration by addition of elements derived from one's internal experience, unwittingly, unconsciously, and intuitively.

PLAY AS A TRANSITIONAL SPACE

Winnicott (1953) defines a psychological space that is located transitionally between the self and the object wherein play takes place. It is in this space, located outside the self, where the repudiated object remains available and responsive, and returns to the infant what he puts out with a degree of modification, that allows the infant to take it back and by using it in its modified version he creates a new construct which the mother takes and uses in play within this transitional space. It is the mother's ability to tolerate the infant's repudiation and remain engaged in this playful interaction that provides the possibility for the child to learn to play. This is a developmental acquisition that promotes learning, creativity, mastery and emotional as well as cognitive growth. In this sense play carries a significant value in its own right, apart from any autoerotic or masturbatory attributes which have been the main focus of attention of the early psychoanalytic writers. In fact Winnicott (1967) explains that when autoerotic activity begins play stops immediately. This is based on the fact that while autoerotic and masturbatory activity are centrally concerned with the self, play by contrast, takes place outside the self and in a transitional space between the self and the object. Winnicott also emphasizes the role of play in promoting developmental progress even in the absence of insight, narrative formation, or self-reflection. Play can be therapeutic and may facilitate psychological progression by itself and regardless of interpretive intervention. In a therapeutic setting it can serve the purpose of trial and error, problem solving, and conflict resolution even without verbal interpretation by the therapist. Psychoanalytic treatment itself may be viewed as a highly developed form of play which facilitates regression in the service of the ego and allows the analyst and the analysand to enter this transitional space in which both members of the dyad can play with puzzling questions, ambiguous entities, and unrealistic fantasies. When the analyst receives the patient's repudiation, holds and contains the affective content, and responds by returning it in a sufficiently modified version that can be used by the patient in forming a new and useable construct, an intersubjective field for this kind of play is provided. This enhances the analysand's ability to play and to use his own creative capacity in the service of the analytic aims. In this sense it might be said that one of the tasks of treatment is to teach our patient to play. This would particularly be necessary in those cases whose early developmental experiences may have been void of the good enough early care which ordinarily should provide empathic attunement, emotional availability, and secure attachment. In the therapeutic setting it is through this kind of playful engagement and empathic attunement that self-reflection, insight and self regulation may be restored and enhanced as the analytic function is, through this process, internalized.

Understanding how one's own mind, or the mind of others works, is not possible without the help of a person who is capable of holding in mind and reflecting one's state of mind. The normative move from the early "actual" or the "psychic equivalence" mode of thinking to the later "pretend" mode and the subsequent integration of these two modes into representational and symbolic thinking may be arrested in children who have not had such a person available or when the content of the mind of their caretaker has been too traumatic to be tolerated as an aspect of reality that could be metabolized. Play therapy can provide an opportunity for these children to learn to reflect upon, understand and beneficially utilize their own mental states as well as those of others and thereby better anticipate and regulate their own emotions and empathically participate in relationships with others.

EVOLVING LEVELS OF PLAY

Infants begin exploring their environment first in primitive sensory-motor reflexive activity. Initial patterns of action and response gradually coalesce to form a repertoire of skills and coordinated behavior which continually expand into increasingly higher levels of complexity and flexibility. Even in the earliest neonatal hours and days infants display preferences for some forms, sounds, colors, lights, and movements. In time, reaching, touching, grabbing and eventually holding, first by one hand and soon by two, in coordination, expand the domain of exploration and allow for a more intimate appreciation of whatever that can be manually grasped, and for still closer inspection, placed in the mouth. By the middle to the end of the second year the toddler can carry a doll and treat it as if it were a baby. This is a level of concrete symbolism that is the result of "actual" thinking or psychic equivalency (Fonagy and Target, 1997), when the child equates his own thoughts with reality. By the fourth and fifth year when the child has reached higher levels of self and object constancy and is aware of gender differences, he is capable of differentiating pretend from reality. By now peers can be included in play, but there is no playing together even when other children are involved. The rules are self-made and egocentric and everybody can win. By age seven and eight rules begin to matter but are not always stable or clear until age ten or eleven. By age twelve, when formal operations are available, rules are stable and the preadolescent can apply them consistently. Rivalry and competition with oedipal and pre-oedipal themes dominate many forms of play throughout childhood and beyond. In early childhood play is often free flowing and without firm rules or limits but beginning in latency games become more organized, standardized, and more tightly structured. By adolescence games are highly organized, more complex, and arduously pursued. Individual aspirations, self-esteem, and group identification in team membership gain increasing prominence as skill, persistence and resiliency also become sources of pride and aspiration. Many of these features and persuasions extend far into adulthood and continue to provide valuable peer affiliation, socialization, group identification, and camaraderie in varying forms of hobbies, recreational activities, stress reduction, or perhaps even professional pursuit of games and sports.

Elements of competition and rivalry affect different children differently based on their character, life experience, and their developmental achievements. For example, at age eight Alex has a reputation at home and in school for his dramatic temper tantrums. He is easily frustrated and becomes violent when things don't go his way. He can only play with children who are younger and whom he can boss and control. He has no friends and can't tolerate losing. He is unable to finish any games if he is not winning and is used to introducing his own new rules as he goes, in order to ensure that he is always ahead.

Seven-year-old Ben is a good swimmer and loves the attention and affirmation he receives for his prowess and his willingness to work hard and long, trying to improve his time, again and again. Soon however, he runs into competition with a newcomer in his age group who is quite exceptional in his ability and repeatedly out performs Ben. Ben is distraught and discouraged as he finally and mournfully decides to give up swimming competition and to vacate his high standing and relinquish his ranking and prestige. He no longer finds the endless hours of exhausting practice worth the results he is forced to accept. We discuss these developments while Ben does his best, with his parents' support, to recapture his first-place standing, to no avail. He decides to stop and his parents and coaches support his decision after much deliberation. In time he is able to reassess his situation and confines his swimming to casual recreation. He spends more time hiking and fishing which brings him closer to his uncles and cousins and gives him exposures to more social and family activities he had been missing for a long time. His parents are sympathetic and pleased with his ability to respond to a tough challenge thoughtfully and realistically, while adjusting his routine to find new and rewarding outlets for healthy competition and acquisition of new skills. The parents believe that he has gained from a difficult experience and are pleased how he has been able to use our sessions to constructively negotiate his dilemma.

Chrissy was a shy but very intelligent fifth grader, the only daughter and the oldest of her parents' four children, each about two years apart in age. She was beset by self-blame and shame when she repeatedly underperformed on tests and mysteriously sabotaged herself by making minor mistakes that she knew she should not have. Being the best and at the top of her class was very important to her since she knew she was capable and worked hard to be her academic best. Chrissy was becoming increasingly anxious, compulsive, and restricted in her extracurricular activities as she was driving harder and harder to prevent her inexplicable errors which too often resulted in lower grades. It was in the course of playing card games and checkers that we observed together how difficult it was for her to allow herself to get ahead or win. Each time she did well or had a lucky hand she became anxious, lost concentration, and could not perform as well as she knew she could. Associations to her play material and reconstruction uncovered frightening hatred and murderous impulses, disguised in dreams and fantasy toward her three siblings and her parents whom she unconsciously felt were leaving her out and depriving her of what she wanted to be exclusively hers. While consciously she took grudging pride in helping her parents in caring for the younger siblings, unconsciously she felt robbed, enslaved, slighted, and denigrated. For her rage, envy, and forbidden wishes, unconsciously she felt guilty and deserving of punishment and suffering. Even more intense were her unconscious envy, rivalry, and hatred toward her mother whom she feared (wished) she might destroy and replace as a greedy and dangerous rival who had monopolized the affection and power of the father whose company Chrissy craved and who was often away at work and on trips. Chrissy's unresolved oedipal conflicts created unconscious guilt, lowered self esteem, anxiety, and inhibition of her aggression and intellectual ability. She needed to defeat herself rather than chancing the unspeakable dangers of allowing herself the forbidden gratification of an oedipal victory.

CONCLUDING REMARKS

The significance of play as a developmental need, promoter and facilitator, as well as an important component of normality and requirement for mental health has clearly been established and confirmed rather recently, through psychoanalytic observations, clinical experience and research. Play therapy as a technical modality in treating children has been widely and successfully applied since the early pioneers of child analysis began working with young children. In psychoanalytic treatment of children play is utilized as a substitute for free association which is the essential instrument of analysis in treatment of adults. Because of the pretend quality of play material and its relative distance from the center of the self experience, material exposed in the course of play activity tends to invoke relatively little resistance and may therefore be more easily addressed in the form of running commentary, clarification, confrontation, and eventually interpretation. The form and content of play reflects the child's developmental level of maturity as well as psychosexual conflicts, whether pre-oedipal or oedipal and may serve as a potent aid and confirmatory device in making differential diagnoses. It can help clarify questions regarding the qualitative and quantitative aspects of pathology and functional impairment. Similar to dreams, play can be used as a royal road to the unconscious in order to access the realm of repressed fantasies and primitive drives. Play has a unique role in mastering loss and trauma, working through unresolved conflict, acquiring new skills, as well as using and enhancing imagination and creativity. It helps in testing reality and accommodating to demanding challenges of reality through anticipatory strategizing and the use of trial and error.

Learning to play takes place in a transitional space, outside the self and between the self and the object. It requires the presence of a care taker who is able to return to the child what has been repudiated, with a sufficient degree of modification that allows the child to receive and in turn return it with a degree of modification effected by him. The caregiver's receptive availability and empathic accommodation enhances the emergence of meaning, intersubjectivity, reflective capacity, and the ability to, in time know one's own mind as well as the mind of others.

Inside as well as outside the treatment setting play can be reparative, corrective, constructive, growth promoting, and instrumental in conflict resolution, even without verbal or narrative accounting of its content or any interpretive intervention. In treatment setting we strive for eventual verbalization of the latent content as the fragmented or disguised elements in the material become integrated and begin to rise to a level between the preconscious and consciousness.

In examining the peek-a-boo game I have suggested that the emergence of laughter as a new capacity in relationship to playful recovery of a nearly lost object creates a predictable and controlled premise of suspense, ambiguity, anxiety, and pending danger that is abruptly terminated when the concealed object is revealed, thereby inducing an explosion of expulsive tension and profound delight in achieving relief. I have traced this set of central dynamics in the context of other games but particularly in the underpinnings of humor, in general, and the place of the punch line in jokes, in particular. I have explained that humor requires the capacity to think in a pretend mode and being able to hold in mind more than one concrete and egocentric version of reality simultaneously. When developmental deficits or trauma impede the emergence of this capacity, self-reflection, affect regulation and appreciation of the state of mind of others as well as one's own mind, will be impeded. The capacity to use play in a creative and progressively productive manner will be impeded. In the case of those who present to us, in treatment, with such developmental arrests we provide the holding, containing, and transformative experiences that allow for the emergence and plastic productivity of play, leading to the integration of the split-off aspects of disavowed or un-metabolized past experiences. It is in this sense that we invoke Winnicott's (1967) observation that the analytic experience itself can be thought of as a higher level of play.

Chapter Five

Normal and Pathological Playfulness

Salman Akhtar

> "As we travel the difficult path from primitive to sophisticated expression, the best outcome is to be able to choose our own behavior, depending on what circumstances require. Ideally, we learn to adopt, quite genuinely, the consciousness of the accountant, or the poet, or anything in between." —Stephen Appelbaum, *Evocativeness: Moving and Persuasive Interventions in Psychotherapy*

Allow me to begin this contribution on the notion of playfulness by talking about a revolver. Yes, you read it right: a revolver. The story goes like this: Donald Winnicott was to present a paper to the British Psychoanalytic Society. After being introduced, he walked up to the podium, opened his briefcase, took out his paper and also a revolver which he carefully placed on the lectern. A hush fell over the audience. Winnicott began reading his paper and, after a few minutes, stopped and said something like this: "In case you are wondering what this revolver is doing here, let me tell you. It is intended for the person who, instead of discussing my ideas, would begin his remarks by declaring that what I am presenting is not psychoanalysis." The audience laughed, a bit awkwardly to be sure. Winnicott then went on with reading his paper.

This anecdote is radiant with a deft admixture of light-heartedness, bold yet restrained expression of an instinctual agenda and, with a wink to all the parties involved in the interaction, a thinning of the boundary between reality and unreality. It depicts playfulness in all its glory. But let me not get ahead of myself. Instead let me lay out the plan of this discourse. I will begin by elucidating the phenomenon of playfulness and its various drive-based, ego-anchored, and object-relational constituents. Then I will trace the developmental origins of the capacity for playfulness. Following this, I will move into the realm of psychopathology and discuss the relationship of playfulness to character organization, its potential overlap with "manic defense" (Klein,

1935; Winnicott, 1935), and five specific types of pathological playfulness. I will also illustrate the role of playfulness in analytic technique with the help of some clinical vignettes. I will conclude by pulling this material together and raising some questions for us to consider.

NORMAL PLAYFULNESS

The meaning of the word "play" seems self-evident yet upon closer look turns out to be surprisingly multifaceted. "Play" can mean "a recreational activity," "a particular maneuver in a game," "brisk, fitful, or light movement" (e.g., the gem presented a dazzling play of colors), "unimpeded motion" (e.g., the piston had a lot of play), "the stage presentation of a story," "to fiddle with something," and so on (*Webster's Collegiate Dictionary*, 1998, p. 892). Additional connotations of "play" are evident in the contexts of theatre ("playing a role"), music ("playing an instrument") and sexuality ("foreplay," "playing around," "playing the field," "playboy") as well as in the sphere of language via exaggeration ("to play up a point") and humor (through "wordplay"). With the exception of philandering, acts involved in these wide-ranging contexts are harmless, amusing, and enjoyable. They also have an element of freshness and make-believe quality. The mental operation underlying them is akin to what Peter Fonagy and Mary Target (1996) have termed "pretend mode." This consists of the knowledge that internal experience might not reflect the facts of external reality and the separation of internal and external reality with the accompanying assumption that an internal state has no actual impact upon the external reality.

These attributes of "play" discerned through its linguistic versatility also feature in psychoanalytic writings on the subject. However, the gaze is deeper here. The founder of psychoanalysis, Sigmund Freud, noted the subtleties of play—largely involving words and visual images—in the creation of dreams (1900) and jokes (1905). Addressing child's play, Freud (1908) wrote the following remarkable passage:

> Might we not say that every child at play behaves like a creative writer, in that he creates a world of his own, or, rather, rearranges the things of his world in a new way which pleases him? It would be wrong to think he does not take that world seriously; on the contrary, he takes his play very seriously and he expends large amounts of emotion on it. The opposite of play is not what is serious but what is real. In spite of all the emotion with which he cathects his world of play, the child distinguishes it quite well from reality. (pp. 143–44)

An implication of this proposal is that play (and its trait counterpart, playfulness) is not supposed to have consequences in reality. There is a quality of transience as well as fantasy to it. Indeed, Freud (1911) traced the origin of fantasizing to childhood play and, in a celebrated observation of the *fort-da* game of his eighteen-month-old grandson (1920), discovered the adaptive purposes of playfulness.

Subsequent contributions to the psychoanalytic understanding of play (Ferenczi, 1932; Waelder, 1933; Fenichel, 1946; Alexander, 1958; Erikson, 1950; Winnicott, 1971) underscored the fact that play serves many purposes. These include mastery of conflict, reworking of trauma, comprehension of external reality, and fine-tuning of ego skills. These contributions have, however, remained focused upon children's play and give the adult personality attribute of playfulness short shift. The work of Donald Winnicott (1953, 1971) constitutes a major exception. He described the "transitional realm" or the "intermediate area of experience" where reality and unreality are put aside, imagination is born, and paradox reigns supreme. Once developed, this psychic "area" remains available for the rest of life. It is the location of cultural experience. Poetry, fiction, metaphor, games, faith, and religious belief all reside here and so does playfulness. In being playful, an individual takes a temporary leave from the constraints of reality, knowingly enjoys the pleasure of "absurdity," and, in the process, lets his authentic self emerge.

Emphasizing the ego-replenishing features of such an attitude and paraphrasing Freud (1900), Erik Erikson (1950) has called play "the royal road to the understanding of the infantile ego at synthesis" (p. 209). He regards play as an ego function and an attempt to synchronize the somatic and the social strands of the self. According to Erikson, "When man plays he must intermingle with things and people in an uninvolved and light fashion. He must do something which he has chosen to do without being compelled but urgent interests or impelled by strong passion; he must feel entertained and free of any fear or hope of serious consequences. He is on vacation from social and economic reality" (1950, p. 212).

Erikson underscores how moments of playfulness allow a periodical stepping out from the strictures of reality (including gravity and time) and can be seen in social settings and in love life. Freed from "the compulsions of conscience and impulsions of irrationality" (p. 214), man can feel authentically one with his ego. Through play, he can express his inner agenda in an aim-inhibited and socially acceptable way. The pleasure of discharge brings about ego-relaxation. Later reflection (conscious or preconscious) upon what underlies the play deepens the ego's reach and makes self-knowledge possible. A remark about the nature of poetry made by Nobel Prize winning Irish poet, Seamus Heaney, captures this point with remarkable precision. Heaney (1995) declared that in writing (and reading) poetry, the movement is always from "delight to wisdom" (p. 5) and not the other way round.

The mention of poetry serves as a bridge to cross over from the island of play, about which much has been written, to the nation of playfulness about which psychoanalytic literature is relatively silent. The word does not appear in the index to the *Standard Edition* of Freud's writings and in any of the twenty-seven psychoanalytic glossaries published so far (see Akhtar, 2009, for a critical review of them). A search of the *PEP Web,* the computerized compendium of psychoanalytic literature reveals only seven papers with "playfulness" in their titles over the last one hundred and twenty years (Auerhahn and Laub, 1987; Moran, 1987; Shengold, 1988; Ehrenberg, 1990; Feiner, 1990, 1992; Solnit, 1998;). What I have to say about playfulness is derived from Winnicott's (1953, 1960, 1971) contributions, the seven papers mentioned above, and my clinical and social experience.

The first point that needs to be made is that "play" is an act and "playfulness" is an attitude, which is harder to define. Psychoanalytic literature shows various authors fumbling in an effort to describe "playfulness." George Moran (1987) explicitly states that he found "the notion of playfulness difficult to define" (p. 15) though three qualities do occur consistently with it. These include (i) light-heartedness, (ii) a pleasure-oriented flexibility in commitment to reality, and (iii) the retention of the knowledge that one is not being "serious." Mortimer Ostow (1987) notes that while "play" and "playfulness" are free from the restrictions of logic, "the tendency to play and the tendency to be playful are not necessarily correlated" (p. 195). He makes an emphatic distinction between them, stating that a playful attitude is actually the converse of play. "The fully engaged player disengages himself from reality, enjoys the disengagement, but obtains even greater pleasure by reintroducing a small amount of reality. The playful attitude on the other hand takes full cognizance of reality but, by treating it as if it were a joke, alternates, to some degree, its accompanying pain or stress" (p. 195).

The need to bear the burdens that come from accepting reality and the possibility to derive enjoyment from debunking reality bring up scenarios of early development that contribute to the genesis of playfulness.

DEVELOPMENTAL ORIGINS

The origins of playfulness can be traced to the earliest period of infancy when the social referencing and pleasure in the discovery of new relational and conceptual patterns make their first appearance (Emde, 1991). The child's obvious delight in exploring the mother's face, hair, and necklace, etc., observing his own hand movements, delightedly responding to the cooing noises of the mother and of his own are all early prototypes from which the later, more complex and subtle phenomenon of playfulness would evolve. An important step in this development is mother's introduction of the peek-a-boo game. This facilitates the tolerance of her absence in a judiciously dosed, pleasurable way (Kleeman, 1967) and shows the child that real-unreal confusion ("has the mother gone" or "is she still there?") can be used for ego-enriching purposes. The rupture of relatedness (via mother's disappearance) is coupled with the joy of reunion (via her reappearance) and mutuality (in the increasingly solid retention of the shared knowledge that she *will* reappear). Initially passive in their interaction, the child gradually adopts a more active role in the game. He anticipates it and, at times, even initiates it.

While all this is well recognized, three psychoanalytic contributions need special mention. Winnicott (1953, 1960, 1971) holds the child's capacity for playfulness to be a major sign of healthy development. Playfulness is a poem written by the true self. Winnicott's (1989) "squiggle game,"[1] a technique of working with children in psychotherapy, is anchored in this conviction. Essentially, it consists of the therapist drawing a wave-like line or figure on a paper and inviting the child patient to add to it or to draw something of his own, to which the therapist can add. He and the child then take turns to "complete" some sort of a picture from their random "drawings." The result of this game could be likened to dreams, since it was a representation of the unconscious. While the game is initiated by the therapist, the two partners must remain equally active in playing it. Spontaneity and surprise are necessary elements to such interaction.

Echoes of Winnicott's (1953) emphasis upon the "gentlemanly agreement" between the parents and child that his attachment to his "transitional object" will not be questioned are also to be found in Martin Stein's (1985) observation on the birth of the capacity for irony. Stein writes,

> We urge the child to eat his breakfast; he responds with a defiant "No!" and may make his point even clearer by dumping his cereal on the floor. The wily mother, or father as the case may be, changes the procedure. She says, with mock severity, "Don't you dare eat that cereal!" The child looks at her mischievously and immediately proceeds to wolf down his breakfast, as if in defiance. The mother portrays a kind of mock horror, perhaps even exclaiming, "You bad child!" Both laugh gleefully, enjoying the process. This is clearly ironic. The command, "Don't you dare eat that cereal!" and the scolding, "You bad child!" are understood by the child, correctly, as meaning the opposite. He is pleased by being treated not as a stupid literal baby, but rather as an intelligent being who is capable of understanding a joke. (p. 50)

George Moran (1987) offers confirmatory evidence for such thinking from The Study Group on Developmental Disturbances at the Anna Freud Centre in London. Moran underscores the impact of the parents' biological bond with their children upon their readily identifying with the latter's needs and frustrations and attempting to lessen them by all means including playfulness.

> Playful parents find many inventive ways to lighten the demands which they make on the child. In the case of infants, playful parents will try to enhance the infant's feeling of competence and mastery. They may, for example, let their baby hold the bottle and attempt to put it into his own mouth, coming to the baby's aid at the appropriate moment. Such parents will protect their child's nascent frustration tolerance by endeavoring to minimize interference with the child's pursuit of pleasure. Playful mothers may contort themselves while changing a nappy or dressing their babies. Such parents will invent playful interactions to mediate a large variety of tasks. (p. 16)

Subtle forms of such interactional patterns persist through latency and adolescence. Games played in the home's backyard, joint dare-devilry at amusement parks, family vacations, and even mutually-shared home cleaning projects can provide the nidus of parent-child playfulness and lead to the internalization and consolidation of this capacity on the growing child's part. Moving on from a potentially "hard wired" substrate through an interactional pattern to a communicative trait, playfulness comes to be a part of the subsequent adult's character. However, this assumes that the development has gone well. This, as we know, is not always the case.

FIVE PSYCHOPATHOLOGICAL SYNDROMES

The foregoing survey of literature reveals that "playfulness" is variously regarded to be an area of the mind, a potential attitude, an interactive pattern, a manner of communication, and a character trait. While no attempt has been made to correlate playfulness with specific character constellations, three possibilities seem to exist: (i) those who can be playful and retain the ability to put their playfulness aside; (ii) those who cannot be playful, and (iii) those who can not stop being playful. Individuals in the first category are closest to mental health though "higher level" (Kernberg, 1970) hysterical personalities might also behave in a similar fashion. Individuals in the second category are obsessional, depressive, paranoid, or schizoid though their inability to be playful arises from differing levels of psychic conflicts and different types of ego rigidity. The individuals in the third category are chronic pranksters and those with burdensome effusiveness; they are "hypomanic characters" (Akhtar, 1988). The last two categories reflect psychopathology. Andre Green's (2005) reminder is pertinent in this context. "It is true that the great majority of the meanings attached to play are positive, but we cannot forget that play is also associated with cheating, from which it is inseparable: to play into somebody's hands, to be caught in someone else's play, or to be trapped. I think that all these expressions can be seen as perversions of play" (pp. 15–16).

My own way of looking at psychopathology involving playfulness[2] is to categorize it into: (i) deficient playfulness; (ii) pseudo-playfulness; (iii) inhibited playfulness; (iv) derailed playfulness, and (v) malignant playfulness.

Deficient Playfulness

This is witnessed in the rhythmic and twirling behaviors of autistic children. The sensation-dominated use of "autistic objects" (Tustin, 1980) by psychotic children also belongs in this category. These objects, usually small and hard (e.g., keys, little metallic cars), are deployed as scaffolds to stabilize the mind. "They may have no fantasy whatsoever associated with them, or they may be associated with extremely crude fantasies which are very close to bodily sensations" (Tustin, 1980, p. 27). Their loss is felt as a loss of a body part and hence they are immediately replaced. Play with such objects has a ritualistic quality and the child has a rigidly intense preoccupation with them. The appearance of "playfulness" is deceptive under such circumstances. The repetitive activities of autistic children are "relatively mindless in terms of fantasies, illusion, or a mental or behavioral effort to explore, practice, or try on roles having elaborate defensive and adaptive capacities" (Solnit, 1987, p. 211). Playfulness, in contrast, is based upon symbolizing capacity and facilitates the solution of conflicts in an exploratory, make-believe manner.

Pseudo-Playfulness

Individuals with a relentless tendency to joke, pun, rhyme, and act impulsively belong in this category. Their sunny meddlesomeness arises from sustained "manic defense" (Klein, 1935; Winnicott, 1935) and is different from genuine playfulness. The possibility of self-knowledge is impeded by manic defense (i.e., the trio of idealization, denial of dependence, and omnipotence) and enhanced by playfulness. Manic defense erases links to psychic reality and especially the depressive anxiety that is inherent in emotional development. Playfulness, in contrast, permits a well-titrated discharge of id derivatives that can be reflected upon to gain insight into the affective and relational state of the self. Moreover, playfulness is a source of joy for all the parties involved in it whereas manic defense tends to amuse only the subject and that too in a frenetic and ego-depleting way.

Inhibited Playfulness

An individual's capacity to be playful can become inhibited owing to many reasons. The fear of unintended breakthrough of aggression keeps the paranoid individual unduly vigilant, robbing his communication of levity and spontaneity (Akhtar, 1990). The intense reaction formations of the obsessional have a similar result though here the situation is compounded by the pervasive use of intellectualization; the latter is opposed to the elements that are critical to playfulness especially paradox and metaphor. The ego-rigidity and social discomfort of the schizoid also makes playfulness difficult. However, some schizoid individuals can relax with a select few in a sort of "enlarge autism among people of similar persuasion" (Kretschner, 1925, p. 162). Often this requires the help of alcohol.

Similarly, some highly "logical" obsessional adults and analytically-deprived, sad children can "borrow" the capacity to be playful from others. While unable to be playful on their own, such individuals can respond to an active playmate" by showing increased imagination, trying on new roles, and letting fantasy life emerge into consciousness (Solnit, 1987, 1998). This phenomenon might be termed "induced playfulness."[3]

Derailed Playfulness

Ordinarily the attitude of playfulness consists of a light-hearted, enjoyable, and transient relaxation of reality-unreality boundary alongside a will-titrated diffusion of the ego by id derivatives, especially of the pregenital variety. At times, however, its make-believe quality begins to disappear. The suspension of reality in the service of enjoyable regression is lost and play is replaced by activity with real consequences. The ego-id balance shifts and direct instinctual gratification is sought. Such "derailed playfulness" is evident in children who are playing with each other, teasing, bursting out in laughter, and even wrestling, till suddenly they lose perspective and start fighting for real. They transgress the "rules" of the game and disregard its context. A daydream of camaraderie has now turned into a nightmare of bitter rivalry.

Similar scenarios can arise in the context of sexual perversions. Indeed it is possible to envision the pregenital pleasures of foreplay, the idealized thrills of perversion, and the breakthrough of actual violence (toward self or others) during lovemaking on a hierarchal continuum of playfulness. Foreplay involves undressing, facing each other naked, and stimulating each other in ways other than genital to genital contact. Shedding one's shame over nakedness and gently overcoming the partner's shame are important tasks here (Kernberg, 1991). Yet another important aspect of foreplay is the emergence into consciousness of pregenital drive derivatives (e.g., sucking, biting, licking, showing, looking, squeezing, and smelling). Fears regarding the real and imaginary blemishes of one's body also have to be put aside. For all this, genuine self-regard and trust in the partner's goodness is needed and so is a robust capacity for playfulness. In perversion too, the two partners enter into an unspoken agreement of suspending judgment for a while. Thus seemingly sadomasochistic activities like handcuffing, wax-dripping, paddling, whipping, boot-licking, and even "stronger" acts, including bondage and discipline (Stoller, 1973) retain a pretend quality and remain enjoyable. The difference between pregenital indulgences of foreplay and sexual practices considered perverse, however, lies in the degree of ego-autonomy and reality testing that is maintained; Lili Peller (1954) says that an activity ceases to be play when it cannot be stopped at will. Acts in foreplay are optional and under ego control; acts in sexual perversion are mandatory and id-driven. A naked man frolicking in his wife's panties right in front of her eyes, teasing her fondly, as she bursts out laughing, before they settle on sexual intercourse or after they have had it, is being playful. A cross-dresser who is totally unable to have any pleasure without public demonstration of a vestimentary transformation of the self and then too can achieve orgasm only through masturbation has a problem. The curious masquerade of transvestism remains less psychopathological, however, than the morbid mutilations associated with transsexualism. While it is a matter of degree, the realm is one of "derailed playfulness" to be sure.

Malignant Playfulness

A much more malignant corruption of playfulness is seen among serial killers. Often these deeply troubled (and troubling) individuals "play" with the victims before torturing and murdering them. Needless to add, the "game" is bloody and all one-sided. Their tendency to play "hide and seek" with their official nemeses (e.g., cops, detectives, FBI) is also mutual only in their imagination. The mocking challenges they pose to legal authorities, by leaving provocative clues and fabricating individualized monikers, betray unconscious guilt and a deep-seated wish to be punished. There is also the variable of grandiosity and a defensively evolved sense of invulnerability involved here. However, what strikes me more is the element of a bizarre and, frankly, a bit tragic, playfulness in all this. Serial killers appear desperately hungry for a playful father-son relationship, something that most of them have lacked in their backgrounds (Stone, 2001; Hare, McPherson, and Forth, 1988; Innes, 2006). By teasing the cops, they are initiating a playful interaction with them.[4]

Having reviewed the phenomena of normal and pathological playfulness and the developmental considerations pertinent to them, we are now prepared to tackle the role of playfulness in the therapeutic situation.

THE ROLE OF PLAYFULNESS IN CLINICAL WORK

Donald Winnicott (1967) made pioneering observations on the role of playfulness in psychotherapy and his brilliant but outrageous protégé, Masud Khan, applied some of these ideas to the work of adult psychoanalysis (Hopkins, 2000). More recently, Ehrenberg (1990), Mahon (2004) and Coen

(2005) have made significant contributions to this realm. Winnicott, for whom the capacity to play was the hallmark of mental health, declared that "Psychotherapy has to do with two people playing. The corollary of this is that when playing is not possible then the work done by the therapist is directed toward bringing the patient from a state of not being able to play into a state of being able to play" (1967, p. 38).

Such ever-present and subtle role of playfulness in the clinical situation is a far cry from the use of formal "play technique" (Klein, 1923) in the treatment of children, regardless of whether one equates the child's play with the adult's free-association or not, and regardless of whether one's interpretive efforts are preceded by educative and ego-preparatory remarks (A. Freud, 1929) or not. Winnicott's concern—and mine—is not "play" as an activity but "playfulness" as an attitude, even though the latter can only be discerned through the units of action in the clinical dyad. At the risk of repeating myself, such attitude is one of light-heartedness, blurring of the reality-unreality boundary, imaginativeness, and linguistic innovation. According to Darlene Ehrenberg (1990), "in playfulness, words do not stand for what they literally mean, and paradox is often a critical element" (p. 76). She adds that "playfulness" with others assumes a sense of mutuality and, in a dialectical fashion, strengthens that mutuality. Both parties involved in a playful interaction derive pleasure from it. Ehrenberg notes that "Playfulness can include the use of humor and irony, affectionate kinds of teasing, banter and repartee, joint fantasy, and a host of other possibilities. Because it can be effective as a means to communicate on multiple levels simultaneously, and can allow for transcending communicative barriers, it can work to cut through distance, and to expand the range of communication" (p. 76).

Moreover, all parties involved in the "playful" interaction instantly and intuitively recognize its nature. A look at the following clinical vignette would attest to this.

CLINICAL VIGNETTE 1

Sy Goldman, a bright corporate attorney in his forties, is in analysis with me.[5] His chronically, even it subtly, frustrating childhood experience with his cold and "proper" mother has left him resentful and inconsolable: "I am a person for whom ninety-percent is not enough," he says. His disdain for his bumbling father has also contributed to an inward sense of weakness and, despite success and accolades, feeling bereft in this world. He hates being a Jew and has concocted all sorts of ways to come across as a Gentile.

We work well together. Time passes. Layer by layer, his distress unfolds. Holding, "affirmative interventions" (Killingmo, 1989) coupled with interpretations proper and reconstructions gradually help him. He begins to feel better. He becomes more confident overall and especially in his identity as a Jew. He joins a synagogue. However, he retains "soft spots" and is vulnerable to regressions. One day, while preparing for a dinner speech at a prestigious club, he says to me "Mind you, I am not ashamed of being a Jew." I spontaneously respond, "That is something Richard Nixon might have said." Sy instantly knows what I mean, bursts out into laughter, saying, "Fuck you for calling me Nixon. . . . That's really helpful!"

In this instance, both the patient and I instantly knew what had happened. We shared the insight that this defense interpretation provided. We also experienced a sense of mutuality and pleasure.

CLINICAL VIGNETTE 2

Sarah Korn, a fifty-or-so-year-old real estate agent, is given to talking profusely and incessantly in her sessions. She is always socially busy and overbooked. Her mind is cluttered though without ever eliminating the one preoccupation she claims to be tortured by and this pertains to her "boring" husband. Day after day, week after week, and month after month, I hear accounts of situations where he appeared uninterested, uninteresting, mindless, and "boring." When I question her need to repeat this, Sarah stops for a while but shows little actual curiosity regarding what might underlie this pattern. Gradually things change. My patience bears fruit and my interventions take hold. Now the transference re-creation of a self-absorbed mother who had little mental space for the little Sarah comes to our attention. As an adult, Sarah is driven to make sure that I will listen, take her in and keep her there (i.e., in my mind). The need to repeat betrays the dread of my having forgotten what she had told me. Sarah's manic defense lessens though the characterological propensity in this direction does not entirely leave her.

One day, she comes in, lies down on the couch, and says, "I have nothing to say today," and I instantly respond "but my fear is that you will still talk." Sarah burst out laughing and says, "You know, you are right. I cannot stay quiet for too long." And the session proceeds in a somewhat more meaningful way.

Like the previous clinical vignette, this one demonstrates the mutuality-building (and, of course, arising from previously existing mutuality) impact of a well-timed, light-hearted comment. The enhanced sense of our "being in this together" and sharing the knowledge of where we might beneficially go next permits further interpretive deepening of the clinical material. Undoubtedly such exchanges can only take place if the clinical situation is experienced as a "felicitous space" (Bachelard, 1969) or "a safe place necessary to allow the flowering of useful thoughts" (Loewald, 1987, p. 177). A development of this sort, in turn, depends on the mutual fit between the analyst and the analysand, the affective state of their moment to moment relatedness, and the analyst's having renounced a rigid clinging to "proper" technique. According to Corradi Fiumara (2009), "It is a question of overcoming rigidity and advancing toward the sort of spontaneity that allows for psychic leaps. It sounds paradoxical to say that immediate reactions function in the domain of rigidity, while creative actions involve the capacity to leap into staying still, into waiting for the good inspiration" (2009, p. 69).

Not all goes well all the time, however. The analyst's playfulness can fail to find a receptive partner in the patient, resulting in a serious "disruption" (Akhtar, 2007) of the clinical process, or, if one is fortunate, merely a moment of awkwardness.

CLINICAL VIGNETTE 3

Barbara Wilkins, a thirty-five-year-old librarian, is quite schizoid. She has few friends and is generally mistrustful of people. She is secretive though rationalizes it on the grounds, "who would be interested in me." In her treatment too, Barbara is reticent and often quiet for long lengths of time. A year or so in our halting and staccato collaboration, she comes, lies down on the couch, reports that she had a dream (her first in the course of our work) but immediately adds that she has "completely forgotten it." Seeing her lapse into her usual silence, I say, "Well in that case, why don't you make one up?" I am upbeat but Barbara does not respond. She remains quiet. Her silence comes across as stony and cold.

Here my playful attempt to pull the patient into the "intermediate area of experience" (Winnicott, 1953) failed miserably. Was it because it was ill-timed and too rushed? Was it because my comment itself was a cheery denial of having felt let down at her "offering" a dream and then taking it back by saying that she forgot it? In other words, did my playfulness reflect a "manic defense" against hurt and hostility on my part? To what extent did the patient's characterological mistrust of spontaneity contribute to the failure of this intervention? Questions like these must be raised inwardly if genuine progress is to be made in the future work with rigid and withdrawn patients.

Stanley Coen's (2005) observations and suggestions come to our rescue in this regard. He reports the rather disastrous consequences of a prematurely play remark with a very controlled analysand and warns against beginning "treatment by attempting to draw a schizoid patient into play engagement" (p. 827). With characteristic clinical sensitivity, Coen states:

> When a schizoid patient is very serious, concrete, and terrified, shut down, the analyst must respect these terrors and needs for avoidance, protection, control, domination, rejection. The obvious question is when and how to shift into other therapeutic approaches. How long is the analyst's initial welcome, affirmation, validation, tolerance of the schizoid patient's imperative need for control and acceptance to last? The short answer is for the entire length of the treatment. But within the analyst's acceptance of the patient, creative, playful ways must be found to invite the patient to join in sharing a common world. (p. 827)

The idea is to enliven the patient's rigid and calcified persona, enhance "mentalization" (Fonagy and Target, 1997), and make what is pathological a bit curious, even humorous, given its anachronistic stance. The analyst's playfulness can become an irreverent challenge to the patient's fantasized omnipotence, fragility, or both. This is especially true in the case of schizoid patients. With less withdrawn patients, especially if they are psychologically minded, the analyst's witty and imaginative prodding can work like an interpretation while yielding pleasure for the analyst and the patient alike.

CLINICAL VIGNETTE 4

John Widroff, a sixty-year-old internist, is in psychotherapy with me. He has suffered many losses as a child, though his previous treatments did not unearth some of them. Psychologically sophisticated but sentimental, John cries readily in movies and upon hearing songs about separation. Vulnerable to loss, he preemptively rejects love. When his wife tells him that she loves him, he habitually responds by saying "no, you don't." Within our work too, the same pattern emerges though subtly and with less anxious aggressivity. He likes me, recognizes that I am good to him but finds my interventions "too kind." He attributes them to my being a "good guy" and my possessing some sort of "Eastern wisdom." I note the multiply determined nature of these observations (including, of course, their potentially derogatory implications) but regard them as falling within the overall range of what Freud (1912) called "unobjectionable positive transference." We go on with trying to understand how his traumatic childhood separations from important people have shaped his character.

One day, he asks me why is it that he dreads separation but loves songs and poems about it. I respond, "Come on! You know that there is a difference between a rooster that's run over by a farmer's truck and an elegantly prepared chicken dish." John laughs, looks at me admiringly and, more importantly, knowingly with a broad and sunny smile over his face, he asks me, "Did you just make that up?" I say, "Yes," also with a smile.

Once again, we can see how light-heartedness, imaginativeness, and a momentary blurring of professional work and joking results in expansion of ego dominance over the inner world. And, this is what playfulness in the therapeutic situation is about: a shared capacity of the partners in the clinical dyad to create new and surprising ways to advance their work, ways that yield pleasure and enjoyment for both parties. Analysis is not fun and games but it does not have to be ponderous and dull either. The ego-freedom that we want our patients to experience in their lives outside of the treatment situations must be fostered within it.

This brings up the tricky issue of responding to playfulness on the patient's part. Psychoanalytic orthodoxy pressures us to not respond in kind and indeed there might be occasions when remaining impassive is best. It is safe to assume that such stance is based upon the analyst's "diagnosing" the patient's behavior as "pseudo-playfulness" and largely defensive. However, the imperative to conform to some "ideal" way of analyzing must not lead the analyst to become automaton-like. He must have enough freedom to momentarily join in the patient's playfulness and then, as the session proceeds, decide whether that interaction needs to be brought up for scrutiny, shelved away for later reference, or regarded as an "unobjectionable" and useful ingredient of the "working alliance" (Greenson, 1965) between him and the patient.

The possibility of "countertransference enactment" is ever present in such moments. Becoming playful (Feiner, 1979; Jacobs, 1986) might occur as a collusion with the patient's conscious or unconscious avoidance of a difficult issue in transference or in his life outside of treatment. At such times, the analytic playfulness can preclude the needed expression of the affect and/or fantasy that is troubling the patient. Consequently, the analyst must monitor the impact of his participation upon the analytic process and realize that his playfulness can be experienced by some patients as seductive, teasing, provocative, or dismissive. What also remains true is that such monitoring on the analyst's part can itself reveal important data about the state of transference, countertransference, and the nuanced intrapsychic agenda linking the two partners in the clinical dyad at any given time.

CONCLUDING REMARKS

In this chapter, I have attempted to elucidate the concept of playfulness. I have described it as a character trait and/or interactional pattern comprised of light-heartedness, spontaneity, pleasure experienced in the context of mutuality, and a transient suspension of the reality-unreality boundary. I have traced the development of playfulness back to the matrix of early parent-child relationship and even to certain "hard-wired" constitutional capacities of the child. I have noted that, like any other mental capacity, playfulness is subject to the encroachment of psychopathology. To highlight this point, I have described five psychopathological syndromes: (i) deficient playfulness, (ii) pseudo-playfulness, (iii) inhibited playfulness, (iv) derailed playfulness, and (v) malignant playfulness. Finally, I have tried to demonstrate the application of these ideas to the therapeutic situation and, with the help of illustrative vignettes, showed the uses, advantages, and risks of playfulness within the clinical dyad.

Despite covering considerable ground, I am aware that many important areas pertaining to playfulness have remained unaddressed in this contribution. The first such area pertains to *gender*. While differences in the patterns and specific activities of play in the two sexes have been documented (Gilligan, 1982) little in psychoanalytic literature sheds light upon the similarities and differences between the two genders vis-à-vis playfulness. Is it possible that men are more playful with men and women with women? After all, the dimmed light upon reality can stir up more intense sexual impulses in the context of heterosexual relationships than can be contained within the confines of playfulness. But if this is so, are there differences between heterosexual and homosexual individuals in regards to playfulness? Could it be that heterosexual men and women are more comfortably playful with their respective sexes but homosexual men and women with those of the opposite sex? Do we really know this? And, what might be social and clinical implications of it?

A related area is that of *culture*. All sorts of questions arise as one pays attention to this variable. For instance, are there cultures (e.g., Latin American) that permit more playfulness than other (e.g., Germanic)? Is it a matter of "more" or "less" playfulness or do different cultures have different forms of playfulness? Can one be playful with one's elders to a comparable extent in different cultures? What about playfulness across the boundaries of race, ethnicity, religion, and social class? And, is the extent of playfulness permissible at the workplace comparable in different cultures? Clearly more thought is needed here.

Finally, there is the role of the *public media*. While idiosyncratic factors of individual experience, especially during the formative years of childhood, determine the blossoming or withering away of playfulness in a given individual, the constant bombardment of senses by the media also has a role here. A less than ponderous tone to the newspaper coverage, a frolicsome air on the morning television shows, a rib-tickling monologue on talk shows, and a mandatory sense of levity injected into television commercials go a long way in creating "induced playfulness" in the audience. A public media climate that is unerringly dour might have the opposite impact. Media and the celebrities that populate it uphold a modal, if not ideal, way of behavior and invite identification with it. Consequently, playful media makes us a little more playful.

All in all, playfulness turns out to be far more complex a phenomenon than it superficially appears. It is a deft mixture of light-hearted spontaneity, bold paradox and harmless pleasure. The episode involving Winnicott's revolver at the beginning of this contribution contained all these elements and so does the following sharp retort by Gandhi. Upon being asked by an American news reporter as to what did he think about Western civilization, Gandhi said, "I think that will be a good idea!"

NOTES

1. Less known is Winnicott's (1942) "spatula game." This consists of putting a shiny spatula within the reach of an infant and observing how he reacts to it. Under normal circumstances the infant's response consists of three steps: (i) noticing the spatula, reaching for it and then, in a moment of hesitation, gauging the mother's response, as if seeking her permission to proceed further; (ii) picking the spatula up and mouthing it; and, (iii) dropping it, as if by mistake. If the spatula is offered again, the child is pleased and repeats the same sequence, though with greater intentionality. Absence or unevenness of the sequence suggests some disturbance within the infant or, more likely, within the infant-mother dyad.

2. While Winnicott did not describe psychopathology of *playfulness*, in a posthumously published paper (Winnicott, Shepherd, and Davis, 1989, pp. 59–63), he did delineate seven types of pathology of *play*. These included: (i) loss of capacity to play associated with mistrust; (ii) stereotypical and rigid play; (iii) flight into daydreaming; (iv) excessive sensualization of play; (v) dominating play; (vi) playing as a compliance to authority, and (vii) flight to strenuous physical exercise.

3. Domestic pets can also elicit playfulness from those who are otherwise dour. A striking example of this is to be found in the fact that Freud, who was tone-deaf and hated music, would start humming under his breath and even singing while playing with his favorite dog, Jo-fi (Gay, 1988).

4. A similar dynamic is evident in Osama bin Laden's choice of September 11 as the date for the attack against the United States. By flaunting the established nationwide emergency contact number, 911, bin Laden was being sadistically "playful."

5. Two matters of style need clarification here. First, all the patients reported upon in this contribution have been given full names rather than the usual "Mr. A, Ms B, etc." Though the names are fictitious, their use gives the report a warmer and more human quality. Second, all clinical vignettes are written in the present tense in order to give them an "experience-near" quality.

Chapter Six

Remembering, Replaying, and Working Through: The Transformation of Trauma in Children's Play

Monisha C. Akhtar

> "When the child is overwhelmed by some dangerous, unpleasant reality, and especially when taken by surprise, he may resort to play. He may disavow the reality of his experience or the traumatic perceptions by making them play, not reality." —Jacob Arlow, "Trauma, Play, and Perversion"

In his seminal paper, *Remembering, Repeating and Working Through*, Freud (1914a) observes that, "the patient does not remember anything of what he has forgotten and repressed, but acts it out. He reproduces it not as a memory but as an action; he repeats it without, of course, knowing that he is repeating it" (p. 149). Freud thus delineates what analysts then and today have come to uphold as a major tenet of psychoanalytic thinking and technique. Within the clinical realm, it means simply the following: the patient repeats and brings to bear via transference that which has been repressed and forgotten. The symptoms and anxieties appear gradually, in the "here and now," and repetitively. The analytic dyad explores via transference and defense interpretations, the patient's particular configuration of neurotic symptoms, their underlying meanings, conflicts, and anxieties. Repetition of the symptoms leads to the patient remembering and gaining insight. The patient's consistent verbalizations of this insight and its utilization toward behavioral change have come to be regarded by some as hallmarks of good and stable mental health and a precursor to termination from analytic treatment.

Following Freud many analysts expanded and elaborated on the nature of remembering (Frank, 1969), the role of insight (Abrams, 1981, A. Freud, 1981), and the role of other therapeutic factors in treatment (Caspary, 1993,

Altman, 1994). The explosion of theoretical and technical contributions to the field has led to new and varied understanding of self and object relations, emphasis upon the role of affect and empathy, and transition from a predominantly one person to two-person model for analytic work and interaction. However, despite these advances in both the theoretical and technical realms, analysts still maintain that adult analytic work rests on three cardinal psychoanalytic principles, i.e., free association, interpretation, and insight. These primary formulations also influenced analysts who worked primarily with children. Unlike their adult counterparts, however, child analysts had to modify their technique, as the customary tools of the analytic frame and process were not readily available to them for their use. Their young patients did not readily resort to verbal expression and free associate, nor did they follow the official analytic dictums and confine themselves to the analytic couch. Instead, working with children introduced a whole new genre of analytic thinking and technique with play as its central tool. This has gradually led to a plethora of literature on play, highlighting its theoretical and clinical status, its functional objective, and the controversies regarding its interpretation within the analytic frame.

THE ROLE OF PLAY IN CLINICAL WORK WITH CHILDREN

Hug-Helmuth (1919) was the first child analyst to introduce the use of play in working with children. Though doubts regarding her work as a child analyst have been raised, it is agreed that she was "responsible for a large number of valuable initiatives in various directions, which were taken up by others and converted into a methodology and technique of child analysis" (Holder, 2005, p. 23). Since then two key models of working with children and the use of play have dominated the child analytic work. These involve the work of Melanie Klein (1921, 1923, 1926, and 1932) and Anna Freud (1926, 1927, 1936). They developed their theories and techniques almost simultaneously but with varying emphasis on the use of play and its interpretation. Both Melanie Klein and Anna Freud acknowledged the central importance of play in working with children. Both underscored the significance of verbalizing insight in child work. However, in contrast to Anna Freud, Melanie Klein attributed symbolic meanings, derived from inner instinctual pressures and their corresponding "phantasies," to a child's play. She interpreted the child's play "directly" by linking it to these underlying "phantasies." For instance, when a child deliberately made two toy cars collide aggressively, she saw it as representing his view of parental sexual intercourse. Anna Freud, on the other hand, emphasized the role of the child's immediate reality in play and during treatment. She also gave greater importance to the fact that play, at least in part, reflected the ego's strivings toward mastery of external and internal difficulties. She offered interpretations in a more tentative manner and felt that some educative and "preparatory" work with the child was needed before interpretations could be given. Despite the differences in their theoretical and technical formulations, the influence of Melanie Klein and Anna Freud on child work continues to reverberate till today.

Donald Winnicott further elaborated the role of play in working with children in his conceptualizations of the transitional object, the "use" of an object, and the interactional nature of play within the clinical setting. Winnicott, (1953, 1967, 1968, 1969, 1971) placed great emphasis upon play and playfulness both in the clinical and social setting. He proposed the concept of an "intermediate area of experience" where concerns of reality and non-reality did not matter and where imagination reigned supreme. This area was the proper locale for creativity as "psychotherapy takes place in the overlap of two areas of playing, that of the patient and that of the therapist. Psychotherapy has to do with two people playing together. The corollary of this is that where playing is not possible then the work done by the therapist is directed toward bringing the patient from a state of not being able to play into a state of being able to play" (1967, p. 38).

The functional utility of play has captured and captivated the literary and research imaginations of psychologists and psychoanalysts for decades. The former commented on the adaptive nature of play, highlighting its importance in skills building (as in developing fine and gross motor skills), sensory knowledge and exploration of roles, development of cognitive, problem solving and social skills as well as language development (Hughes, 2003). They also examined play's role in the development of a structured mind, based on a hierarchical organization of increasingly complex information, reflecting the integration of new knowledge and experiences into existing schemas of reference. Two complementary processes, namely, assimilation and accommodation (Piaget, 1962), exist in order to take in information from the outside world and facilitate ongoing adaptation to their environment. Piaget distinguished three main categories of play. The earliest he called "practice play" referring to pre-symbolic activities. This is followed by "symbolic play," and finally, "social play" in which the child moves to play governed by specific and agreed upon rules. In contrast, psychodynamic theories of play have focused more on the meaning and function of play. According to these views, play is a behavior that permits children to communicate and to master fears and anxieties. Through symbolic and fantasy play, it allows the child to bring these underlying fears and anxieties to consciousness and work through them in the course of their game.

Waelder (1933) articulated this position and provided a comprehensive theory of play, which highlighted (in addition to wish fulfillment) the child's desire to gain mastery and cope with anxieties and fears especially when faced with overpowering situations. To this, Peller (1954) added that "all play brings wish fulfillment, pleasure, elation, a feeling of euphoria, well-being." (p. 180). However, Peller did not regard play as a direct manifestation of the pleasure principle (though the child's innate capacity to play and derive pleasure from it has since then, been confirmed by contemporary neuroscience research (Panksepp, 1998). From a psychodynamic perspective, play was seen as "an attempt to compensate for anxieties and deficiencies, to obtain pleasure at a minimum risk (p, 180)." However, as Peller notes later, play did not always function as play and nor was it always pleasurable. This was especially noted when play became repetitive in nature and the child was unable to stop playing when he wanted to.

Arlow (1987) elucidated this point further by examining the deleterious impact of trauma on the development of play and the formation of character traits that remain resistant to treatment. In his analytic work with five young boys who had all experienced significant trauma during early childhood, Arlow noted the re-emergence of repetitious play behaviors during adolescence that were reenactments of their earlier trauma. These behaviors were seen as attempts to render their traumatic experiences unreal through the medium of play. The failure of the ego to master the trauma leads to the development of character traits and perverse practices.

The classical formulation of play behavior continued to dominate the child analytic scene for decades. In recent years, however, object relations theory, self-psychology and relational perspectives have made inroads into this literature. This has sharpened the questions that already existed regarding the specific elements in the "play space," (whether in the child, therapist, or both) which lead to a positive therapeutic result.

CONTEMPORARY PERSPECTIVES

Contemporary observers, having embraced innovative trends in psychoanalytic thinking, have broadened the ongoing dialogue by emphasizing the role of the therapist in the clinical situation. Further elucidating this point, Ornstein (1984) writes, "play is like a window through which the investigator or therapist can take a glimpse at the workings of the mind" (p. 1). This is similar to a dream but unlike a dream, "the therapist can also respond, interact with the player and thereby affect its outcome" (p. 1).

Frankel (1998) has elaborated further on the role of mutuality in child therapy. He underscores the co-creation that occurs between the child and their therapist and suggests that the renegotiation of self-other relationships through play renders it therapeutic in and of itself. This renders play, according to Frankel, "not as preparation or as a vehicle to deliver other essential processes, but as itself an essential process of therapy" (p. 2)

Expanding on this idea of play as a primary form of development, Krimendahl, in her paper, *Metaphor in Child Psychoanalysis: Not Simply a Means to an End* (1998) writes, "dramatic play should be viewed, not simply as a parameter for adapting adult psychoanalytic technique to a population with less mature verbal and cognitive skills, but as a route to therapeutic change in itself" (p. 1). Elaborating on this, Krimendahl highlights the working within the play metaphor and writes:

> I believe that for some older children, therapeutic change may occur through the patient's interaction with the analyst solely within the play metaphor. The analyst's function is to expand and deepen the story that is there, suggesting alternate possibilities and greater complexity in representations of self and other. Although verbalizations are used, including the interpretation of the child's relational patterns within the metaphor, interpretation is more an adjunctive technique than a primary one. (p. 3)

While Krimendahl's position on play continues to occupy a central position in contemporary child analytic work and is echoed by others as well (Birch, 1997), the role of verbalization in the clinical process has not entirely disappeared. Gilmore (2005) feels that "the transformation that child analysis facilitates and which the child patient anticipates is achieved primarily through verbalization while in the state of playing" (p. 13). This "state of playing" (Gilmore, 2005) is unique to the analytic dyad and contains elements of conscious and unconscious exchange that result in a positive therapeutic reaction. More recently, the benefit of exploring the analyst's countertransference with children has also been examined (Bonovitz, 2009). The therapist's personal childhood memories accompanied by fantasies and their affective states can be translated into symbolic play and add to the understanding of the child's mind. Regardless of these controversies, the central role of play in child therapy is indisputable and the burgeoning literature on this is evidence of its key position in the technique of child analysis. In working with traumatized children, however, the picture becomes more complicated. In such cases, obsessive-compulsive rituals and frozen modes of behavior do not appear like play and adults can quickly notice the transition from play to the use of play as a phobic defense.

THE PLAY OF TRAUMATIZED CHILDREN

The repetitive and defensive nature of play in traumatized children was documented extensively by Terr (1979) in her seminal work with the Chowchilla tragedy, during which a busload of children were kidnapped and buried alive underground for several hours before being discovered. Terr documented both the short-term as well as the long-term effects of such trauma, especially on the children's capacity to play. She noted that the "major defenses in traumatic play were turning passive into active, displacement, identification with the aggressor, denial and isolation of affect. Much of the play was simply repetition of a traumatic episode" (p. 17). Terr's work with the children of the Chowchilla tragedy brought to the forefront many of the issues related to trauma and working with traumatized children and had vast implications for theory and technique. It highlighted the effect of a single trauma on a child's development and predated many of the current clinical and theoretical concerns. Some of these included the impact of trauma on a child's capacity to achieve object constancy, to regulate affects, develop age appropriate frustration tolerance, have a sense of self, and develop appropriate social and interpersonal skills.

The consequent explosion of research on this topic attests to the ubiquitous nature of trauma, to the growing concern in the professional communities to understand and mitigate the effects of trauma, and to the need to evolve nuanced techniques for the use of practicing clinicians. Elucidation of the issue of trauma and play within the analytic community further highlighted these issues and identified the implicit tensions between different strands of thought. At the heart of these theoretical debates are questions such as what constitutes a trauma, what is its etiology, and what is the role of external reality versus internal conflicts in its experience. While most agree to the following definition of trauma, as "any experience, which calls up distressing affects—such as those of fright, anxiety, shame, or physical pain" (Breur and Freud 1895, p. 6), disagreements about the role of external reality versus internal factors continue to appear in the psychoanalytic literature. The former position attributes all traumas as resulting from the impact of outside events, big or small, and disregards the role of the individual's internal world (with its compromise formations and internal conflicts) that might be traumatic in and of itself. The latter group on the other hand puts greater premium on internal psychological processes that cause immense distress and disregard the profound influence of an individual's immediate environment and external reality. To this theoretical conundrum, Sugarman (2003) offers another perspective. He combines both approaches, favoring neither, recognizing the capacity of the brain to filter, organize and structure information at different levels. In addition, he recognizes, as do others (e.g., Busch, 2005), that traumatic experiences and memories also become part of one's internal conflicts in reaction to which an entire venue of defenses develop and operate quite unconsciously such as the psychological process of not wanting to know the trauma.

In working with children, trauma specialists like van der Kolk, McFarlane, and Weisaeth (1996) have also broadened and deepened our understanding of how traumatic experiences impact and are stored in the brain. The notion that traumatic memories are encoded differently in the brain has both implications for recall during treatment as well as the technical considerations in working with traumatized children. Within the context of play technique, the repetitive re-enactments of games (related to traumatic events) suggest the possibility that children might face re-traumatization within the clinical situation. Traumatic memories coded in a different part of the brain utilize memory processes that are not readily available for verbal expression. Supporters of this position (Terr, 1988) use the distinction between procedural (implicit) versus declarative (explicit) memory to argue for technical interventions that do not privilege verbal expression as a marker of insight and therapeutic gain. They emphasize the emotional interaction between the child and their therapist as the focal point of any therapeutic action. The re-experiencing of procedural memories in the analytic relationship is at the core of this work.

In contrast, there are those analysts who believe that the inability of a patient to put something into words is evidence of an underlying defense and resistance (Bohleber, 2007). They emphasize the role of interpretation in facilitating self-reflection and thinking. Their argument is based upon recent evidence (Gaensbauer, 1995; Bauer and Wewerka, 1995) which suggests that traumatic memories are not markedly different from other memory processes, and preverbal traumas are remembered both procedurally and declaratively. This controversy has an impact upon clinical work with children, especially in realm of play. With the therapeutic relationship now at the center of the work, questions regarding the transformative power of play itself can then be raised. Elucidating the importance of play in mastering trauma and promoting conscious self-reflection, Sugarman (2008) writes, "Language is less often a useful vehicle for promoting insight than behavioral enactments and assisting children in developing a narrative in their play helps them consider multiple relationship paradigm's, articulate affect states, distinguish different emotions, and learn the difference between acting on and speaking about feelings" (p. 806).

Play, in and of itself, can have a significant mutative impact on children in analysis, including those suffering from cumulative trauma (Sugarman, 2003, 2008) Not entirely disregarding the need for verbally mediated clinical work, Sugarman, offers a slightly different perspective in working with traumatized children. He suggests that perhaps the work of play can be viewed as establishing a process of insightfulness. This technical approach is geared toward helping a child develop an interest in how his or her mind works (Fonagy, Gergely et al., 2002). This is consistent with the work of many (Mayes and Cohen, 1996) who favor understanding the process versus the content, which they believe enhances affect regulation, sharpens self-other differentiation, and improves reality testing.

Advances in psychoanalytic thinking have also added and refined the original definition of trauma and contributed further to clinical work and theory. Today, the differences between an acute and a slowly evolving trauma are better recognized with the former referring to "shock" trauma and the latter to "strain" (Kris, 1956) or "cumulative" (Khan, 1963) trauma. In acute trauma, the "protective shield" is ruptured with unbearable affects, which overwhelms the ego, resulting in a state of helplessness. Trauma can also result in fixations and character pathologies, when they are un-metabolized and remain frozen, so to speak, in mute internal states. The outcome of trauma is determined by several factors including the child's constitution, his or her age at trauma, the severity of trauma, and the resiliency of the child. Some, however, hold that the occurrence of a "shock" trauma of enormous significance such as the Holocaust causes severe ego disruption leading to dissociative amnesia, repetitive behaviors, and, in some cases, neurobiological changes (Terr, 1979). Attempting to "analyze" defenses in such situations might be experienced as un-emphatic and thus be detrimental to the treatment. Furthermore, trauma can impact the development of affect and impulse regulation, and in turn, can contribute to aggressive and impulsive behaviors (Damasio, 1994).[1]

These theoretical advances in the definition of trauma have added greatly to the dialogue on treatment, especially in the area of play. In this context, the goal of now helping young children develop mentalizing functions, (Fonagy, Gergely et al., 2002; Fonagy et al., 1993) emerges prominently in not only facilitating the gradual emergence of insightfulness (Sugarman, 2008) but also in helping the children structure and organize their minds in more constructive ways. This process also allows for the development of a vast range of skills from affect regulation to development of empathy and from frustration tolerance to possessing and maintaining a more integrated coherent sense of self. The ability of a child to understand how his or her mind works develops within the functional space of play, within the treatment setting, and outside of it as well. While this is seen as helpful in child analytic work, it is also recognized that not all children have the necessary cognitive end emotional foundation to work at these levels. In such cases, working within the context of play, with what is available and is at the surface (Busch, 1993), is as a central contributor to therapeutic action (Sugarman, 2008).

While traumatized children use play to cope with stress using displacement, identifications with the aggressor, turning passive into active, and denials they also benefit from when their analysts facilitate their imaginary play. Conscious recall of traumatic memories is not always possible with young children and sometime self-reflective capacities, indicative of mentalizing processes (Fonagy and Target, 1996) may be inhibited or denied to avoid painful affects. Developmental incapacities as well as conflicts might affect the degree to which conscious verbalization of internal states can be expected in young patients. Working through play and encouraging the development of a narrative becomes a necessary step to help these children access their internal fears, anxieties, and wishes over time (Cohen and Solnit, 1993; Slade, 1994). Appearing within the emotional interaction with their therapist, their narrative unfolds with the therapist as both an observer and participant. In fact, as Sugarman (2003) notes, "the ability to play and to fantasize freely becomes a guidepost or sign of analytic progress and mental health in the child (p. 343). Recognizing the gradual process of understanding and integration, Pretorius (2007) recommends a phase specific approach to working with trauma. In his analysis of a six-year-old boy with a history of significant strain trauma, Pretorius provides a step-by-step approach to facilitate the gradual emergence and metabolism of affective states. The child's reenactment of early traumatic memories in displacement leads to affective arousal, which is worked through and gradually assimilated. Pretorius, like many others (e.g., Frankel, 1998) in the field emphasizes the therapeutic alliance established with his young patient, in the context of which self-other representations can be recognized and renegotiated to attain higher and more integrated self-other representations.

TWO CLINICAL ILLUSTRATIONS

The foregoing survey of literature establishes the complex and transformative connection between play and trauma. It highlights the central role of play in working with children and the evolution of contemporary thought on the play techniques in child analysis. The following two vignettes illustrate this connection further, drawing attention to the therapist's engagement with the patient, the role of reenactments and the gradual emergence of traumatized memories. The repetitive nature of traumatic play including the child's displeasure in play and yet being unable to stop is apparent. The vignettes illustrate how the therapist functions both as observer and participant and how for the young patient, aspects of affect regulation, frustration tolerance, and acquisition of skills are impacted by their participation in the play. Transformations in play that occur as a consequence of the therapist's participation in the game are elaborated upon to further elucidate the relationship between trauma and play.

The Trauma of Maternal Absence: The Case of Elly

Elly, a three-year-old Caucasian girl, was referred to me by her schoolteacher, who noticed marked changes in Elly's behavior following a return from a recent visit to her father's home. Her parents, who had divorced when she was barely a month old, maintained joint custody over their only offspring. Each parent had remarried and Elly spent weekend, holidays, and sometimes long stretches during the summer months shuffling between the two homes. Not surprisingly, adjustments were always hard for Elly upon her return but this time it was exceptionally difficult. Her teacher became concerned when Elly turned to hitting her head on the wall, fighting with her peers and overall becoming quite unmanageable. At home, Elly had taken to destroying all her toys, pulling the arms and legs of the dolls she played with and periodically withdrawing from her family, looking quite morose and sad.

My initial impression of Elly was that of a charming little girl, who smiled readily and easily separated from her mother. Accompanying me to my office, she was curious about the toys that I might have though once we entered the playroom she maintained a high level of activity during our initial sessions, moving rapidly between games, never staying long enough on any one activity for us to become fully engaged. This pattern of frenzied nonengagement continued for several weeks till one day she picked up the game of "Sorry" (meant for older children). This game requires the player to move a dice, the number of spaces based on a number displayed on a card, drawn from a deck of cards, and involves some strategy. The player has an option of defeating their opponent with their well thought out moves. The game with this element of revenge and possible victory elicits a great deal of laughter from older kids who gleefully exercise their right to defeat their opponent while loudly stating that they are "Sorry." The game is played on a board with four sides. The players take turns, picking up a card and then moving along the sides of the board, to get to their home plate. Elly, did not understand any of the rules of playing the games. She could read the numbers and had some rudimentary knowledge of the ranking of the numbers. For several weeks, we played the game in a repetitive manner, moving the dice at random, without any particular pattern in mind. I later came to understand this as a reenactment, though during the initial stages its meaning was quite unclear. I was aware of my personal reactions (my anxiety and wish to impose some meaning into our work also informed me of Elly's internal state) and my initial attempts to contain Elly's agitated and disorganized internal state and its behavioral manifestation. Recognizing it as projected parts of Elly's chaotic inner world, I gradually relaxed and Elly and I began to spend more time "playing Sorry."

The following vignette from a session during this period illustrates how Elly made use of this game to convey a complex set of fears, wishes and anxieties. These feelings could not be verbalized but found expression in actions that metaphorically captured the essence of Elly's despair and internal turmoil; the latter were not available for conscious recall but certainly actively present during our sessions, in play.

I had returned from a weeklong break and was meeting Elly for our usual Monday afternoon session. Moving quickly to the shelf of games, Elly pulled the game (Sorry) and placed it on a table that I use for playing games. Sitting down, she removed all the pegs (four pegs in colors of red, green, blue and red) and said that she wanted to play with all of them. I reminded her that I too would need some of the pegs so I could join in the game. She responded by nodding her head but holding on to her two favorite colors, blue and red, and handing me the remaining two sets of colored pegs, green and yellow. I asked Elly what she wanted me to do, waiting for my part to unfold in the narrative. She responded by saying "you know what to do," and laughed out aloud. We both place our pegs in their designated circles. After some to-and-fro chatter about the dice and circles, we proceeded to play the game, with no rules. Quickly, the game reverted to her counting the numbers on the board (with some help from me) accompanied by gleeful laughter on her part when she had a number that was higher than mine. Then, as we began to go round the board, and her players were ahead of my players, she said "can you see me?" and "can you hear me now?" This happened repeatedly. Surprised and not knowing what to make of this, I said that yes, I could see her and then I waited and asked what she wanted me to hear. She ignored my question and moved ahead with a higher number, laughing and then asked again, with an expectant yet anxious tone, "can you see me now?" and, "can you hear me now?" We continued in this manner, this repetition in the game appearing throughout and taking up much of our session time. On several occasions, this was accompanied by her covering her ears with her hands, shaking her head and screaming, and I remained ineffective in my attempts to try and understand and participate.

Following this session, during a meeting with the parents, I asked them if they had noticed similar behaviors at home. Though they had not seen similar behavior at home, they informed me of Elly's repeated separations from her mother, which began when she was a year old. While visiting her father, she would be pulled away from her mother, all the time crying and screaming for her mother. She would then not be allowed to see her mother or hear from her for the duration of the visit to her father's home. This could last as long as two months. On the rare occasion that her mother's phone calls got through, Elly would respond by just screaming in a loud and uncontrollable manner. I began to now understand that Elly's communication during this game (as demonstrated by "can you see me?" and "can you hear me now?") had something to do with early maternal loss, and repeated separations. In our work, it was triggered when I was away. At first masked by her highly disorganized and agitated behavior and manner of playing, it could now emerge in the form of a game (reminiscent of hide and seek). Elly had no words to talk about her painful feelings but she could demonstrate them to me. And that is what the game allowed her to do.

A few sessions later following a period when I was away from the office, Elly asked to play Sorry. As we sat down to play, she once again asked "can you see me, can you see me now?," and "can you hear me?" I said, "I can see why you ask me that, every time. I think you want to know whether I remembered you even when I don't see you. Like when I am gone and we did not meet." When Elly kept quiet but appeared to be listening, I proceeded to add that even though people sometimes do not see each other, they still remember them, like when her mother went to work, she knew exactly what Elly looked like and things about her as she did with her younger brother. But, I added, if Jason, (her younger brother who was 8 months old) who was so small, did not see his mother he could get very confused. "Little children," I said, "could not remember the way bigger kids and big people could. They need some help."

During the following weeks, Elly's use of this game continued to playfully expand on variations of being seen and hearing but she seemed less concerned about my response. Instead, we moved into more variations of the game, with some preliminary attempts to incorporate some structure. Though she never verbalized the loss of her mother, including her fears and anxieties, my contextualizing of our experience, referencing what I had learned from her parents about her early losses, allowed for a gradual amelioration of intense affect and feelings. During subsequent separations, Elly's anxiety diminished and with some additional containing gestures on my part (making a calendar and marking the days we would see each other, drawing a figure and then cutting it in half of which she kept one and I the other), Elly's interest in this game eventually subsided. Though the game appeared later on in our work, we never played the game with the same twist of "now you see it and now you don't," again.

The Trauma of Fluid Boundaries: The Case of Molly

Molly, a cherubic looking eight year old, had witnessed her six-year-old brother suffer a tragic accident two years ago in which he sustained a serious head injury. Subsequently, her parents became excessively preoccupied in the care of their impaired child, which left Molly pretty much to cope with the traumatic event alone. A year or so later, Molly, who had till then done fairly well in school began to experience difficulties. Teachers began to complain about her boisterous behavior, failure to follow rules, and the propensity to get into fights. This was also beginning to occur at home as well, which finally led her parents to seek a consultation with me.

It was clear that Molly was not happy to come for therapy. She protested loudly in the waiting room and continued to do so as she accompanied me reluctantly to my office. Her protests turned to sneers as she viewed with contempt the array of games and other child oriented things that I had in a corner of my room. This continued for many weeks as she continued with her verbal deriding and chastising of what she felt was a less than optimal situation.

One day, having learned from her parents that she had been an active and accomplished soccer player (a game which she had since her brother's accident refused to participate in), I brought in a soccer ball. It caught her eye immediately (as I had hoped it would) but not without some suspicion. She was curious about my level of experience and since I had none, I acknowledged woefully my inadequacies, indicating that she probably knew a lot more about the game. Molly perked up with this admission of both my lack of skill as well as recognition of her relative superiority. Soon we began to engage in a game of soccer. It was clear that Molly knew the game well and was quite skilled and well versed in the rules and etiquette of the game. It was also clear that I knew nothing about the game and this seemed to both delight Molly immensely (as I observed her smile widen when I confessed to this) as well as gave her material to make me the target of all her hostility and aggression. Though this had appeared earlier in our verbal encounters, her capacity to receive and tolerate any interpretation was quite absent.

Molly and I now began to play "soccer" on a regular basis. Our game was a simple one. Establishing some boundaries in the room, which served as our goals, we had to deftly bypass the other player and make our winning points. Molly was quite adept at bypassing me and very quickly had amassed a sizeable number of goals. I, on the other hand struggled, as both my level of expertise and her superior blocking maneuvers thwarted my attempts to score any goals. Our game proceeded in this manner, with me commenting favorably on her moves, trying to follow suit and then failing miserably. What compounded the situation were Molly's relatively undisguised attempts to throw the ball directly at me, either catching me off guard or in some cases, wanting to hurt me directly. I now took turns being both the player, defending myself, as well as the participant observer who commented on her game, and drawing attention to her undisguised attempts to destroy and annihilate me. Setting limits and establishing rules became the first order of "play business" to help in affect regulation and frustration tolerance. As I informed Molly, I needed some rules as I had never played the game before and we both needed the same set of rules that were fair and preserved the integrity of the game. Molly, with her long history of playing this game and priding herself on her knowledge, could now suspend temporarily her desire to inflict pain (arising from underlying guilt and a desire to be punished as she had witnessed the tragic accident). Appealing to her sense of "fair play" allowed us to proceed to understanding those moments when she found herself reverting to a less structured form of play. During such moments, I would suspend my play and ask for clarification, commenting on either a change in rules, or my not knowing the rules. Gradually, we could begin to incorporate such moments of derailment in play to our ongoing game. Interpretation of underlying guilt was temporarily suspended as Molly and I continued to work through a complex set of negotiations, which involved limit setting, affect regulation, and frustration tolerance.

As our work progressed, our game of soccer now became a more pleasurable activity which began with a playful set up of the space, followed by a good humored exchange of who would win and with how many points and moving onto a less affectively charged game itself. With these changes, I could now introduce some interpretative speculation regarding Molly's shifts in behavior. For example, when during a particular exchange, I was caught off guard by a ball thrown at me, I could now draw her attention to this and comment on what had just happened. Keeping my tone even and light, and referring only to her behavior, I would temporarily halt the game and remark on what had just happened. In the playful exchange that ensued, Molly at first dodged my attempts to draw attention to her underlying feelings, by deflecting, changing the topic or engaging in another soccer move. Gradually, however, through a smorgasbord of clinical techniques, playful bantering, and rhetorical questioning, we would arrive at some sort of understanding. As Molly's participation in the game became less governed by rage and anger, we could begin to entertain other possibilities for her loss of control, and the anger that she directed toward me.

Later, Molly transitioned to playing with dolls and within this play, began to reveal a long history of trauma related to maternal loss and neglect and culminating with the more recent tragedy in her life. Encouraging imaginary play within the session, we began the exploration of early childhood memories. A narrative of early maternal absence emerged. A year into our work, Molly reenacted a scene in which a mother leaves her two-year-old daughter in her stroller and walks away, to look at clothes in a department store. The little girl, after a few minutes, walks behind her mother, her voice barely audible, asking the mother to pick her up. When I commented on how the little girl must have been scared and confused when left like that, without her mother, Molly seemed surprised. I added that children sometimes get so scared that they either just become quiet or do something to make sure someone hears them, like when Molly would throw me a curve ball during our soccer games, thinking I had not paid attention to her. Referencing our past activity drew a smile from her but it also served to further strengthen the fact that Molly's behavior was resulting from all kinds of underlying feelings, that we could understand them, as we had in the past and that it would not hurt her or me in the process. This session was followed by a series of sessions in which other memories of being abandoned and neglected were enacted. Furthermore, memories of severe parental strife also appeared adding to a picture of trauma that was more nuanced and complicated. Meanwhile, we learned that Molly's father, who encouraged his children to participate in a variety of sports, had become a central figure in her early childhood years. Molly's participation in sports was a natural outcome of his involvement as well as her physical aptitude. While this served to gratify many of her feelings, it never quite compensated for the loss of her primary love object, and Molly longed to be close to her mother. This also became more apparent in our transference as Molly became curious and more thoughtful about me.

Molly could not comprehend her mother's obsession with her brain-impaired brother, but she did experience her unavailability and absence in her life. This compounded her survivor guilt feelings though her verbalizations of such feelings along with the acknowledgement of shame, jealousy, and revenge (since her brother was seen as being the favored child) did not appear till much later in our work. We worked for over four years, understanding and gradually incorporating hitherto unaccepted parts of her self, tolerating painful affects and acknowledging the current realities in her life. Feedback from her parents confirmed that she was indeed doing better with her friends and in school though her behavior at home continued to be problematic from time to time.

DISCUSSION

"Play of the preschool child, and the mental activity similar to it in the adult, is necessary to the growth of a healthy self. Seen in this way, the play of the child is not mere diversion. It is vital to the evolution of mature psychic life" (Meares, 1992, p. 61). Play is a quintessential tool in the compendium of techniques available to the child analyst. The repetitive nature of play of traumatized children in the clinical situation has elicited a variety of technical interventions. These range from asking the child to stop playing the game like Terr (1990) to those who use limit setting or action interpretation (Sugarman, 2008) as a precursor to a more in depth understanding of the meaning of the play. Recognizing that play is essential to development, most child analysts now give credit the therapeutic alliance as the fulcrum of therapeutic change and advocate the development of insightfulness (Sugarman, 2008) in working with traumatized children. Role of interpretations to develop insight are seen by many as an adjunctive tool in this process though helping the child develop an understanding of how their mind works is now viewed as essential to a good treatment outcome.

The vignettes described briefly in this paper illustrate aspects of playing and working with two children who had experienced cumulative trauma. The children reenacted aspects of their traumatic memories during therapy. In the course of our interactive play, a narrative of shared meanings, affect modulation and the mental representation of intolerable psychic experiences became part of the analytic exchange (Gilmore, 2005; Pretorius, 2007). Their initial inability to play was evidence of internal chaos, disorganization and affect deregulation and the therapist's participation in facilitating the process of being able to play (Sugarman, 2008) was crucial to the therapeutic progress. The setting of rules and establishing some boundaries, while seen as an essential part of the work, was only applicable with Molly, who had the cognitive and emotional maturity to handle these restrictions on her behavior. This form of "action interpretation" (Sugarman, 2008) is necessary as it fosters a feeling of safety for the child, containing his or her aggression and promoting an initial awareness that he or she cannot cause damage to themselves or others. Many analysts recognize the importance of physical limit setting with words, which help the child to mentalize and to think about how one thinks and does things. Words alone however do not have the same impact and need to be accompanied by limit setting. The work in fantasy play later elicited more underlying painful affects, which could then be worked through within the analytic space. It is also important to recognize that the action interpretations have to do with the therapist and patient interaction only. In the playing of the game itself (as in Elly's case), the absence of any adherence to rules may in itself be communicative.

In both children there was evidence of trauma. For Elly, the pre-verbal cumulative trauma related to repeated separations from her mother without ongoing contact caused enormous disruptions in attaining object constancy, affect regulation, and an inability to tolerate painful internal states and processes. When a triggering event later in her life led to the reenactments of earlier (procedurally coded) traumatic memories, both inside the clinical situation as well as outside, Elly became disorganized and out of control. But Elly's reenactment of the traumatic memory, during the course of our "playing," helped integrate some aspects of repetition and reenactment. It also communicated what was not available to her in words. Triggered by my absence, Elly could begin to engage in imaginary play that permitted us both to become participants in an experience that had clearly overwhelmed her developing ego at one time. As both participant and observer, I had the task of making sense of what Elly was trying to convey to me as well as convey to Elly what I thought she was trying to tell me. Of course, my meeting with her parents also facilitated this process. They provided me with information regarding maternal loss at a crucial period in Elly's development. My collaborative venture with Elly, conducted within the confines of our "playing," eventually led to increased insightfulness (Sugarman, 2008) on both our parts, and facilitated the process of therapeutic change.

In Molly's case, witnessing her brother's accident triggered acute reactions in her as well as in her parents. She had no insight into the rage and other feelings that consumed her but its impact on her life was clearly evident. Our game of soccer tapped into an inherent strength that Molly had, as she was an accomplished soccer player (her parents had informed me of this), even relative to her brother, who now could no longer play. Molly's intense physical expressions of rage defended against feelings of shame, guilt, and sadness. In the course of our playing the game of soccer (which is defined by rules of play as well), Molly could reclaim (with my participation in limit setting) a more healthy superego structure where rules and limit setting facilitate social skills development. This also helped facilitate an internal as well as interpersonal state (between Molly and myself) to move into more fantasy play. The danger of feeling out of control with impulses of wanting to physically hurt me were never verbalized by either Molly or me. Instead, within the context of our play, transformations in this behavior began to occur with Molly displaying control over her behavior and more empathy for me during the game itself. This initial management of her behavior established the necessary constraints to allow us to work through other aspects of her underlying dynamics.

CONCLUDING REMARKS

In conclusion, it can be stated that the work with trauma in children incorporates many evolving conceptualizations of both technique and theory. The following considerations bear being kept in mind in this regard.

1. Traumatic memories emerge gradually and in displacement, primarily through imaginary play. The use of a narrative, facilitated by the therapist's participation allows for reconstruction of the traumatic memories.
2. The therapists' emotional interaction with their patient can serve as the mode of mutative action. In this respect, being attuned to the child's emotional state, waiting patiently yet with certain structural guidelines to contain affective moments is helpful.
3. Sometimes therapists may choose to bring a physical object pertinent to their young patients concerns in order to engage and facilitate the process of play.
4. A gradually progressive movement in therapeutic gains can be seen with each acquisition of healthy affective modulation, frustration tolerance, self-other definition, and recognition of interpersonal boundaries and space.
5. Traumatic memories are encoded in a different part of the brain (procedural and implicit) and may not always be accessible to verbal exploration. Recall during analytic treatment can occur with triggering events either inside the clinical situation or outside of it.

6. The repetition of behaviors during play is not always pleasurable and may convey the child's wishes, fears, and anxieties. Sometimes, limit setting (action interpretation) may be necessary so that therapeutic work can continue. The therapist's ability to function as a safe holding environment for the young child conveys a feeling that the child's affect is tolerable and cannot hurt anyone, including himself or herself. The role of the therapist, perhaps as a developmental object in some cases, may be necessary to foster the therapeutic alliance as well as provide an analytic space for ongoing exchange.
7. The patient's verbalization of underlying distress, traumatic episode and memory, and related feelings is not always possible, nor always desirable to achieve. The gradual containment of affect and mastery of physical space (internal as well as external) is indicative of therapeutic gains.
8. Meeting with the parents is a useful (and necessary) adjunct to the analytic work with children. It allows the therapist to inquire about their perceptions as well as obtain important information regarding early childhood environment. Furthermore, it allows them to determine if the child is doing better outside, in school, and at home. Sudden and unexpected departures from expected behaviors points need to be noted as they may serve as markers for emerging trends in play.

Transformations in play and the use of objects appear to be markers of a metabolizing process that perhaps occurs in the presence of a wide assortment of clinical tools. These include a "holding environment, "containment of affect," some commentary on a child's current realities, and interpretation proper. It is difficult to conclude the extent to which these transformations in play occur as a result of treatment or maturational and developmental changes. Suffice it to say that the work of play in trauma is a challenging and multilayered task between two people where the co-construction of a narrative emerges gradually and is informed by many different sources. Helping these children achieve a "state of being able to play" allows them to enjoy the activity in a more developmentally appropriate manner and in the service of ego mastery.

NOTE

1. The relationship between shock traumas and subsequent play related activities has been further elaborated in chapter 9 in this book.

Part III

Sociocultural Aspects

Chapter Seven

Cultural Pathways to Understanding Children's Play: Mythology and Folklore

Daniel M. A. Freeman

> "Observations of infants and children from cultures radically different from the Northern European and North American culture belt indicate that where there is a far more prolonged symbiotic mothering in more communal societies, often with multiple mothering, transitional objects are not nearly so much in evidence." —Alan Roland, *Cultural Pluralism and Psychoanalysis*

As a result of revolutions in communications and travel during the past century, our world has been rapidly shrinking and progressively becoming, as Marshall McLuhan (1962) predicted forty-eight years ago, a single interconnected "global village." Travel, urbanization, global commerce, intercontinental migrations, and especially the movies and the electronic media have transcended cultural boundaries. Societies that previously were unfamiliar with one another have become electronic neighbors who can be instantaneously interconnected by Skype or through cell phone. We now work with colleagues, teach students, and treat patients from unfamiliar cultures, and are more aware of the need to broaden our understanding.[1] Just as in play therapy and in psychotherapy, where clinicians put aside their perspectives in order to focus on how their patients or clients perceive things within their own life experiences, we need to set aside cultural assumptions in any cross-cultural interaction and see things through the window of other people's own worlds. As clinicians, we know that the storyline of manifest play, dreams, or fantasies cannot be understood at face value. We seek to understand the personal associative meanings and connotations that have metaphorically been condensed and are defensively disguised behind an individual's symbolic representations. A similar freedom from assumptions about meanings is essential when we seek to understand the connotation of events, fantasies, or ideas from the perspective of another culture's worldview.

Since play and other transitional creative processes are pivotal during ontogenesis, insight into how creative play and fantasy have contributed to intrapsychic development and adaptation in a particular culture could be very helpful in trying to understand people from that society. Individual intrapsychic development progresses along a number of developmental lines (A. Freud, 1963) and through a series of epigenetic stages of and reorganization (Erikson, 1950). The anthropologist Anthony F. C. Wallace (1956, 1961) studied how, in response to changing circumstances, entire cultures similarly go through successive adaptive reorganizations which he referred to as "maze-way re-syntheses." It would be extremely valuable if we could have a readily accessible data bank that would offer us insights and provide an understanding of unique patterns of fantasy play and interactive experiences that have shaped and reflect intrapsychic development and interpersonal processes in an unfamiliar culture that we may currently be seeking to understand.

ETHNOGRAPHIC STUDIES

It is perhaps surprising and certainly disappointing that there is a lack of adequate comprehensive data concerning children's play and the development of intrapsychic functioning in most traditional anthropological ethnographic literature. Children and children's play were infrequently studied. There is, however, another body of cross-cultural data that can be very helpful. We do have extensive archives and libraries of traditional sacred mythology and secular folklore from many cultures. Secular folktales and sacred myths are refined distillates portraying shared intrapsychic fantasy and play, at successive stages of development through the life cycle. They have been consensually condensed into narratives that are told and retold, are dramatized in plays and in ritual enactments, fill core emotional needs for their audiences, and have been refined and passed on through successive generations. As Freud suspected, but never had a chance to fully explore beyond Western culture,[2] the symbolized narratives and dreams of a culture's mythology can serve as a royal road to understanding shared memories and fantasies that underlie a culture's worldview and values, in the same way that an individual's dreams can be a royal road to understanding individual ontogenesis and intrapsychic functioning.[3] Unfortunately we have only limited ethnographic data that focuses specifically on children's own experiential perspectives, associations, and fantasies during their play and the role of their play in ontogenesis. Anthropologists and folklorists have collected a great deal of valuable data concerning adult languages, worldviews, religious rituals, organized games, and even adults' manifest infant care and child rearing techniques. However, their data does not generally report anthropologists' experiences in the field as they related with children, or children's own perceptions about themselves and their world at different stages of their development. In some cases this was due to the orientation of the researcher. In others, it may be explained by the fact that in many cross-cultural situations it is difficult for an adult outsider to obtain participatory data concerning child or adolescent play using traditional anthropological fieldwork methodologies.

Helen B. Schwartzman (1978, 2001), an anthropologist who was studying children's play, extensively surveyed this problem in 1978 and again in 2001. She reviewed in detail how children had appeared on the pages of the *American Anthropologist* (anthropology's major journal) during a century of studies, from 1898 to 1998, and found that children had generally been "marginalized subjects for anthropological research." Anthropologists had collected extensive data concerning ecology, group organization, kinship structures, language structure, and folk wisdom. They gathered art and artifacts for museums, recorded descriptions of adult ceremonial rituals, and collected folktales and sacred mythology for literary archives. She noted that adult child-rearing precepts and practices had been observed and recorded, but almost none of the ethnographers had taken time to talk and play with children, or to collect data about children's imaginary worlds and dreams. Sometimes observations were recorded concerning structured games, but the ethnographers did not explore what children were thinking and feeling in their play. Schwartzman (1978) referred to Piaget's important methodological contribution (1932) that had not yet been picked up by most anthropologists:

> Piaget's method of acquiring information . . . was unique . . . for he broke with tradition by assuming that the child was the expert and he [Piaget] was the student. . . . His statement to each informant was . . . 'Let's play together. You'll teach me the rules and I'll play with you.'

Schwartzman concluded that most researchers had viewed children and adolescents as being "adults in training . . . rather than focusing on the experience of children as children." Ethnographers apparently had tended to feel that it would seem fruitless to ask a child to tell them about their culture, since children could not be expected to have relevant knowledge and experience. Instead, they had focused on adults, whom they assumed to be the knowledgeable authorities concerning the culture and in the best position to serve as expert "informants."[4]

Several other factors may also have contributed to the relative lack of anthropological data concerning children's fantasies and the perspectives that underlie their play. Cultural barriers may make it difficult for an outsider to enter into a shared alliance with children in order to explore and gather the kind of associative data that we, in the West, gather in play therapy and in research. It is sometimes much easier for ethnographers who are friendly and interested in a culture to develop trusting relationships with adults, and to learn about parental and grandparental perspectives concerning children, than it is for an outsider to become extensively involved in children's play. Whereas adults in many cultures are able to become comfortable relating to someone who is interested in learning about their lives and traditions, they may not understand why anyone would want to "demean" their own "dignity" by getting down on the floor, letting children take the lead, and engaging in childish play. Children, on their part, may also be uncomfortable and guarded in relating to an unknown outsider adult—who is not only a stranger but also culturally very dissimilar to adults with whom the child is familiar. In some cultures, relating casually and openly expressing associations and feelings in any unstructured relationship may be dystonic for adults and children. In other cultures, children may be perceived to be occupants of one or another of a number of completely discrete categories or dissimilar states of being, without apparent continuity from one state to the next—comparable, for example, to an insect egg that is seen as quite unlike a caterpillar, totally different than a pupa or chrysalis, and certainly not similar to a moth or butterfly (P. A. Freeman, 1971). Also, as Schwartzman (2001) pointed out, it is unfortunate that where cross-cultural data concerning children are available, in many instances the data were gathered by a Western social scientist trying to experimentally test out and confirm a particular Western hypothesis. In these instances, preference has generally been given to studying complex stylized rule-structured competitive enactments such as recurring action games, rather than introspective exploratory and creative forms of play. These researchers tended to study manifest behavior without attention to motivations, conflicts and meanings or how the observed play or game was subjectively experienced. Though several kinds of Western-based questions were "tested" on various non-Western people, the records of these observations tell more about the worldview of the researcher than about subjective motivations or the functions of game behaviors for the players.

FOLKTALES AND SHARED DAYDREAMS

Although there is a lack of real-time direct participant-observer interactional data that we would like to have concerning children's transitional processes and formative play, many cultures offer us a potentially valuable, alternate, derivative, route of access to fantasies underlying their play. A culture's traditional shared sacred mythology and folk narratives, passed from generation to generation, are symbolically disguised retrospectively summarized autobiographical condensations of memories of key formative conflicts and developmental experiences. These collectively synthesized stories are derived from fantasy narratives, originally arising in children's transitional processes (Winnicott, 1971) and early symbolic imaginary play, and then modified and elaborated upon in interpersonal play in subsequent stages of development. Inputs from parents' and grandparents' storytelling and sacred rituals offered culturally endorsed symbols, icons, heroes, and rogues that contributed to shaping the fantasies and shared narratives. Individual narratives were creatively pooled during shared make-believe play and game enactments of late childhood and adolescence. Insofar as a culture remained relatively stable (so that children's developmental experiences were similar to those of previous and subsequent generations), major themes tended to be carried forward from generation to generation in secular folklore and in hallowed sacred myths.

These consensually-shaped stories are group-created symbolized portrayals of shared memories of fantasies and of make-believe play, woven into the form of cultural narratives that "feel" "real." They portray people's deepest understanding of their lives' most significant truths, their consensus concerning what "really mattered" and was emotionally crucial as they grew up. The stories allow people an opportunity to revisit memories of mutative life experiences that they have shared with one another—pivotal turning points of developmental reorganization and ontogenetic metamorphosis in their particular culture. Over generations (sometimes millennia), people have refined and retold their sacred and secular narratives, not only to reminisce and to revisit old memories but also to pass on a legacy of experience and wisdom, providing potentially useful roadmaps and insights for their grandchildren and future generations. This symbolized data can help us to understand a culture's underlying core experiences in the same way that fantasies and dreams offer us access, in psychotherapy, to understanding individual psychodynamics. Like dreams, folk narratives have been defensively disguised and arise from condensations, symbolization, and displacements that function as ego-syntonic disguises. But underlying latent connotations can be understood within their associative context—the personal world of the dreamer or the cultural world of the teller of tales and his or her audience. Folk tales and myths have been collectively formulated as syntonic narratives that seem deeply "significant" and "meaningful." The attraction of this data is that it has been symbolized by members of a culture in a form that is syntonic for themselves, is readily accessible and gladly shared, and has left "tracks" or "footprints" in the form of stories and dramatic enactments that have been extensively documented and are archived and available to be studied. This data can significantly contribute when we seek to understand interpersonal relationships, communicate meaningfully, and collaborate with people from other cultures. The tales and myths, avidly collected by ethnographers and folklorists over the last two centuries, have been preserved, and are often catalogued and accessible in libraries and archives, in paperbacks, and/or on the Internet.[5] As cultures change, the stories evolve or they are replaced by new narratives.

FREUD'S VIEW OF CULTURALLY SHARED FANTASIES AND DREAMS

In the 1890s, at the time of his initial discovery of the value of dreams, Freud (1900) realized that myths and dreams were similar symbolized representations of unconscious fantasies, and that they become manifest through similar displacement, condensation, and symbolic representation. He suggested that just as dreams could serve as a royal road to understanding an individual's unconscious, mythology and folktales could offer insight into unconscious processes and conflicts shared by members of a particular group. He used familiar Greek and Biblical stories—Oedipus (1900 and 1912), Narcissus (1914), and Moses (1914 and 1939)—to illustrate and convey his ideas. He was also very interested in how children's play related to fantasy. In *Creative Writers and Day Dreaming* (1908), he described how "every child at play behaves like a creative writer, in that he creates a world of his own, or rather, rearranges the things of his world in a new way which pleases him" (p. 143). He suggested that play, like creative writing, could serve to present situations that, if real, would cause little pleasure but through imaginative activity can be both exciting and enjoyable.

In 1909, David Ernst Oppenheim, a professor of classical literature who was interested in folklore and had attended Freud's lectures, sent Freud a copy of an article he had written and dedicated to Freud on dreams in several European folktales. In the article, Oppenheim referred to Freud's psychoanalytic observations and said that the symbolism in these folktales "coincides completely with that accepted by psychoanalysis" (p. 25). Freud wrote back, proposing that they collaborate:

> I have long been haunted by the idea that our studies on the content of the neuroses might be destined to solve the riddle of the formation of myths, and that the nucleus of mythology is nothing other than what we speak of as "the nuclear complex of the neuroses." . . . Two of my pupils . . . have ventured upon an attempt to invade the territory of mythology and to make conquest in it with the help of the technique of psychoanalysis and its angle of approach. But we are amateurs and have every

> reason to be afraid of mistakes. We are lacking in academic training and familiarity with the material. Thus we are looking about for an enquirer . . . who possesses the specialized knowledge and is ready to apply to it the psychoanalytic armory that we will gladly put at his command. . . . Can it be that you are willing to be this man we are looking for? (p. 14)

Oppenheim agreed, sent Freud a number of secular European folktales, and they collaborated in drafting a paper on *Dreams in Folklore* (1911).[6] Discussing the folktales, Freud wrote,

> It is very much more convenient to study dream symbolism in folklore than in actual dreams. Dreams are obliged to conceal things . . . these comic (folkloric) anecdotes, however, . . . are intended as communications . . . meant to give pleasure to the person who tells them as well as to the listener, and therefore interpretation is added quite unashamedly to the (underlying unconscious) symbol. These stories delight in stripping off the veiling symbols. . . . It seems . . . that behind these . . . facades are concealed mental reactions to impressions of life which are to be taken seriously.[7] (p. 14)

DEVELOPMENT OF FANTASY DRAMAS IN CHILDHOOD AND THEIR SHARED EXTERNALIZATION IN FOLKLORE AND MYTHS

Children's creative playful juggling and rearranging of symbols within transitional states illusion leads children to new insights and new syntheses. Evolving forms of play are crucial as organizing processes at the interface between unconscious fantasy and cultural reality. Derivatives of play's fluid creative thinking, molding of images, and projective identificatory blurring of boundaries continue throughout life. Both myths and dramatized ritual enactments of shared folk narratives can offer access to culturally typical fantasies that originated in childhood imaginary play and in make-believe enactments. In latency and preadolescence, children increasingly move out beyond the interpersonal "subculture" of their own family into greater contact with the larger cultural environment. They seek to team up with like-minded latency and preadolescent peers in order to have allies who are "on their side" and to be safer in relation to real and imagined dangers. In emotionally distancing themselves from previous sources of security and esteem within the family, they seek peer support and a group leader whom they can follow. They tend to idealize a "good" peer group ("my" team) in relation to a "bad" peer group (the opposite team). Peer acceptance is needed and group consensus is sought.

The storylines of children's personal narratives that had been played out in imaginative play are shared and enacted in more structured interpersonal role-playing dramatic games during later childhood and early adolescence, and they contribute to the development of group-shared stories or scripts. They are "scripts" in that the roles have been formulated as potential action responses to be activated in certain circumstances, have been pre-rehearsed in imaginative play, and they have been enacted in interpersonal play to sample "audience" responses. Freud (1908) wrote that the skill of a dramatist or a novelist lies in his ability to imaginatively create a symbolic representational story or script that circumvents individual anxiety and resistance in an audience or readers, while permitting them to playfully participate in a shared make-believe illusion and to vicariously experience emotions which had been repressed and could not usually be discharged outside of a make-believe format. Ritvo (1993) suggested that "Play serves like a theater workshop" (p. 244) and that the creativity of the narrator is in the creative achievement of the ego that invents ways of giving expression to warded off drive derivatives or weaves a tale that disguises or hides them from open view (Solnit et al., 1993). Geertz (1972) described the entire culture of a people is an ensemble of such texts or play contexts. He suggested that shared play is a story people tell themselves about themselves. Potentially dangerous emotions and aggression can be expressed in the safety of the play form, since they are framed as "only play" and practical consequences are removed.

In the broader culture, there are agreed-upon traditions, roles and standards that guide people's actions and interactions. In the small peer group culture of latency and preadolescence, however, traditions and standards are in flux. Actions that are forbidden, and would create shame or guilt in a public forum, can be enacted if they are "played" out (as "just pretend") within loosely structured make-believe role-playing games that are contained by their own rules. Children join with one another in pretend interactions, trying out imaginary roles. Individuals' own personal fantasies and narratives are playfully shared, enacted, molded, and "socialized" in make-believe role-playing interaction with other children. In the course of the play and replays of fantasy enactments, both the narratives and individual roles are tailored and adjusted to become more meaningful for the individuals and the group. In addition, children continue to be imaginatively playful in personal dreaming, daydreaming and abstract make-believe play. As children and young adolescents become aware of their peers' points of view, they are able to view themselves from new perspectives. As they share personal stories, they discover commonalities and tend to merge the common features of their perspectives and insights. They try to accommodate and fit into an emerging consensus with other members of their group, or to fit into their group's deferral to a formula or game-plan proposed by the group leader. As individuals play different roles in fantasy game dramas and in real life interactions, and gain perspective on themselves among others, they try to align congruently with one another. Shared elements of individual narratives tend to converge and be merged. Individuals' personal memories and sense of identity, symbolized in their personal narratives, may be modified and somewhat reformulated in the course of the group's interplay. These peer interchanges (supplemented by increasing participation in broader cultural enactments, rituals, rites of passage, etc.) gradually adjust values, identities and roles within the group, leading toward a shared peer group culture emerging. Similar elements of the narratives gradually become integrated into a co-constructed agreed-upon symbolized version of "our life story."

No single personal perspective or script is likely to appeal equally to, or be syntonic and comfortable for, all members of any group. If a core theme is valued and meaningful to most people, that version of the story is consensually agreed upon and passed on in the culture's oral tradition. Details that are dystonic and themes that evoke anxiety for some members of the group may be fine-tuned and balanced by modifications, by adding mitigating or counterbalancing details, or by shifting the context of the story in order to lessen anxiety and resistance and to keep the storyline safely within the boundaries of make-believe and fantasy. The main components of consensus become integrated to constitute the current group's synthesized worldview and narrative.[8] Individual storytellers may embellish a story with additional personal twists, details, and associations of their own. If a particular detail in one person's narrative is new and resonates with deeper feelings for most people who hear the story, that detail may become incorporated into the group narrative. But a variant will only be passed on as part of the shared story if the particular detail seems to "fit" and "feel right," so that it enhances and clarifies the narrative. If a variant or embellishment seems extraneous, tangential or dystonic and doesn't "resonate" meaningfully for others, it will not be incorporated in the next retelling of the story.

MYTHOLOGY

Myths are collaborative symbolized condensations or syntheses of core "memories" in a group of individuals who have experienced similar formative experiences within a relatively homogeneous cultural milieu, in which parents share a common cultural perspective and philosophy and have used similar child-rearing practices in relating with their children. The stories portray successive stages of children's evolving perceptions, feelings, and object relations in their culture. Episodes of intrapsychic restructuralization in the course of development are often represented as heroic metamorphoses leading to the emergence of a new personality, and may be symbolized as death and rebirth or as the birth of a new generation.

The process of working out the interaction between positive and negative impulses is often portrayed as a story about mythical beings that are transformed back and forth between animal and human form. Negative impulses may be projected onto a beast or wild animal; idealized characteristics are commonly attributed to a cuddly pet or stuffed animal. In some societies, the animal image may be portrayed as more impulse ridden, self centered, and prone to antisocial behavior (for example, a trickster or monster), while the human image is seen as more refined, proper, and loyal to its responsibilities to others. In other cultures, mythical animals are manifestations of divinities and ancestral spirits that at times transform themselves into human form and interact with people. Alternately, there may be human-like angelic and demonic supernatural figures with cosmic or nether-world powers. Nursery rhymes, folk tales, toys and nighttime stories facilitate children's bridging the gap between the real world and a world of fantasy. Most cultures maintain some degree of idealization of cosmic figures and projective attribution of negative impulses to alien and fantasy beings. At first these co-created stories may be passed on as secular folklore tales. Throughout life, people like to return periodically to "replay" old memories, identify with actors "playing" dramatic roles in a ritual or on stage, and identify with secular team "players" engaging in competitive enactments in sports. Key mutative experiences, responses, and successful turning points are often later selectively remembered as "what really mattered" in one's life—crucial events that people want to revisit and share with one another, reminisce upon, and sometimes reenact in symbolic ritual and drama. Ultimately, over a number of generations, the most emotionally significant stories may become refined and valued as hallowed sacred myths.

Since both male and female members of a culture may be listeners and tellers as tales are transmitted from generation to generation, there may be two storylines or "red threads" condensed within a single myth, respectively portraying male and female perspectives at a particular stage of development. In that case, male and female listeners and tellers of a story may at times be having different associations, and may be tuned in to and hearing different story lines. In order for a stable fully elaborated system of mythology to evolve, a society must be relatively homogeneous and stable over time, with consistency of child rearing practices. Rapidly changing polymorphous heterogeneous societies also develop shared narratives, but these stories change from generation to generation and tend to be the products of subcultural groups rather than of society as a whole. Such self-generated fantasy material offers the analyst and psychoanalytic anthropologist access to the subjective experience of individuals—from a perspective inside one's self and one's culture—rather than the perspective of an onlooker viewing a culture from the outside. Although I can touch upon only a small number of stories, I will go into some of the detail in a few instances to illustrate the depth and richness of traditional narratives as shared memories, which—when combined with anthropologists' observations concerning adult child-rearing practices and concerning children's overt actions in play—can offer access to the ontogenesis and unconscious fantasies of people in another culture. As examples, we will explore shared narratives from two non-Western cultures for which we have both ethnographic data concerning child rearing practices and children's behavior, and folklorist documentation of the culture's mythology. We will briefly consider mythology of an Apache tribe whose stories emphasized the development of the heroic male hunter-warrior, and then a portion of traditional Japanese Shinto mythology that focused on the development of the girl who was destined to become the principal deity as the Sun Goddess. When cultures change so that ontogenetic experiences of children differ significantly from those of previous generations, shared fantasies become modified or replaced by newer narratives. In the last section of this chapter, I will briefly mention three recent feature-length animated movies that reflect present-day shared memories of ontogenesis (in Japan, China, and the United States) and offer to creatively update traditional folklore and mythological narratives in new portrayals that have been widely acclaimed in their respective cultures.

PLAINS APACHE (KIOWA APACHE) MYTHOLOGY

Having become interested in anthropology as an undergraduate, I felt that after medical school it might be valuable to become familiar with a non-Western culture as background before immersing myself in Western psychiatric and psychoanalytic training. This also worked out very well for my wife, who was working toward a masters degree in anthropology. We had the opportunity[9] to spend a year living with the Plains Apache tribe in Oklahoma (formerly referred to as "Kiowa Apache" tribe), from July 1964 to June 1965, prior to my adult and child psychiatric and psychoanalytic training.

Myths, like dreams related early in treatment, condense much more than we can initially appreciate. I recall feeling puzzled and somewhat disorientated when we first encountered Apache mythology.[10] Often, there are details in the folklore of an unfamiliar culture that may initially be experienced by an outsider as dystonic or confusing. These seemingly strange or perplexing details reflect unexpected nuances and differences in ontogenesis and intrapsychic functioning in a newly encountered and as-yet unfamiliar cultural world.[11] I also wondered why the Apaches emphasized the importance of telling their stories in a particular sequence, although they were not aware of a reason for this. In certain instances, they knew that the telling of one myth was supposed to be immediately followed by the telling of another (seemingly unrelated) story, so that the second flowed directly from the first. They felt that the traditional sequence had deep significance, but they were not sure why. Because we felt somewhat perplexed during our initial immersion in Apache mythology, we did not pursue it further at that time, and instead learned from and about the Apaches by living and interacting with them and their families. My wife's masters thesis was on "Kiowa Apache Concepts and Attitudes toward the Child" in 1965 (P. A. Freeman, 1971), and I wrote about "Adolescent Crises of the Kiowa Apache Indian Male" (D. M. A. Freeman, 1968).

Ten years later, I was invited to participate in, and to be reporter for, a 1976 American Psychoanalytic Association panel on "Psychoanalysis, Folklore, and Processes of Socialization" with Jacob Arlow, Bryce and Ruth Boyer (who had lived with and studied the Mescalero Apaches), and the folklorist Alan Dundes (D. M. A. Freeman, 1977). In the interim I had become more familiar with intrapsychic and interpersonal development, during my child psychiatric and child psychoanalytic training. I was surprised to discover that, when I looked at Apache myths again from a more comprehensive perspective, the meaning of the seemingly unrelated stories was suddenly clear. What I was reading was an autobiographical portrayal of a sequential developmental continuum. As the stories moved through a series of dangerous challenges and death-and-rebirth transitions and metamorphoses, they portrayed a sequence of developmental stages, each with its concomitant personality reorganization and intrapsychic restructuralization. The myths and folktales reflected a progressive unfolding of individual male and female developmental lines in their culture. Even when the narratives had been defensively symbolized so that they appeared to be about different mythical figures in seemingly unrelated circumstances, they portrayed the Apaches' shared autobiographic perception of the flow of their developmental experiences.[12]

Several parallel Apache cycles of myths portray experiences that traditionally shaped an Apache boy's development from childhood through turbulent adolescent reckless warrior years (which culminated in a vision quest to beseech aid from departed ancestors and supernatural powers), leading to his ultimately settling down and becoming a stable responsible elder once he reached grandparenthood. I will summarize the first portion of the storyline of one of these cycles of myths so that we can see how the shared narratives recapitulate ontogenesis. Occasionally I will briefly refer to collateral details from other parallel story cycles that can enhance and clarify our understanding of the stories.

The Plains Apache story about the hero twins, Fire Boy and Water Boy (McAllister, 1949) begins with their mother's childhood family. She and her family had been starving, but then started to repeatedly inexplicably find food lying on a path. Nistcre, a cannibalistic monster with a body of stone, had been leaving food in order to fatten them, as he was planning to eat them. They realized what was happening and fled, but Nistcre pursued and successively overtook one after another, until only the girl survived. Thunderman rescued her and concealed her. When Nistcre threatened Thunderman, he struck Nistcre with lightning, blowing the monster to bits. Thunderman married the girl and they lived on a hill near a river. When she was pregnant, she told her husband that outside the teepee something was saying, "Look at me! Look at me!" but that she didn't want to look. Thunderman told her to never look. Just before her baby was due to be born, she again heard this voice while her husband was away, and her curiosity got the better of her. When she punched a hole in the teepee covering and looked out, something hit her and killed her, and took her twin babies. It threw the youngest boy into the ashes of the fire and the eldest into the river. When Thunderman returned and found his wife dead, he said, "I told you not to look at the sun. She's jealous of you." (The sun had been his former wife.) Thunderman magically revived his wife and discovered a baby in the fireplace ashes. They called him Fire Boy. Once Fire Boy was old enough to play on his own outside, he went down to the river, called out to his twin, and they played together. Thunderman wondered who his son was playing with. Fire Boy finally admitted he was playing with his brother who lived in the river with his grandfather, Snapping Turtle. Although Thunderman wanted Fire Boy to lure the brother out of the river so that they could catch him, they anticipated that Water Boy would try to fight to get away. Since the brother was wild, had long nails, and would bite, Thunderman gave Fire Boy a thick jacket so as not to be hurt. They captured and carried Water Boy back to their teepee and Thunderman called him "son." But Water Boy continued to cry and wanted to go back to his grandfather, the water monster Snapping Turtle. They put cedar and an aromatic root on the fire to create thick smoke (which was used to treat emotional disorders and to get rid of bad spirits), and talked kindly to him. Thunderman said, "I am your father, and this is your mother and your brother." Water Boy said, "But you threw me away!" Thunderman replied, "No, we didn't throw you away. But we have you back and you must stay with us." Water Boy calmed down, they cut his fingernails, and he began playing with his brother and forgot about his grandfather. The two brothers became great pals and went around doing things together.

In order to orient ourselves before going on to the next story, we need to briefly digress to consider how Apache child-rearing concepts and practices affected an infant and young child, and led to a slowing of a child's rate of progression through the stages of the life cycle, including a prolongation of adolescence (D. M. A. Freeman, 1968). This prolongation was adaptive in that it maximized the daring, initiative, and reckless assertiveness that were advantageous in a warrior-hunter. In their teens and twenties, young Apache men and women were not yet ready to form stable heterosexual attachments. The men were often away from home, and the women were responsible for cooking, tanning hides, making teepees and clothes, caring for infants, and the hard labor of nomadically moving to new campsites. In these active years of their twenties, although they bore children, neither men nor women were adequately emotionally available for the task of caring for children. Initial marriages, in their early thirties, were unstable and temporary. Stable deepening attachment to a spouse and one's family developed only with an advance in years (McAllister, 1937). Final maturation was catalyzed by the advent of the opportunity to serve in a grandparental role.[13] Grandparents assumed this role once a toddler was weaned, at around eighteen months of age.

An infant experienced a dichotomous relationship with his or her mother. On the one hand, infants were in a position of special privilege. They were seen as magically omnipotent, and their mothers were expected to respond immediately to every whimper. However a mother's responses were inconsistent. An Apache mother was traditionally afraid that her infant was omniscient and that he or she was aware of the mother's ambivalent thoughts and impulses to "get away" from the child. They would say, "A baby knows!" A mother feared that if she fell asleep while nursing, the infant would turn into a "water dog lizard" and would bore through her breast into her heart and kill her. She felt a need to "get away" from the infant, and traditionally kept the baby bundled on a cradle-board, hanging near her so that she and the infant could see one another, with the cradleboard often being rocked by a breeze (P. A. Freeman, 1971). The ambivalently favored position of a youngest child led to the severity of his or her fall when the mother became pregnant again and a new baby was on the way, or when the nursing toddler had reached about eighteen months of age. In the midst of the child's rapprochement subphase of separation-individuation (Mahler et al., 1975), at a stage when toddlers become intermittently anxious about issues of autonomy and separateness, and alternately push away from and cling to their mother, the mother could not tolerate the child's ambitendent behavior.[14] The child would suddenly abruptly be rejected and "thrown away." The mother would put a bad-tasting substance on her nipples, withdraw from the child, and (often harshly) say, "Get away!" Fortunately, supportive, loving and empathic substitute relationships were available, and the more mature grandparents would take over the "parenting" role.

In this light, we can understand that the story of Fire Boy and Water Boy illustrates a prolongation of rapprochement turmoil and a delay in neutralization and integration of split-apart images of "good parent" versus "bad parent" and of "good self" versus "bad self." As a result of the traumatic interruption of the child's relationship with the primary object, rapprochement resolution and the move toward stable internal self and object representations was delayed. Adults might seem to be duplicitous cannibalizing monsters (like Nistcre) or benevolent rescuers and protectors (like Thunderman or Snapping Turtle). The child's self was split into a more primitive impulsive aggressive self (Water Boy) and a more mature constructive collaborative self (Fire Boy). Fire Boy was the "younger" twin who had been rescued and grew up in the parental home to become the "good" side of the self in relation to the good parents. Water Boy, was the "older" sibling who remembered he had been thrown away by his parent, and remained angry until he was recognized, rescued, and reassuringly called "son." The beginning of resolution, neutralization, and integration of these polarities, and a move toward stable individuated autonomy, self-constancy and object-constancy, began only when it was mediated by a loving parental figure. A very special relationship of reciprocity and intimacy existed between a grandchild and grandparent, both of whom were dependent upon the active young adult generation to care for their basic needs. They referred to each other as being equivalent, using the identical kinship term (*dah-ton*) for one another. Their relationship offered a new world of special privilege for the child, as the mature grandparent was truly devoted to the child, taught the child about the world, and would rarely refuse a grandchild's request.

The grandparent's storytelling provided mythical figures with whom a child could now identify. In the mythology and in grandparental tales of their own exploits during their youth, stress was laid on winning acclaim by being daring, ignoring cautions, and attempting to accomplish whatever was dangerous and "impossible." Grandparents would say, "My mother said, 'Don't do this; don't do that.' But I did those things and I learned my own way." "I just went ahead—I do anything!" "We're just free. We do what we want!" (D. M. A. Freeman, 1968, 1977). As the story continues, Fire Boy and Water Boy "became great pals" and "went around shooting and doing things together." Identifying with and imaginatively participating in the exploits of their elders' stories, they engaged in heroic adventures, overcoming prehistoric dangers and triumphing over enemies. Whenever cautioned not to go somewhere because of danger, they went there, conquered the danger, and reported back, "We did what you told us not to do . . . but we got the best of them and killed them." Ultimately, however, when warned that they had better stay away from Cyclone, they, as usual, recklessly went out to conquer it but couldn't get the best of Cyclone, and they were never seen again.

This story was to always be followed immediately by the story of an old lady who lived alone. When she went out to find some wood for her fire, she found what seemed to be a clot of blood. When she put it into her pot to cook it and make soup, the clot of blood miraculously turned into a baby! Apaches explained that the clot of blood was all that was left of Fire Boy and Water Boy. The baby grew into a child, Poor Boy, who was clumsy, unkempt, unattractive and snotty, and at first appeared to be the antithesis of competence and of everything that Apaches would value in a child. This orphan represented the poor self image of a lonely rejected child who is rescued by his grandmother when his good and bad sides initially have merged into one.

Yet there appeared to be "something special" about him. As the story continues, it becomes apparent that Poor Boy has magical powers. He performs impossible feats to win the chief's beautiful daughter, though he at first is not ready to consummate his marriage to her. He performed a number of miracles providing food for the tribe in the middle of winter, and distanced himself from impulse-ridden "coyote" trickster aspects of himself that briefly re-emerged. Poor Boy then goes through another metamorphosis. He goes off on a magical journey (vision quest) to the world of the ancestral spirits, and is reborn to become one of the most important and sacred of Apache healers and leaders. Later, when he departs for the sky world, he becomes their most important divine figure, Blue-White Man (McAllister, 1949).

JAPANESE ANCIENT SHINTO AND CURRENT MYTHOLOGIES

We will consider some stories from ancient Japanese Shinto mythology, and then look at how cultural changes have been reflected in modern Japanese shared narratives documented in other media. Sacred Shinto mythology, which had roots in oral traditions dating back to earlier millennia of unrecorded history, was collected and compiled in written form at the beginning of the eighth century AD.[15] Initial stories described "The Age of the Gods" (Aston, 1972). Heaven had emerged as a pure, orderly, united body out of an original state of void or chaos. Earth, however, was still a formless heavier, grosser thing, floating below Heaven like drifting oil or a jellyfish floating on water. A confident young goddess, Izanami, and her new husband, Izanagi, descended from Heaven with a charter to organize and establish Earth as their new home. As they came down the Floating Rainbow Bridge from Heaven, Izanagi reached down and stirred the formless mass with the tip of his Heavenly Jeweled Spear until it began to curdle. He drew up his lance, and sticky glutinous brine dripped from its tip and coagulated to form an island. Descending to the island, the hero and heroine erected a pole called The Pillar of the Center of the Land, and proceeded together with the work of creation, giving birth to the forces of nature, the land, and the gods. They gave birth to Amaterasu, the Sun Goddess, whom they designated to become ruler of the Universe; her consort, the Moon God; and a fierce tempered, wailing, demanding, wicked god, Susano-wo, who was to become ruler of the Nether Land. But suddenly, the mother goddess Izanami was burned while giving birth to the God of Fire, and she died after terrible suffering. The tragic loss of Izanami left her husband and children alone and inconsolable. Furious at the baby who had caused Izanami's death, Izanagi picked up his sword and cut off its head. He was unable to deal with the separation and tried to follow Izanami to the subterranean Land of Darkness, begging her to return to the world of the living. She told him not to enter her house in the Land of Darkness, and said, "I beseech you not to look at me!" Izanagi, however, ignored her warning and looked into her dwelling. When he saw her decomposing body full of maggots and smelled the sickening odor, he became repulsed and terrified, and fled in revulsion and horror. Izanami was mortified and enraged about having been seen by him in this condition, felt violated and deeply shamed and rejected by his reaction of revulsion. She sent the Thunder Gods (or snake deities) and all of the Hideous Female Spirits of Hades to kill him. She also chased after him herself. Izanagi tried to escape with the demons pursuing. He managed to get to the end of the tunnel and blocked the opening with a giant rock. Izanami screamed and cursed at him from behind the rock, saying, "I will strangle to death one thousand of your offspring every day!" Izanagi replied that he didn't care: "I will build fifteen hundred parturition huts and give birth to fifteen hundred babies every day!" (Aston, 1972).

The disruption that had occurred in most children's lives was not the actual death of their mother, but rather the interruption and the loss of the unique intimacy of their symbiotic relationship, often at the time of the birth of a new baby. The birth of a sibling would lead to the abrupt deflation of a young child's sense of shared dyadic omnipotence. Children identified with the image of the needy Izanagi pursuing their lost mother. He embodied the anguish and pain experienced by those who had depended upon her. They wished to hold onto her, and wished for but feared reunion, feeling the same ambivalent impulses as Izanagi was experiencing. Their continuing hurt, angry and demanding feelings led children to fear that it was they who were either the Fire Child or the assertively intrusive and demanding Izanagi who had hurt their mother, and that she had abandoned them because of their aggression. The child would attempt to project his or her feelings of rage and destructive impulses onto the new sibling, blaming and imagining punishment for the Fire Child.[16] The bereaved father, Izanagi, went through a process of trying to purify himself, as one must do after contact with the dead, but he continued to cry. Two principal deities (Amaterasu the Sun Goddess, and her younger brother Susano-wo the Storm God or "Impetuous One") who had been born earlier were now reborn from their father's tears and from the washings of his eyes and nose. Their rebirth refers to their 'psychological birth' or individuation (Mahler et al., 1975) which occurred at this stage.[17] Their individuated personalities that emerged in the new gelling of identity at this stage were distinctly different from one another. Henceforth, female and male story lines interact in a complementary way, but diverge.

The father, Izanagi, built himself an abode of gloom, wishing to withdraw into silence and concealment. He assigned to each child the responsibility for ruling in a realm of their own, and instructed them to go to their respective kingdoms. However, the problem of dealing with separation and loss was much worse for the youngest, Susano-wo. Whereas Amaterasu ascended to become the principal deity in Heaven, her brother Susano-wo would not leave and was unable to be consoled. He continued weeping and groaning. His loud intrusive crying is described as like a typhoon; his rage and uncontrolled behavior were intolerable. No one could stand the noise. His wailing withered the green mountains, and dried up rivers and seas. He was impetuous, violent and destructive, and associated with the deities that work evil. At first his father tried to console him, and asked him what was wrong. But when his father heard that Susano-wo wanted to go to visit his dead mother, the father got very angry, could tolerate it no longer, and banished Susano-wo. Susano-wo said that before departing, he wanted to visit his sister Amaterasu in her realm in Heaven to say goodbye to her. When Amaterasu heard the commotion as the out-of-control "Impetuous One" was approaching, she feared he would try to take control of her land or wreck her kingdom. She put on male clothing, donned a suit of armor, came out with weapons ready to do battle, and issued a battle cry. She stamped the earth, shouted "with an awesome fury," and put forth "her dread manly valor." Susano-wo sued for rapprochement and peace, saying that he was not trying to make any trouble but was only trying to say goodbye. Trying to pull himself together and to rise to a more responsible grownup level, he said that he had no evil intent and promised to behave maturely. He suggested, in fact, that he and Amaterasu be joined in a solemn alliance and that they get together to produce some children, to continue the creation work left unfinished by their parents. Amaterasu agreed. Their procreative acts then occurred with each standing on an opposite side of the wide Holy River of Heaven. Susano-wo gave Amaterasu his sword, which she broke, chewed up, and blew out as a mist or foggy spray to produce three female children. She then gave him her strings of jewels, which he cracked between his teeth and blew out as a misty spray to create five male children[18] (Aston, 1972).

An older girl's and young woman's experiences at two different stages of life, first as an older sister and later as a young mother, are condensed in this story. During childhood, older sisters were called upon to become responsible, to assume a mature "maternal" role, and to accept and forgive the immature demandingness, clinging, and boisterous aggression of younger brothers. The early socialization experiences of a girl differed from those of a boy. Greater emphasis was placed on an expectation that girls should develop affectomotor and postural controls, politeness, deference, reticence, and restraints on their own assertive and autonomous behavior. Girls would identify with a mature maternal role. Boys were permitted greater latitude to be assertive and to express ambivalent feelings and demands for satisfaction. As a result, girls would become more controlled and more "responsible," and, at least on the surface, more able to tolerate separation than their brothers.

Later, like her mother before her, she would be called upon as a young woman to leave her family home and to go off to establish a new family in an unfamiliar foreign environment. In a traditional arranged marriage, she would leave her own parental family to live in her husband's and mother-in-law's home. At first a young wife would be a stranger in her mother-in-law's domain; but ultimately, once she became the mother of her husband's children, she would become the most important figure, the Sun Goddess, of a new family.

Amaterasu tried to serve in the maternal role thrust upon her. She tried to be mature and to handle her feelings. But she too had lost her mother, and like her father she found Susano-wo to be more than she was able to tolerate. She saw him as being like the Fire Child who had already taken her mother away from her, and feared that this brother was wanting to invade her new realm and take that away from her as well! She feared he would try to take control and wreck her kingdom. When Susano-wo sued for peace and promised to try his best to be grown up and be good, she was relieved and accepted his offer. But neither Susano-wo nor Amaterasu had much of an understanding yet about how to be a mature adult or about how to make babies. Susano-wo was so pleased with his "success" that he overreached himself. He was unable to sustain a more grown up level of functioning, and his impetuous and destructive side again broke through. He started to break down boundaries—dikes between rice fields, fences, and walls—and he defecated and urinated on the floor of Amaterasu's sacred New Palace when she is about to celebrate the feast of tasting of first-fruits. As an older sister, the Sun Goddess reacted in a motherly way, accommodating, forgiving and making excuses for the disruptive behavior of an impetuous son. (Boys will be boys. He's trying. He really meant well. Boys are like that. What do you expect?) Everyone else was beside themselves with anger, but Amaterasu at first did not protest Susano-wo's disruptive and destructive acts, and in fact made excuses for him (Philippi, 1968, p. 79). This continued until Susano-wo went too far and committed an act that Amaterasu was unable to tolerate.

At the climax of his impetuous behavior, Susano-wo broke a hole through the roof of the sacred Weaving Hall or temple where the Sun Goddess and other goddesses were weaving the sacred garments of the gods, and he threw the skinned corpse of a dead horse into their sacred chamber (Aston, p. 41). This was a most extreme ultimate act of violation, pollution, and contamination! According to one version, everyone was so startled that a weaving shuttle penetrated the genitals of one of the goddesses and killed her (Philippi, 1968, p. 80). The Sun Goddess became so frightened, incensed, and enraged that she withdrew and sealed herself inside a cave, plunging the world into darkness and winter. In another version, the goddess who was injured and killed was the Sun Goddess herself, and the cave that she entered was her tomb (Aston, 1972, p. 41). Though an older sister has a responsibility to care for younger siblings, Amaterasu was still at a bisexual stage of her own development, uncertain about her gender identity and femininity, uncertain how to procreate, in need of privacy and embarrassed about being intruded upon. She was concerned about messy pollution and contamination. She had begun to understand that babies were created in a sacred chamber, "woven" like sacred cloth inside the women's sacred Weaving Hall or Temple. But her image at this stage was of a process in which only females would participate. She continued to be sensitive and anxious about the impetuous male who did not respect her boundaries, and wouldn't give her space. She feared penetration as an ultimate violation and humiliation, causing injury and contamination, and was not yet familiar with or comfortable about ideas of genital interchange. Amaterasu sought to flee from 'The Impetuous One' who wouldn't respect her privacy, did not respect her request that he not enter and not look, and intruded (like his father, Izanagi). The idea of a male barging in, making a hole in her sacred chamber, throwing something contaminating inside, and penetrating with a shuttle cock was mortifying and terrifying. She hid, slammed the door shut, and sought to seal up her cave forever. Everyone was deprived of the sun's light and warmth and the world was plunged into cold and darkness. This was not unlike Amaterasu's own experience. She too was cold, lost, hurting, and alone. She had lost own her mother, who was also locked in an underground cave forever. The withdrawal of the Sun Goddess plunged the world into darkness, offering evil spirits and ghosts an opportunity to gain control. All manner of calamities occurred.

The gods got together to figure out how to get Amaterasu to come back. They decided to put on a joyful festival, with a sexy sacred goddess (Uzume) doing a raucous striptease dance in front of the mouth of the cave, hoping to pique the Sun Goddess's interest and curiosity. They also welded stars together to form a large mirror. Carried away by divine ecstasy, the dancer pounded her feet, exposed her breasts and then pushed her skirt-band down below her genitals. The crowd roared its approval with laughter. Hearing the sounds of revelry outside the cave, the Sun Goddess wondered what is going on. She was amazed that everyone didn't seem to be sad, and peeked out to find out what was happening. This is what the gods had planned. They held the mirror up in front of her, showing Amaterasu her own reflection, and said, "There is someone out here even superior to you. That's why we're rejoicing and dancing." The Sun Goddess was astonished to behold a bright deity, not knowing that she was seeing her own reflected image, and gradually came forth. Only then did she discover that it was her own image that was beautiful. In another version, the gods praised her more directly, reciting a liturgy in her honor. Amaterasu responded to the warmth of their prayers and praise. As the Sun Goddess stepped part way out of the cave and approached the mirror, the God of Force grasped hold of her hand and drew her out, while another god stretched a sacred rope behind her to prevent her from retreating. They appealed to her, told her that they need her, and begged her not to deprive them of her presence again. Just at the time when she was most conflicted and feeling the worst about herself and her body, Amaterasu was astonished to discover that people thought she was beautiful, saw her as a giver of nurturing warmth and light, missed her, and wanted to draw her toward them. She peeked out, looked into the mirror and discovered to her surprise that she was, in fact, attractive rather than dirty. She heard people saying, "Don't pull away from us—we want you and need you!" They helped her to discover that she was desirable and that she could be light and warmth for everyone if she came out and joined them. They tried to cheer her up and to relieve her of her sadness and mourning by creating joyous music, dancing, and rollicking festivity.

It is important to note that Uzume, the dancing Goddess of Mirth and Joy, was traditionally portrayed in Japanese folk art and sculpture not as a lithe young woman but rather as an older woman. An older woman was more comfortable with her sexuality and served as an example for the young early adolescent girl who was shy and afraid. The young girl watched from a distance, and at first was somewhat surprised to see that mature women seem to enjoy their fertility and sensuality and to be the joyous center of everybody's attention. Amaterasu hadn't yet consolidated her feminine identity and her feelings about herself and her body. Uzume and the others around her helped Amaterasu to feel attractive and to develop a new idea about femininity. Amaterasu came out of the cave and began to become more comfortable in the adventure of discovering herself as a woman.

Mythologies change over time to reflect changes in a culture. As stories are retold and reenacted by successive generations, ancient details may be revised or entire stories replaced by new shared narratives—particularly if a culture is changing relatively rapidly, as has commonly been the case in recent centuries, especially the modern era. Japanese culture was influenced by Buddhist and Confucian ideas from India and China, and—since the nineteenth century—by ideas from the West. Plains Apache culture was influenced by the Kiowa and Comanche tribes, and during the past century by the culture of the Euro-American settlers among whom they now live.

The generation of autobiographical narratives in individual children's imaginative play, the shaping of fantasy dramas in group interpersonal play, and the process of developing and refining consensually shared folktales and mythology continue generation after generation. As Freud (1908) pointed out—talented artistic individuals who have skill in creating symbolic narratives that circumvent anxiety and resistance while permitting playful vicarious participation in repressed emotions experienced within shared illusion, become recognized as the storytellers, novelists, or dramatists whose works meaningfully express a cultural consensus. Older stories may be revised, merged, or become interesting curiosities or hallowed uncanny antiques.

Cultural themes and ontogenetic experiences reflected in shared narratives may be supplemented by documentation in other media. For example, the Japanese are a visually oriented people whose visual art offers us pooled direct mother-child "observational" data that we can correlate with shared fantasies portrayed in folklore and mythology (Kitayama, 2005; Freeman, 2005). Exquisitely sensitive artistic portrayals of intimate mother-infant and mother-child interactions and of children's play in Ukiyo-e woodblock prints during the seventeenth through nineteenth centuries comprise a source of shared-memory data that can offer us insights concerning children's development during that period of Japanese history.[19] In our current world, feature-length animated movies have proven to be an ideal artistic medium, in which mythological and magical animated figures can dramatically enact current culturally shared myth-like ontogenetic fantasy narratives. Creative contemporary teams of Chinese, Japanese, and American storytellers and artists have recently offered myth-like animated feature-length movie narratives that vividly portray culturally shared memories as 'children's stories' which are deeply meaningful not only to children but also to the adults who accompany children to the theater. All three have been enthusiastically received in their respective cultures[20] and in our local theaters. They offer a relatively simple way to gain direct access to current up-to-date culturally shared narratives that portray a girl's latency and adolescent development in today's Japan (Hayao Miyazaki's *Ponyo*), a boy's childhood and adolescent development in modern China (*Lotus Lantern*, updating an ancient mythological story), and a boy's latency and preadolescent conflicts and development in the United States (Spike Jonze's *Where the Wild Things Are*, updating Maurice Sendak's 1963 classic children's story). Each story is portrayed in an animated film that has been on the screen of our local theaters during the past year, and is available on DVD. These superb present-day intuitive narrative constructs are up-to-date "folktale" treasures that epitomize a culture's shared consensus, in exquisitely apt and "meaningful" dramas which epitomize sequential stages of individual development. Synthesizing the available data from ethnographers' observations of adult perspectives and child-rearing practices and their observations of children's play and game behaviors, folklorists' archives of shared fantasies symbolically embodied in traditional mythology and folklore, and current updates or revisions in the form of new culturally shared narratives, can serve as a royal to understanding a culture's shared dreams, shared memories, and shared unconscious fantasies.

NOTES

1. For the past year and a half, for example, over one hundred Chinese mental health professionals at five major universities in China have been participating in an extensive two-

year lecture and seminar training program on psychoanalytic concepts and receiving supervision and psychoanalytic psychotherapy from more than two-hundred American psychoanalysts, through Skype and the Internet, under the auspices of the China American Psychoanalytic Alliance. At such cultural interfaces, we come to recognizing how much we need to grow by learning from one another.

2. Freud focused on Western classical Greek and Biblical myths, with which his colleagues and readers were familiar. He was aware of his lack of familiarity with other cultures' mythology, and wrote "we are amateurs, and have every reason to be afraid of making mistakes. We are lacking in academic training and familiarity with the material" (1911, p. 14). Later, when Freud's students from Japan (Heisaku Kosawa) and India (Girindrasekar Bose) presented non-Western myths to Freud, he seemed intrigued but puzzled by the differences in their frames of reference as he did not have the cultural "associative" material he needed to understand these stories within their cultural contexts.

3. As Moore and Fine (1990) noted, "Psychoanalysis has from the time of its inception been concerned with the study of mythology as an avenue to understanding the workings of the human mind. Freud (1926) explicitly stated that knowledge of mythology was necessary to an analyst's work. Arlow (1961) stressed the myth as a shared fantasy that serves multiple purposes of instinctual gratification, defense, and adaptation for the group and its individual members. In return for renouncing gratification of infantile instinctual wishes, which is necessary for civilized living, the individual is presented with community acceptable versions of the wishes in the form of myth.

4. In her update, Schwartzman (2001) suggested that, during the 1990s, anthropological studies started to become more "child-focused"; and she hoped that this foreshadowed a future "anthropology of children" that would focus on children's perspectives as social actors, with children being "incorporated as both informants and research collaborators" (p. 4).

5. In later sections, we will be considering examples that illustrate these processes in Apache, Japanese, Chinese, and American cultures.

6. This paper was, unfortunately, only published posthumously (Freud and Oppenheim, 1958).

7. Freud's collaboration with Oppenheim was interrupted when Oppenheim went off in a different direction. Freud apparently did not find a Narcissus (1914) or Moses (1914 and 1939).

8. The particular issues that are focused upon and played out in group role-playing games tend to be culture-specific. In societies where previous experiences have led to a considerable degree of unneutralized aggression in late childhood and adolescence, make-believe role-playing enactments in the group may lead to schisms into subgroups, or an assertive leader or bully may become dominant and direct the group's aggression toward a scapegoat within the group or toward outsiders perceived to be enemies. The shared worldview of such groups is affected by and becomes reflected in their culture's folklore and mythology. Alternately, in some adolescent play groups, the interactive experience may lead to a pleasurable illusion of flowing together with others into a feeling of unity and "communitas," reaching a new equilibrium freed from the constraints of the real world. For example, Robert N Freeman (1995) studied "Deadheads"—devotees of "The Grateful Dead" musical group and of "Other People" (a musical group inspired by Grateful Dead). During performances, musicians and audience would merge with one another in play through the music and dancing. "Rules and structures are clearly integral to the play. . . . Other People erect a familiar playground, freeing themselves to frolic in its gaps, challenging themselves to invent fresh games to play within these spaces, and surprising themselves in the moments when the process seems effortless and inevitable. . . . As individuals begin to flow within these systems, they experience the disappearance of apparent structural constraints though full internalization of relevant rule systems" (pp. 52-53).

9. Supported by the University of Oklahoma Medical School and Department of Anthropology.

10. Traditional Plains Apache mythology had been extensively collected in 1933–1934 (McAllister, 1949) from tribal elders who had learned the stories as children in the late 1860s and 1870s, when most traditional Apache cultural systems were still intact. The elders had a tradition of trying to strictly quote and retell the stories *exactly* as, and only as, their own grandparents' had told them. The collected stories therefore dated from a time before the

Apaches had been conquered and before significant culture change had occurred. Many of the stories continued to be alive and relevant in the early 1960s, when an elder explained that, "If a person has good parents or good grandparents, they will tell you the creation story from night to night, and they will take an interest in their children and grandchildren. They will try to instill good things into the children by telling them these stories" (Bittle, 1964 [unpublished notes]).

11. This initial experience has been referred to as "culture shock." These novel aspects of a culture may similarly be puzzling and disorienting when they appear in a patient's associative material and transference, unless their cultural and developmental context is understood.

12. Paul Radin (1956) had made a similar observation concerning Winnebago Indian trickster myths.

13. Elders would encourage a new grandfather to move forward in this final step in maturation into his new nurturing role, saying, "You're a *man* now, not a boy!"

14. This difficult and often-turbulent phase has sometimes been referred to colloquially in our culture as the "terrible twos."

15. The ancient stories were recorded in two official compilations, *Kojiki* (712 AD) and *Nihongi* (or *Nihonshoki*) (720 AD), which later were translated into English by Philippi (1968) and Aston (1972) respectively.

16. Kitayama (1985, 1991) has discussed self-blame for having injured mother as it appears in folk tales and affects personality development.

17. Mythological transitions of death and rebirth symbolically represent developmental reorganization in the child. As children mourn and relinquish their previous attachment to the mother, they form a symbolic internal representation of the relinquished mother as she had been experienced in the preceding developmental stage. Then, in the next stage, they establish a new relationship with a mother who is experienced in a different way, from a more mature individuated perspective. Simultaneously, as the former relationship is relinquished and mourned, there is an intrapsychic reorganization in the child and a reformulation of the child's own sense of identity and self. These changes are often portrayed in myths as the birth of a new generation.

18. This pregenital view of oral procreation contrasts with an image portrayed earlier, in the opening story, of the newlywed Izanagi and Izanami having discovered adult genital procreative interaction.

19. Each fragile Ukiyo-e paper print that was carefully protected and handed down from generation to generation has been preserved and has reached us because the interactions portrayed in the pictures were experienced as very *deeply* meaningful and the prints were therefore treasured by successive generations.

20. The recognition that each of these films has received within their own culture attests to their resonance with shared dreams, fantasies, and memories.

Chapter Eight

Playing for Survival during the Holocaust

Ira Brenner

> "If one in the future would like to discover traces of our life in the ghetto, and there would be no documents or diaries to be found to bear witness, this site will be a genuine symbol of an unrestrainable vitality and an unrelenting will for survival in us." —A Jewish official in the Vilna ghetto upon the opening of a new sports area and playground

Of the roughly six million unanswerable questions that may be asked about the Holocaust, one of the most perplexing pertains to the nature of "play." While it is indeed amply documented through diaries and journals as well as survivor testimonies, photographs, artwork, and poetry, it is not yet possible to have a full understanding of the meaning, purpose, and capacity to play under the conditions of sadistic, dehumanizing, genocidal persecution. A young girl in the Warsaw ghetto simply put it this way: "When I am in play, I forget my hunger. I forget that outside of such evil Germans even exist. Early in the morning I rush to the child care center and I wish that the day would never end, because when it is getting dark, we all have to return home. In my room it is so full with dark shadows and black fear" (Eisen, 1988, p. 101).

An eyewitness report to his superiors in London from Jan Karski, a member of the Polish government in exile who secretly entered the Warsaw ghetto to document the conditions noted:

> Everywhere there was hunger, misery, the atrocious stench of decomposing bodies, the pitiful moans of dying children. We passed a miserable replica of a park—a low square of comparatively clear ground in which a half-dozen nearly leafless trees and a patch of grass had somehow managed to survive. It was fearfully crowded. Mothers huddled close together on benches nursing withered infants. Children, every bone in their skeletons showing through their taut skins, played in heaps and

> swarms. "They play before they die," I heard my companion on the left say, his voice breaking with emotion. Without thinking, the words escaping even before the thought had crystallized—I said: "But these children are not playing. They only make believe it is play." (Karski, 1944, quoted in Eisenberg, 1981, pp. 169–70)

Karski's enigmatic words warrant deeper consideration of what it is these children were doing. In my own work with Judith Kestenberg interviewing child survivors (Kestenberg and Brenner, 1996), it became abundantly clear that they felt robbed of their childhoods and many felt that they either never learned or had lost their capacity to play. When they became parents, many complained that they could not play with their own children. Indeed, Auerhahn and Laub (1987) corroborate this finding through their analytic work with three Holocaust survivors and conclude that the extent to which one can rediscover her lost playfulness is an indicator of her potential to heal.

Anna Freud and Sophie Dann (1951) describe an "experiment" determined by "fate" in which six orphans from Terezin, ages three to three-and-a-half, were treated in a group living situation at "Bulldogs Bank" in 1945. These children, whose parents were murdered by the Nazis, entered the camp under the age of twelve months and were cared for as best as possible in the Ward for Motherless Children. They had no toys, had access only to a bare yard and the only food they had was a pasty, starchy porridge. When they arrived in England, they did not know how to play and were ignorant about the natural world, with the exception of dogs, which reminded them of Nazi guard dogs and terrified them. At first they destroyed their toys and much of the furniture and were aggressive or indifferent toward the adults. However, the group loyalty and libidinal ties to each other were very strong. Over time they chose soft toys as transitional objects which they took to bed and used for masturbating. Although they learned quickly and became more socialized, the very strong ties to one another in lieu of object ties to parents were most noteworthy. To extrapolate from these findings, the older ghetto and camp children of latency age who were on their own quite likely developed very strong bonds with each other also in order to survive, adding another important dimension to the significance of the nature of their "play" (Freud and Dann, 1951).

The games that ghetto children played reflected what they saw and lived with such as "aktion" (a sudden raid upon the prisoners ending in murder or deportation), "breaking into hiding places," "massacre" or "returning the clothing to the dead" (Eisen, 1988). Latency-aged children were regularly seen in the streets playing with corpses, tickling them to see if they would move, checking to see if they were breathing and incorporating them into their play. Even if one of them were to drop dead in their midst, they would continue with their play. In a sense, there was a grotesque transformation of their play into a "play," which could be thought of as improvisational street theater performed by dying children. In contrast, a child survivor who escaped from the detention camp, Rivesalte, in the foothills of the Pyrenees in the south of France, described more typical play, that of *Three Musketeers* with his fellow young inmates. At age twelve, on the cusp of adolescence and not having been exposed to death, this optimistic boy and his friends were "pretending we were the heroes encountering and, of course, always winning over the evil Cardinal Richlieu and his henchman. That was early in the winter of 1940/41 before the worst to happen reached us directly. That it was early in the Holocaust denouement was probably the factor that allowed us to still play" (Parens, 2004, p. 49). Now reflecting upon his young life with the wisdom of a senior psychoanalyst, Henri Parens observed: "We could fight evil even if only in play, that medium which children use naturally to cope with fear, with anxiety and stress. We played it, we played it, and we played it. It must have worked fairly effectively for us, otherwise we would have soon abandoned the game" (Parens, 2004, p. 49). Parens escaped from the camp, never to see his protective and loving mother again and noted that even upon his transatlantic voyage to freedom and safety in America, he still had not known about the horrors of Auschwitz. It appears that this form of play was not yet saturated with the inevitability of death as with the ghetto children. Furthermore, at his age, the emergence of sexuality was in the air. (On his voyage, he later described his first sexual experience with an older girl who submitted to three boys in succession.) Indeed, Parens tells us that "The other way we tried to go on living was by dancing." Musically inclined at a young age, he sang and thus provided the music for their precious moments. Music was important to prisoners of all ages.

NIGHTLY CONCERTS

There was a secret tunnel under a Nazi concentration camp where something very unexpected took place. This tunnel connected the "infirmary" with the morgue. It allowed the S.S. doctors to murder their ill or injured "patients" and unobtrusively have them transported to the pathology lab where their bodies could be desecrated in the name of "science." Fraudulent death certificates were crafted here to mask their crimes. Then their remains would be incinerated in the crematoria at the far end of the campus. Their ashes were then dumped in the river which separated the facility from a beautiful park where the locals loved to picnic with their families on Sunday afternoons after church. This disposal system allowed for the quiet, systematic removal of unwanted or useless prisoners who lost their value as human slaves, without arousing mass panic and a possible uprising of the other inmates.

The main product of this closed and secret society, just a short train ride from the center of Hitler's universe in Berlin, was the manufacturing of bricks and building materials for the new world that was being eagerly constructed by the architects and builders of the Third Reich. Strategically located near a quarry which provided the raw materials and the river which enabled efficient transport of the finished products by boat, the Sachsenhausen camp in Oranienburg, Germany, was a vital part of the war effort. In this way, those enemies of the Reich who were deemed "life unworthy of life" and taken there could redeem themselves by working to death or providing entertainment for the overlords whose sadism is now legendary.[1] I might add here that during my first visit to this camp before its overhaul in preparation for tourism I was also shown the remains of a huge bakery which was also a source of German pride. In addition, I saw the rusting remains of the crematoria which were eerily sinking into the ground like a lopsided and doomed sailing vessel. So it was here at Sachsenhausen that they baked bricks, bread, and bodies.

But it was a story related to the tunnel that I learned from my guide that day which is especially relevant to this chapter. On this particularly gray, rainy day there was a biting wind which ripped through the open expanse, or appelplatz, where prisoners in their thinly clad uniforms were forced together to stand at attention for as long as and as often as commanded, or face dire consequences. It was so cold, wet, and bleak that day that it felt impossible not to shiver and long to seek shelter somewhere inside. But here at Sachsenhausen there was no respite. It was even worse inside. In the morgue, the white tile, the stainless steel and the concrete were as cold as ice. It left little to the imagination as gruesome life-sized photos of dissected inmates hung on the walls. I was then asked if I wanted to see the tunnel in question and rather numbly agreed. We descended a ramp into the dank darkness which was illuminated by bare light bulbs overhead. In this quiet echo chamber under the chamber of horrors, I learned that a bizarre occurrence would occur regularly there at night. As the report went, a group of musically talented prisoners would secretly gather with their smuggled instruments and quietly but defiantly play their repertoire, risking their lives for those moments of sanity, solidarity, and mournful expression of their souls. Unbeknownst to them, however, the guards were quite aware of these secret concerts but curiously did not forbid or punish them for it. On the contrary, they, too, secretly entered the tunnel but from the far end and unbeknownst to the inmates surreptitiously listened to the nightly concerts. So, for those brief, transcendent moments, there was no perpetrator and no victim hopelessly locked into their respective roles of predator and prey. There were just two groups of people joined together in the very human activity of making and listening to the sounds of music, under most bizarre conditions.

Such a story, as unbelievable as it seems, has been portrayed on a one-to-one basis in the highly acclaimed film *The Pianist* where Adrian Brody, a concert pianist and persecuted Jew in wartime Warsaw, softens the heart of his would-be S.S. executioner who discovers him hiding in an abandoned house barely clinging to life as he is starving to death in the freezing cold winter. The German master commands the wretched Jew to play the decaying piano that is left behind in the house. The hidden Jew is so weak and frozen with both terror and the cold that his fingers barely move at first. Given the capricious abuse of power that so often characterized the Nazi, it is unclear to the viewer whether the S.S. man will shoot Brody on the spot for lying about being a concert pianist until he marshals a superhuman effort to be able to play. Suddenly, in the midst of the bombed-out rubble of the city in the bleak winter night, this utterly horrendous and crazed, caged animal of a man produces exalted music. The officer is quietly but clearly moved by this unexpected treat of music and unexpectedly hides him from the other soldiers, provides him with some food and even gives him his overcoat. We know the old adage "Music soothes the savage breast" and the Biblical story of how young David calmed down the irascible King Saul with his music. Under these conditions, the capacity of the weaker, oppressed other to soothe the perpetrator, at least temporarily, is illustrated in the context of genocidal persecution.

A MUSICAL FAD IN THE GHETTO

An entry in the Łódź Chronicle written by Oskar Rosenfeld, one of its authors, on Wednesday, August 25, 1943, describes a musical "fad" that swept through the ghetto. It may have started when a child took two small pieces of wood between his fingers and created a pleasing clicking sound:

> For several days now the streets and courtyards of the ghetto have been filled with a noise like a clatter of wooden shoe . . . an observer soon discusses that this "clattering" is produced by boys who have invented a new pastime, an entertainment. More precisely, the children of the ghetto have invented a new toy. All the various amusing toys and noisemakers . . . are things our youngsters must, of course, do without . . . and so on their own they invent toys to replace all the things that delight children everywhere and are unavailable here.
>
> The ghetto toy in the summer of 1943: Two small slabs of wood—hard wood if possible! One slab is held between the forefinger and the middle finger, the other between the middle finger and the ring finger. The little finger presses against the other fingers squeezing them so hard that the slabs are rigidly fixed in position and can thus be struck against one other by means of a skillful motion. Naturally the artistic talents of the toy carver and performer can be refined to a very high level. . . .

> The streets of the Litzmannstadt ghetto [the Germans renamed Łódź to Litzmannstadt and Aryanized it] are filled with clicking, drumming, banging . . . barefoot boys scurried past you, performing their music right under your nose, with great earnestness, as though their lives depended on it. Here the musical instinct of Eastern European Jews is cultivated to the full. An area that has given the world so many musicians, chiefly violinists—just think of Hubermann, Heifetz, Elman, Milstein and Menuhin—now presents a new line of artists." (Dobroszycki, 1984, pp. 373–74)

Here we see the desperate inventiveness of these doomed children who communicate to one another and to all the grownups in the ghetto that they are still alive. Like the cacophony of a swarm of crickets they make their music and their fervent defiance known to all.

An entry about a month before, on Saturday, July 24, 1943, provides another view of these massively traumatized and starving children's ingenuity under most devastating conditions. This report describes their creation of playing cards from cigarette boxes:

> The so-called Belgian cigarettes have been a disappointment to smokers in the ghetto, even those who have smoked poor quality tobacco all their lives. Countless packs with their gaudy colors and equally gaudy names could not alter the devastating judgment that has been passed on the quality of the cigarettes. . . . Since every object in the ghetto, no matter how worthless, acquires some value, even those boxes have come to be cherished. The smoker does not throw them out. He saves them and makes sure that they do not go to waste. Children beg for those boxes, children's hands reach out for them.
>
> Outside the ghetto, children receive beautiful and appropriate playthings as presents . . . our children collect empty cigarette boxes. They remove the colorful tops and stack them in a pile until they have a whole deck of cards. Playing cards.
>
> And they play. They count the cards and deal them out. They arrange them by color and name. Green, orange, yellow, brown, even black. They play games that they invent by themselves. They devise systems, they let their imagination take over. (Dobroszycki, 1984, pp. 360–61)

The importance of toys and other inanimate objects is quite well known (Winnicott, 1953; Volkan, 1981; and Akhtar, 2003) and under these conditions they became even more highly prized (Kestenberg and Brenner, 1996; Brenner, 2009). About a year later, the Łódź ghetto was finally liquidated and the wretched survivors were sent to their final destinations, the extermination camps of Chelmno and Auschwitz. There, the remnants of a once vibrant Jewish community were reduced to ash and smoke.

THE FAMILY CAMP

Described as "one of the most diabolical inventions of a Nazi mind" (Eisen, 1988, p. 47), the Family Camp B-IIb, was created in 1943 when approximately 5,000 Czech Jews were forced to the Auschwitz/Birkenau extermination camp from Theresienstadt. Theresienstadt was the so-called model camp which was known for its cultural and arts programs for adults and children. Terezin, an eighteenth century, walled fortress town, was transformed into Theresienstadt, the "gift from the Fuhrer to the Jews," according to Heimlich Himmler. Literally advertised as a refuge which would protect them and help them prepare for their move to Palestine, terrified and well-to-do Czech Jews paid tens of thousands of marks to gain entry. We now know that the "final solution' to the Jewish question was not migration but genocide and that this model camp was designed to hide the inconceivable truth. Even the International Red Cross which visited the camp in 1944 was either fooled by this cynical ruse or was too intimidated to accurately report its findings. The ancient walled city, which never housed more than 8,000 people, became the desperate, crammed quarters to about 60,000 prisoners at a time which, after a "deportation to the east' made room for the next transport. Of the 15,000 children sent to Auschwitz from Theresienstadt, only one hundred survived and none of these was under the age of fourteen.

Although its prisoners found a way of extending and preserving their human dignity for as long as possible, it too had its horrors and was eventually to be totally liquidated. In order to avoid panic and possible trouble from the prisoners who had been ousted from the relative luxury of Theresienstadt to the depths of hell in Auschwitz, Adolf Eichmann continued the elaborate deception to the end, commissioning the painting of a giant mural of Snow White and the Seven Dwarfs in the children's barracks at Hut 31. A German-Jewish star athlete by the name of Fredy Hirsch who developed a youth program at Theresienstadt was among the deportees. He was then to become the "head of the children's day block" and oversaw the building of a playground and creation of a daily schedule of activities for the children which numbered about five hundred. He was even able to procure better food for them, such as milk and eggs. Seeing the children playing openly and freely had puzzled, surprised and confused the inmates. As one Auschwitz survivor who had escaped named Rudolph Vrba had said, "I saw them set aside a barrack for the children, a nursery, no less, in the shadow of the crematorium. I saw a blonde, athletic man of about thirty [Fredy Hirsch] organizing games, then lessons." Tragically, however, when the Family Camp was liquidated and all the prisoners were gassed and cremated, Fredy Hirsch committed suicide by poisoning himself. He was forewarned by the underground resistance about what was to happen and could not believe it given the favorable treatment they had received. He was asked to lead an uprising in the Family Camp which had no chance of succeeding and he could not bear to see the children murdered in either manner. Perhaps like Janus Korczak who could not live without his charges and accompanied the children of his remarkable orphanage in the Warsaw ghetto on their train ride to certain death, Hirsch, too, saw no purpose without his children. Hirsch's children were led to the gas chambers and as they were taking off their clothes, they spontaneously started singing the Czech and the Israeli national anthems. The cold facts of the Family Camp are documented in the Auschwitz Chronicle this way:

> September 8, 1943: 5,006 Jews are transported from Theresienstadt with an RSHA [Reich Security Central Office of the SS] transport. In the transport, there are 2,293 men and boys given numbers 146694-148986, and 2,713 women and girls given numbers 58471-61183 (Czech, 1990, p. 483).

> February 29, 1944: The Director of the Jewish Section, IV-B4 of the RSHA, SS Lieutenant Colonel Adolf Eichmann, views the Theresienstadt Family Camp during his stay in Auschwitz in Camp B-IIb in Birkenau. Dr. Leo Janowitz, the former Director of the Central Secretariat in the Theresienstadt ghetto, and Fredy Hirsch, a teacher and children's attendant in Camp B-IIb report to him. Eichmann also converses with Miriam Edelstein informing her that her husband, the former senior of the Jewish community in the Theresienstadt ghetto, the so-called Jewish Eldest, is most probably in Germany. Meanwhile, Jacob Edelstein, after his arrival in December, 1943, in Auschwitz I, has been imprisoned in Block 11 together with his closest coworkers (Czech, 1990, pp. 590–91).

> March 7, 1944: With the end of the six-month stay of the first group of Jews from the Theresienstadt Family Camp B-IIb and the instructions of the RSHA to kill them, it is decided to liquidate them. To prevent unrest, it should appear that the camp inmates were being transferred to labor camps in the Reich interior. Consequently, all prisoners who are healthy and are able to work are transferred to the quarantine B-IIa in Birkenau. First men are brought over and put up in special blocks; later the women are also brought over and put in other blocks. They are allowed to take their entire belongings with them which they brought in boxes and suitcases from Theresienstadt. For this period the blocks in the quarantine are ordered closed (Czech, 1990, p. 593).

> March 8, 1944: The prisoner Fredy Hirsch, teacher and caregiver of the children in Camp B-IIb, commits suicide because he cannot protect the women and children from destruction and does not want to be a passive witness. Around 8:00 p.m., Camp B-IIa is put under curfew. A large number of S.S. men from Auschwitz II and the political department arrive in the camp. Capos and block commanders whom the S.S. men trust somewhat are called for support. Half an S.S. company with dogs surround the camp. Around 10:00 p.m. twelve trucks covered with tarps drive up. The Jews are ordered to leave the heavy luggage in the barracks and are promised that it will be brought to the train. To maintain order and quiet, 40 people at a time are left on the truck loading platform and the trucks leaving Camp B-IIa do not turn left, i.e., direct route to the crematoriums, but right so it looks as though they are driving to the train station. This operation lasts several hours. First the men are

> driven to Crematorium 3, then the women to Crematorium 2. After waiting several hours for their departure, the Jews in one of the blocks become anxious and around 2:00 a.m. start to sing a Czech folksong. In the next block singing also begins. Startled, the S.S. men begin to fire warning shots. The Jews are forbidden to sing under the threat that the transport will be stopped. The disrobing rooms in the crematoria have been prepared in such a manner that the waiting prisoners hope to the end that they are leaving for a labor camp. Only the order to disrobe makes it clear that they are in the crematorium. The women who are already in the gas chamber are still waiting for the others, singing the Internationale and the Hatikvah at that time, the Jewish national anthem and the Czech national anthem and a partisan song. Toward morning, 3,791 Jewish prisoners from Theresienstadt—men, women and children—are killed in Crematoriums 2 and 3. (Czech, 1990, pp. 594–95)

While the sight of seeing children play was an inspiration and a source of rejuvenation for the beleaguered and doomed population of adults, there soon developed great concerns in the ghettos about the creation of such playgrounds as they would have made round-ups by the S.S. quite effortless. The children would be localized and "concentrated" in such an area, making them much more easily captured, like being baited in a trap. Still, it was incomprehensible to most that their Nazi captors were sending them to extermination camps, to be killed *en masse* like annoying or useless insects. Indeed, even those in Auschwitz, like Hirsch, found it inconceivable until the last minute. The utterly cynical and merciless exploitation of displaced, dehumanized and demoralized civilians could not be hidden from the older children, however, who saw the degradation and murder of their elders. Their reliance on their own ego strength and their own judgment, even when it countermanded their parents' values, may have made the difference between life and death for some (Kestenberg and Brenner, 1996). Their capacity to adapt more creatively and flexibly to the conditions than the grownups has been thought to have been mediated through their surreal form of "play."

MORE REFLECTIONS

Dr. Adina Blady Szwajger, who worked in the Warsaw Children's Hospital, poignantly described how, prior to the destruction of the Warsaw ghetto, the sick and dying children were seeing the world "with the eyes of adults." These "ageless creatures" from four to twelve years of age who were precociously aware of their impending deaths had profoundly serious eyes which expressed "the sorrow of 2,000 years of Jewish diaspora" (Szwajger, 1990). Yet some of these children had retained a capacity for play. For example, she described one boy who screamed in constant pain due to contractions in his extremities until a staff member would place a pencil between his nearly useless fingers. At such times he would calm down and draw pictures from his memory and imagination. Toddlers played in a makeshift playground there pretending to be grownups lighting the Shabbat candles on Friday night and cooking soup with "real potatoes."

Toddlers and latency age children in the Warsaw ghetto would imitate in their play what they witnessed, such as funerals and raids by their Nazi captors. And, as noted earlier, if a child would drop dead during their play, they would continue in their fantasy world seemingly unaffected by the latest fatality in their midst (Eisen, 1988). Their attempts at mastery were noted at the death camps also, where "children played block alster (block elder), roll call, caps off and even gas chambers. They played what they needed to understand and what they did understand was the horror of an adult world gone mad" (Kestenberg and Brenner, 1996, p. 135). The depiction of this play in the cinema was poignantly portrayed in the film *Life Is Beautiful* where a father, played by Roberto Benigni, tried to help his son survive by telling him that it was all a game and that if he could earn enough points, tanks would come into the camp and rescue him.

Amongst older children, writing diaries and poetry were quite prevalent in hiding and in the camps. Anne Frank's diary is by far the most well known one. Development continued and sexual interest was evident but often not spoken of (Nir, 1989; Kestenberg and Brenner, 1996). Themes of despair and hope were omnipresent themes in the poetry and reading them aloud was reported to have boosted the spirits of all who listened (Sender, 1986). Most notably,

> the children of Terezin left a remarkable legacy in their poetry and art . . . [with the help of their] teachers who defied camp rules to offer . . . art therapy in the guise of art lessons, to teach literature and to organize poetry contests, recitation and cultural programs in the girls' and boys' dormitories. . . . One such teacher was Friedl Dicker-Brandeis . . . of the Bauhaus in Weimar, Germany . . . [who] brought what art materials she could to the camp . . . [and] saw the children needed a form of artistic expression as a way to moderate the chaos of their lives. (Volavkova, 1978, VII)

Of those who survived, many child survivors further developed their creative abilities in the realms of painting and sculpture as well as writing. Here are some representative poems written by children in Theresienstadt:

The Little Mouse

A mousie sat upon a shelf,
Catching fleas in his coat of fur.
But he couldn't catch her—what chagrin!
She'd hidden 'way inside his skin.
He turned and wriggled, knew no rest,
That flea was such a nasty pest!

His daddy came
And searched his coat
He caught the flea and off he ran
To cook her in the frying pan.
The little mouse cried, "Come and see!
For lunch we've got a nice, fat flea!"
Koleba, 1944, in Volavkova, 1978, p. 41

The Jewish prisoners' identification with being treated like vermin and their own identification with the aggressor in their treatment of insects is humorously described in this poem. Themes of hunger, hiding, getting caught, and getting burned alive are encapsulated here.

A ten-year-old girl, Gabrielle Silten, who was also in Theresienstadt, described her relationship with rats this way: "In the spaces between the beams [in the attics] lived rats with their families. We would walk on the beams to get to the spaces where the rat families lived (or sometimes just to walk on the beams) and then poke at them and watch them jump. Surprisingly, they never harmed us or attacked us at all" (Friedman, 1982, p. 61).

This young girl and her friends played the game of "aktion" with the rats who, like the Jews, never fought back. This identification with the Nazi aggressor persisted in an aging child survivor who would periodically perform "selections" on the yellowing, dying leaves of my plants, insisting with great urgency they be removed from the healthy leaves (Brenner, 2004).

Homesick

I lived in the ghetto here for more than a year.
In Terezin, in the black town now,
And when I remember my old home so dear,
I can love it more than I did, somehow.
Ah, home, home.
Why did they tear me away?
Here the weak die easy as a feather
And when they die, they die forever.
Anonymous, 1943, in Volavkova, 1978, p. 46

This child seems to have grasped one of the essential factors of death, that is, the permanent and irreversible nature of object loss.

The Butterfly

The last, the very last,
So richly, brightly, dazzlingly yellow.
Perhaps if the sun's tears would sing
Against a white stone . . .
Such, such a yellow
Is carried lightly 'way up high.
It went away I'm sure because it wished to
Kiss the world goodbye.

> For seven weeks I've lived in here,
> Penned up inside this ghetto.
> But I have found what I love here.
> The dandelions call to me
> And the white chestnut branches in the court.
> Only I never saw another butterfly.
> That butterfly was the last one.
> Butterflies don't live in here,
> In the ghetto.
> Pavel Friedman, 1942, in Volavkova, 1978, p. 39

Wanting to fly to freedom but being trapped, the struggle for survival is painfully represented through his appreciation of the simple beauty of nature. This boy died in Auschwitz.

DISCUSSION

In this brief sampling of creativity and play during the Holocaust, I have focused mostly on the plight of children which, until fairly recently, was a largely untold story (Dwork, 1991; Glassner and Krell, 2006; Marks, 1993; Moskowitz, 1983; Kestenberg and Brenner, 1996). The approximately 1.5 million children who perished were killed in every way imaginable: they were stabbed, starved, suffocated, and shot. They were abandoned in knapsacks on the way to slave labor camps, sent into hiding where some were sexually abused, drugged, drowned, smashed against walls, run over, frozen, or died of infectious diseases. And, of course, they were gassed and cremated. Their cries could signal of the presence of Jews in hiding under floorboards or behind false walls. Their discovery by raiding S.S. troops would lead to the certain death of all who were caught. Moreover, any healthy grownups with a child on the selection ramp at a death camp would immediately be sent to the left, directly to the gas chambers. Children, therefore, became a liability of lethal proportions. And, so, the young offspring who, under "expectable" conditions (Hartmann, 1939) would represent the hope and future of any group, became deadly baggage for their parents and an utterly useless commodity for the Third Reich. Indeed, their extermination was especially important to those whose mission it was to cleanse Europe and the world of the Jewish menace, i.e., to make it "Judenrein." In this climate of death, dying, and impending death or living in the constant terror of being caught and sent to death, the children tried to adapt in ways that were characteristic of their ages, stages of development and state of health.

With what we currently know about the child's developmental acquisition of the awareness and meaning of death in others and for himself, it is clear that within a certain range there is considerable individual variation based on experience and psychodynamic factors (Brenner, 2010). Furthermore, precocious exposure to death well before the child's maturational capacity to comprehend it may be traumatic in and of itself and may be thought of as the inverse of a fixation (Kestenberg and Brenner, 1988). As such, the function of play under these most dire conditions of the ghetto might in part help the child learn more quickly about what awaits him in very short order.

Akhtar, in his definition of "play" (2009), which synthesizes the contributions of Freud (1920), Waelder (1933), Erikson (1950), Winnicott (1942, 1953, 1971), Balint (1959) and others, states: "Play enriches life and enjoyment of playing is a hallmark of the growing child's mental health. Playing was the result of acting from the center, so to speak, and fearlessly being imaginative and innovative . . . a spirit which would not torment itself with questions of reality and unreality; instead it will peacefully accept the paradox that some activities are neither real or unreal" (p. 211).

This definition might better apply to the type of play that Parens described where, for example, he and his friends might spontaneously go into character and become the *Three Musketeers* if they encountered one another on the way to the latrine. However, I would contend that it does not apply to the previously mentioned ghetto games, such as "aktion" and "returning the clothing of the dead." Here, the complex activity seems to go beyond the binary distinction between reality and fantasy, beyond being a life-enriching activity indicative of mental health and to be, as Freud stated, "beyond the pleasure principle" (Freud, 1920).

From this perspective it might be seen as a child's ego's best effort at managing an overwhelming upsurge of pressure from Thanatos, the death instinct. The repetitive enactments of real life activities, which were far more macabre than fantasy, incorporated the well known defense of identification with the aggressor, reflected an attempt at turning passive into active, and also seemed to have an additional level of significance. What exactly did Karski mean when he blurted out "But these children are not playing—they only make believe it's play"? And what did the Łódź Chronicle writer mean when he described the boys and their musical toys as playing "as though their lives depended on it"? Could it be that indeed the children were more aware of the inevitability of their deaths than their parents? They "did not simply copy the atrocity surrounding them; rather they imposed on reality their own construction and interpretation. And, in fact, all surviving evidence indicates that the children had a clear grasp of reality and were aware of their fate. Play of the Holocaust, however, reflected this reality in a 'bent' form fitting the players' existing level of cognitive functioning" (Eisen, 1988, p. 114).

If this were the case, how might we understand how they could have acquired an appreciation of reality at a much earlier age than might have been expected? Perhaps a deeper consideration of the nature of this "improvisational theater" and its relationship to reality might offer a clue. And, perhaps there might even be a clue derived from the ambiguity (Adler, 1989) of the analytic situation.

A number of years ago, an analysand who was trying to make sense of the complex nature of the analytic relationship, commented in passing that it had the quality of a Pirandello play. This woman, a gifted academic with wide-ranging interests and knowledge, said that it felt like "a play within a play within a play." In her metaphor, she was alluding to this ambiguity from which analysis is such a powerful modality. The reality of the "frame" of the analytic situation is one level. The fundamental rule, the "signposts" of neutrality, anonymity and abstinence which are most aberrant in human relationships and contribute to the creation of the asymmetry is another level. Under these conditions, the transference may be cultivated in a way which enables the projection of the analysand's internal world to become visible, comprehensible, and interpretable. In the process, the analysand's reality testing becomes strengthened. But then, of course, there is another level to contend with, and that is the unconscious communication between the two which exerts an additional influence in the transference/countertransference matrix, manifesting itself in the enactments throughout analysis. Through interpretation, containment and co-creation, it then becomes possible for deeper meaning, understanding and strengthening of one's sense of inner and outer reality to occur.

For Luigi Pirandello, the Pulitzer prize–winning playwright and novelist who was deeply affected by the horrors of World War I in his native Italy, much of his work dealt with the multiple layers of consciousness, reality, relativity, and self-deception in a chaotic world governed by "arcane" forces. A contemporary of Freud and a playwright like Shakespeare, for whom "the world is a stage," Pirandello saw all experience as theatrical. The quest to understand the mysteries of the world through one's consciousness and self-awareness are major themes in his work. The essence of the creative process, as he saw it, consisted of spontaneita (spontaneity), sincerita (the most honest effort to represent things as authentically as possible), and smania di vivera (the "mania to live"), which psychoanalysts might reductionistically think of as the manic defense (Winnicott, 1935; Akhtar, 2001). Pirandello recognized the twentieth century preoccupation with consciousness and was quite aware of unconscious forces which he saw as multidimensional. He wrote extensively about death, as it most profoundly represented those dark, arcane forces at work, which are always waiting to become manifest and induce people to become totally authentic and truthful about themselves.

As Pirandello thought of theater as "a form of life itself" and a true and proper "active life," he most likely would have seen the ghetto games as a necessary part of existence which, driven by the children's "mania for life," was a true creative process characterized by their spontaneita and sincerita. They were a cohesive group of sick, starving, and dying children, deciding on who would get to play the coveted rule of Nazi commandant in charge of the raids and rounding up of Jews. That decision process in and of itself was yet another drama within the drama. They were loitering on street corners littered with detritus, filth, and, to add to the authenticity of their performance, would not infrequently find a dead body nearby to incorporate into their scenarios. Perhaps it may have been a corpse of someone who was known to them or perhaps one of their relatives; yet another drama within the drama and another level of reality for them to contend with. Then the doomed child would handle the dead body in the context of the play, trying to determine if there was any life left in it and learn more about death; another drama ensues within the larger game, and on and on. And then how would it be decided when the performance would be over for the day? Would a real life "aktion" actually occur?

The strength of the group would empower each child, and by verbalizing, symbolizing, and representing the unrepresentable through repetitive enactments, they could learn what lay in wait for them. They could become more prepared to survive another day and perhaps outlive the masters of death whose own fate would eventually be out of their hands too, as a result of the advancing Allied Forces. From this rather complex process perhaps the children met their deaths with a wisdom and understanding that far exceeded what any child should ever have to know.

CONCLUDING REMARKS

It has been said that play "became an instinctual form for understanding the absurd and accommodating to the irrational. . . . The children suffered, cried, laid down their broken bodies and died; sometimes they played. They played for the few moments they were given with the vehemence and desperation that only the doomed can have" (Eisen, 1988, p. 122). In addition to this observation, it seems that from the descriptions and kinds of play in children in hiding, in ghettos and in death camps, that it was complex and multiply determined, owing to their life and death circumstances, their health, and their stages of development. Perhaps the saturation of their "play" with death is analogous to Volkan's description of the malignant regression in cultural rituals in societies under totalitarian and terrorist rule (2006), where aggression infuses and contaminates what were once lighthearted traditions. Here, in the children's play of the ghetto, their "making believe" they were just playing had the quality of improvisational street theater of desperate and dying children who were trying to comprehend what was happening around them. The ideas put forth by Pirandello about levels of reality in the creative process might help deepen our understanding of this phenomenon.

NOTE

1. Visitors to this camp, which since the reunification of Germany is much more accessible to the West, now enter a modern visitors' center and may rent audio phone guides, like in an art museum. With these self-guided tours, they will hear stories about such notorious criminals as Iron Gustav.

Chapter Nine

Play and Creativity

Lucy Daniels

> "Just as the personalities of adults develop through their experience in living, so those of children develop through their play. . . . By enriching themselves, children gradually enlarge their capacity to see the richness of the externally real world. Play is the continuous evidence of creativity." —Donald Winnicott, "Why Children Play"

"Now," Donald Winnicott declared at the opening of *Playing: Creative Activity and the Search for Self* (1971), "I shall discuss an important feature of playing. This is that in playing, and perhaps only in playing, the child or adult is free to be creative" (p. 53). Like so much of Winnicott's writing, this impresses me as simple, direct, and open to or even inviting further thought on the part of the reader. And, because such statements are imperfect as well as more complicated than easily meets the eye, he has inspired other psychoanalysts to explore (each with his own unique perspective) the arena introduced. Not the least of the advances made in this opening is that of considering playing a lifelong capacity, one not just associated with childhood. Certainly we all know seniors who both pursue creative endeavors and play with grandchildren. Sometimes years of enlightening experience result in their being even more creative in later years. At the same time, as will be considered in detail below, I question the necessity of associating either playing or creating with "free." "Driven" is sometimes characteristic of both.

Of course, Winnicott first set the stage for this with his paper, *Transitional Objects and Transitional Phenomena* (1953), presenting the concept of the baby's first not-me object being used to assist separation from mother. The important conditions necessary for this creation on the baby's part include toleration/acceptance of an irresolvable paradox (the object is both already there *and* created by the child; it is both "real" or external *and* an illusion). This object must survive instinctual loving and aggression without change. It is not a hallucination. And essential for this to take place is what Winnicott, in later papers, labels "potential space." This hypothetical area of mutual creativity between infant and mother (or later, between artist and creation) is only "potential" because its availability depends on "good enough" (neither perfect nor inferior) mentoring.

As significant as the concepts of transitional object and transitional phenomena are themselves, they have also initiated many more valuable thoughts/discoveries regarding play and creativity. Among these, Winnicott's paper, *The Capacity to Be Alone* (1958) discusses the important conditions necessary for the creation/existence of "potential space." Essentially, when this exists, the child/adult is able to be himself and work and play with the security of a significant other present but not intruding. This is, I would say and will demonstrate later, as essential for the creating adult as for free play in childhood. But being relaxed enough to be him/herself is very different from using creating to search for the self. Such searching not only lacks freedom but distracts from creating and tends to deaden its products. In addition, the freedom Winnicott speaks of should not be taken lightly. Or too seriously. The significance of this relationship or trust is huge but to be acknowledged, not obeyed.

At the same time there is self-discovery. Many artists report that creating often surprises them with self-knowledge never available before. In reference to this, world-renowned sculptor, Louise Bourgeois (still productive at ninety-eight) has declared that art is her therapy because it allows exorcism of her problems and their pain. As she puts it "Every day you have to abandon your past or accept it; and then, if you cannot accept it, you become a sculptor" (1995). And in further explanation of this she added in later, "I am saying in my sculpture today what I could not make out in the past. It was fear that kept me from understanding. My sculpture allows me to re-experience the fear, to give it physicality so I am able to hack away at it" (1999, p. 412). Helene Brandt, another well known New York sculptor and colleague of Bourgeois finds herself always enlightened by creating. Her metal work has developed from cages to flying birds to park decorations to using preserved plants to create an array of objects. And in the process, Brandt declares, she is nearly always surprised by both her creative products and what they reveal to her about herself.[1]

In *On Not Being Able To Paint*, Marion Milner (1957) uses a view similar to Winnicott's to consider creativity in a variety of fields. And a unique and valuable aspect of Milner's work is that she discusses all of this from the perspective of her own serious personal pursuits. In the Appendix of *On Not Being Able To Paint*, for instance, she says,

> The writing of this book turned out to be an attempt to discover, within the limits of a special field, something of the nature of the forces that bring order out of

> chaos. . . . But finally, as a result of this study, and also as a result of writing a clinical paper on aspects of symbol formation, I had found a definition which seemed to be at least a workable tool: that is, that psychic creativeness is the capacity for making a symbol. Thus, creativeness in the arts is making a symbol for feeling and creativeness in science is making a symbol for knowing. (p. 148)

Susan Deri in *Symbolization and Creativity* (1984) discusses the capacity for symbolization as a condition necessary for human life, with creating just one example of this. In her view, symbolizing simply amounts to being able to apply some order/understanding/meaning to chaos. It does so by simultaneously connecting and separating, and by expressing something that is absent in a way that is neither immediate nor the raw feeling itself. So, the American flag symbolizes our country, and a rainbow can symbolize serenity after turbulence. But Deri also speaks to the uniqueness of individuals' symbols in works of art, whether the words and phrases chosen by a poet, the tenor and rhythm used by a musician, or the colors and images selected by a painter. She stresses the significance of the dialogue between creator and art object across the distance that separates them. When this dialogue arrives at a well articulated "good fit" between the artist's concept and the created object, Deri refers to this as a "presentational symbol."

In discussing various problems with symbolization Deri illustrates how destructive early life experience and defensiveness can undermine the capacity to symbolize effectively in several ways. For instance, rather than conveying meaning (and meaning *can* be scary and hard to bear), symbols can be used to conceal meaning (cryptosymbolism). Desymbolization is the result when the preconscious form of a memory, feeling, wishing, etc. and the psychic form of its content are wiped out or repressed. And when this happens, there is usually missymbolization (inept representation) as a result of the increased strength of the blocked emotions.

Significant among the problems Deri focuses on are those of people she labels "avid introjectors." These are individuals who, early in life, had to behave as young adults due to the mother's fears or insistence that they take care of her needs. As a result, Deri points out, while most of such individuals tend to be very intelligent and, therefore, become skilled and creative symbolizers, this is only true on an *internal* basis. Any wish to express this creativity externally is likely to be blocked due to their having learned in early life to regard self-expression as forbidden or destructive. Such individuals, according to Deri, are especially likely to benefit from the "potential space" experience of psychoanalysis. Because there their external expression can be facilitated and more easily accepted (by analysand as well as analyst).

Other analysts have looked at the issues that impair playing and creativity without specifically addressing the causes of deficits in symbolization. Phyllis Greenacre (1969, 1970), who basically viewed creating as a libidinal endeavor, a "love affair with the world" that enables individuals to fulfill rather than have to resolve Oedipal wishes, also viewed ineffective creation as due to needing a fetish as a patch to prevent castration. Similarly, Melanie Klein (1958) regarded the individual in the depressive position as capable of three-ness (symbol, symbolized and interpreting subject) whereas one fixated in the paranoid-schizoid position would lack the capacity to distinguish symbol from symbolized.

More recently Thomas Ogden (1993) has focused on the creativity of both the artist and the adult living in the world. In *On Potential Space*, he lists the prerequisites for both potential space and the dialectic process which he regards as essential for effective symbolization to be possible. His list includes:

1. Playing, creating, transformational phenomena, psychotherapy, and "cultural experience" all occur in "potential space."
2. The essential feature of "potential space" is the *paradox and acceptance of the paradox*.
3. To exist, "potential space" needs to be filled with illusion, playing, symbols.
4. For this to take place requires a *dialectical process* in which two opposing concepts create, inform, preserve, and negate each other.
5. But, as Ogden emphasizes, "potential space" must *always* be potential, never actual. Though the dialectical process moves toward integration, integration is never completed, because each new integration creates a new dialectical process with new dynamic tension. *Meaning* accrues from difference; there can be no meaning in a completely homogeneous field.
6. This dialectical process is mainly involved in the creation of subjectivity or degrees of self-awareness, ranging from the most subtle sense of I-ness to the capacity for intentional self-reflection. Ultimately subjectivity is a reflection of the differentiation of the symbol, symbolized, and interpreting subject. The emergence of this subject makes it possible for a person to wish (or long for something).
7. Going back to Winnicott, Ogden points out that "I-ness" is made possible by the other, thus resulting in Two-ness or "the capacity to be alone in the presence of another." But Ogden adds that the transitional object is much more than a milestone in the process of separation-individuation. More significantly, he points out, it is a reflection of the capacity to maintain a psychological dialectical process or "Three-ness"—the separateness of *symbol*, *symbolized*, and *subject*. *Potential space lies between symbol and the symbolized* (between one's thought and what one is thinking about or between one's feeling and that which one is responding to). The achievement of the capacity to distinguish *symbol* and *symbolized* is the achievement of subjectivity. From this point on, *symbolic function* involves the

interrelating of *symbol* (the thought), *symbolized* (that which is thought about), and *thinker* (interpreting self). And "potential space" ceases to exist when any two of these become de-differentiated.

8. Ogden then describes the creativity problems that result from different failures to differentiate:

    a. When fantasy overcomes reality—As when a voice inside the head is *not* experienced as a hallucination but as an actual person speaking. Or when the therapist is experienced as not *like* the patient's mother but *as* the patient's mother.
    b. When reality overrides fantasy—As when a child is unable to use imagination in play and, instead, focuses on staid reality or when an adult patient is unable to dream or regards any dream experience as senseless.
    c. When reality and fantasy are dissociated—As in "splitting of the ego" according to Freud (1940), when the subject both knows and does not know something about which he/she is uncomfortable. Such is the case with fetishes or perversions or any situation where there is fear and denial of meaning deemed dangerous.
    d. When, due to severe stress, neither fantasy nor reality is conceptualized. This occurs when perception remains raw experience that is not attributed meaning. Meaning is simply never created because the subject feels utterly helpless to tolerate it.

QUESTIONS ABOUT PLAYING AND CREATING

In his consideration of the creative process, Winnicott (1971) associates playing and creating. But while these two may sometimes occur together, they are not at all the same. In fact, I disagree with Winnicott's opening statement on two fronts—that play is a prerequisite for creating and that both are associated with freedom. At the same time, as the theories just quoted demonstrate, Winnicott's perspective has been very valuable in triggering further more complex consideration of these issues by others.

So, how do playing and creating differ? Winnicott (1971) himself defines playing as follows: "To control what is outside, one has to *do* things, not simply to think or to wish. Playing is doing." Playing, then, is acting. But, of course, there can be all kinds of actions—repetitive, stereotyped, ranging all the way to imaginative and fantasy-based.

Winnicott and others seem pretty much in agreement that creating involves making something new/original as well as that such creations typically bridge internal and external reality. In addition Winnicott cites the need for "potential space," which suggests a sense of safeness for there to be the freedom to create.

And it is here, in my view, that reality disagrees with Winnicott. Furthermore, it seems to me that Ogden's (1993) paper provides robust material at odds with such a "safe" or "free" view of creating as well. Indeed, the conditions for creating seem to me to be complex. For instance, we are all familiar with the saying, "Necessity is the mother of invention" and remember how penicillin was an outgrowth of the infections associated with injuries in World War II as well as how Salk vaccine was developed due to polio epidemics. In addition psychoanalytic therapists and most of those who have undergone psychoanalysis know all too well how pain is frequently the driver to new self knowledge. I would agree with Ogden that arriving at a successful creation often involves tremendous struggle. Furthermore, I cannot regard either playing or creating as "safe." Rather, I see Winnicott's use of "free" in association with them as meaning "not too consciously scared or defended" in relation to taking the risks involved.

PLAYING AS WRITER AND PSYCHOTHERAPIST

Personally, being both a psychotherapist (of adults and children) and a writer (with some success, including a best seller at twenty-two and becoming the youngest Guggenheim Fellow ever—all before years of writer's block, I have been able to view play and creating from two quite different perspectives. As a result, the role of symbolization has further expanded for me (beyond these two perspectives) to consider yet another example of potential space, the dream, as well as the facilitation of this additional potential space in psychotherapy.

As a psychotherapist, one of my most riveting experiences is the surprise that frequently accompanies creative moments in psychotherapy play. In short, I'm never prepared for the discovery that the child's "perfunctory" play brings to awareness. Two examples follow.

Ted

Ted was a ten-year-old whose family had recently been transferred to Raleigh from a northern U.S. city. He had a sister three years younger, and both parents worked. They brought Ted to me for assessment and possible treatment because he was performing poorly at school (whereas he had been a good student in first and second grade) and was moody, disgruntled, and often disobedient at home, especially in relation to his father. He had long had a severe stuttering problem. He no longer took interest in family outings or games and didn't really have friends yet at school or in the neighborhood.

We agreed that I would take two or three sessions for evaluation, then meet with the parents again.

In the play room Ted investigated my toys but was basically silent. When I asked a question or suggested an activity, he nodded "no." All of this despite my having carefully explained the confidentiality of our sessions, that the point of meeting with me was for him to be able to talk about things he didn't want to share with his parents. Before long he took my Play-Doh and began pounding the doll house and its inhabitants with clumps of it. I didn't intervene as he did this repeatedly, sometimes shifting his aim to other parts of the playroom or its walls. But toward the end of our time, I commented on how he seemed to like having the strength to hit things with the doh and then helped him collect it into its cans.

The next two sessions, despite a few more questions on my part were essentially the same. Only a slight change in his manner which seemed silently friendlier and cooperative in terms of restoring the Play-Doh to its cans. So, I was not hopeful in reporting back to Ted's parents. But they were thrilled! In just three sessions I had cured Ted's stuttering! Which gave the parents the courage to talk with me about another major problem: the father's physical abusiveness. And that was the beginning of an eighteen-month individual and family therapy stint that proved very successful for both Ted and his parents.

Patsy

A quite different case, but with its own surprising developments was that of Patsy, the six-year-old child of divorced parents. I only saw the father once, and then only because I insisted that he attend the initial session. After that I met with Patsy twice a week and her mother every two weeks. The reason for their seeking therapy was that Patsy, like a few other little girls, had been sexually molested by a male employee at her day care center. The main symptom related to this was that Patsy, a beautiful little girl with blue eyes and long dark hair, insisted she was a boy. Nevertheless, she mostly wanted to play dolls—sometimes in the doll house but more often with my closer-to-life-sized baby dolls. There were no indications in any of this of her feeling masculine. Still, whether wearing a dress or overalls, she insisted she was a boy. She was very active in our play—dressing, feeding and rocking the babies, but she also insisted that I was the mother. In the sessions with Patsy's mother, I learned that Patsy slept with her nightly and that this was a comfort the mother did not want to end. I also learned about other stressors in her life, including the terrible experience she'd had giving birth to Patsy. She described the horror of being cut open for a C-section and that she still had the scars. When I asked, she acknowledged that she had told Patsy about this. And that, of course, altered my approach a bit. Besides suggesting to the mother that she gradually help Patsy to be a bigger girl by sleeping in her own bed, I brought into our play sessions my books about how babies are made. There was little or no negative reaction from Patsy on either of these points. In fact, if anything, her mothering in our sessions increased. Sometimes she would bring the birth story to me to read once more and two of the dolls were converted to babies. Then one day she asked me to take off her dress.

"Why would I do that?" I asked, "Nobody undresses in here." "Please!" she pleaded. "I *have* to take off my dress! I *have* to!" "Patsy, we can't do that here. It would not be good for me to help you undress." "Yes! Yes! Please!" She was weeping and shaking her fists at me. "But before we do anything else, let's try to understand *why* it's *so* important to you today to undress."

Still weeping and with an intensely pleading tone, she declared, "Because I can't stay a boy in this dress!"

So, our play had brought Patsy to where her boy fantasy had weakened. In the course of the next two weeks we talked, as we played, about that as well as about why, at some level, it had been so necessary for her to not be a girl. She told me about how her mother had been cut open to have her, and we talked about that in relation to my books about how babies are made. After that, in only a few more weeks of playing house and babies, Patsy was easily talking about being a girl and how she wanted to have real babies of her own when she grew up.

While both of these cases ended relatively successfully in my view, neither moved in a way I would have predicted. The safety of the play room (in part, perhaps, due to the absence of parents), I believe, provided the potential space for each child to project what needed to come out. In both of these situations the results were positive. But, perhaps because of my own problems with writer's block, I am always on the lookout for whatever may be the new discovery in play to be experienced as traumatic. This has not tended to be the case in my therapeutic play sessions. Or, at least, if it is—as with Patsy, the working through tends to arrive at a freeing and constructive conclusion.

In the case of creating, however, I think it is much more possible that effective symbolization, while beneficial to the work, can produce trauma for the psyche of the creator. Especially because, unlike the therapy situation, there is typically no supportive other present. Albert Rothenberg (1990) has written about this in the case of John Cheever's relapse back into alcoholism in the process of writing *Bullet Park* which brought much closer to consciousness than previously his antagonism and murderous jealousy toward his only brother whom he also loved. Perhaps I am particularly concerned about this because of the effects on myself of publishing my first short story at age fifteen and publishing a best-selling novel as a twenty-two-year-old high school dropout still recovering after a five-year hospitalization for anorexia nervosa. Though I had no conscious understanding of it at the time, the short story success intensely exacerbated my anorexia. Similarly, the publication of my international bestseller, *Caleb My Son* (1956, 1957), the Guggenheim fellowship it won me, and then publishing its project, my second novel, *High On A Hill* (1961), was followed by nearly twenty years of writer's block. Both, I came to understand in psychoanalysis much later, had to do with events in my early life that had left me afraid of and horrified by the strength of my voice.[2] Nevertheless, twenty-five-years later, when at the urging of my psychoanalyst, I did resume writing, I discovered something that I now regard as another very valuable form of potential space.

In the fifth year of my analysis, (when I had just completed doctoral training in clinical psychology), my analyst confronted me one day by asking, "What about your writing?" My first response was to insist angrily that I was *not* a writer. When he pointed out that this was at odds with my record in reality, I told him that I had deliberately given up writing for my own good so as to no longer humiliate myself by laboring as a slave to my parents at something I was no good at. But in time when, after more discussion, I did return to this transitional object abandoned by me earlier, I made valuable discoveries that enhanced both the writing and myself.

The analyst was right, of course. In terms of psychoanalysis, my having abandoned my transitional process *did* need to be confronted. Why had I done that? Also, as I did begin writing again, I soon realized that it was still important to me. I had imposed a huge deprivation on myself; writing hadn't just lost its significance as a fading, no longer needed, transitional object. There *were* problems associated with writing, however, problems that interfered with the work's effectiveness. And as I labored to overcome these, I discovered what I now regard as another most valuable "potential space"—the dream.

You could say that the writing flaws *were* symbols. But they were also real. I would now call them cryptosymbols, ways that I unconsciously "saved" myself from a repeat of previous traumatic success with writing by remaining an inadequate underdog. So, writing was *not* potential space for me. However, as I labored to retrieve the transitional object so valued by me earlier, I began to have dreams in which the problem at the basis of the creating was symbolized so that I could recognize and think about it as had never been possible with the manuscript alone. By thinking about the problem thus symbolized, I could be present for myself in the process of writing. Another valuable aspect of this potential space is that as I grew and, with more freedom, had new problems to face, these too, could be symbolized. And, of course, this continually vitalized me as well as the writing, because the dream symbols' personal meanings made me able to think about myself as never before. Examples of this process over time follow:

Early on in August 1982, when I was beginning an autobiographical novel that I found to be flawed with woodenness and weakness, I dreamed I was sitting on a toilet in a mental institution and straining but unable to urinate. The commode was very high off the floor. Like a throne. I was able to understand from this image that I found my writing as disgraceful as urine and connected to the mental institution where I'd written my first novel. The commode high off the floor symbolized how I felt I had inherited writing from my father and grandfather. I kept on working at writing despite the "wooden," "weak," and "shallow" flaws that distressed me. And I talked about this at length in analysis. Then in August 1989, I dreamed that I was on Dr. H's couch telling him about having drunk two-and-a-half glasses of wine, an amount I considered a little too much. Suddenly I noticed that my right hand was in a cast and, then, that this was responsible for a good feeling all over my body, a kind of white light goodness that enveloped me. From this I was able to understand that as hard as I was working to be effective at writing, my unconscious needed to keep me a crippled writer. Why? So that my father (now dead several years) could find me lovable. *That* was why the flaws were so persistent. With more thought I could see that this also kept me a "lovable underdog" like the dachshund who'd been my only companion locked outside in the yard as a small child. Armed with this self-understanding, I continued writing.

In January 1994, as I worked to convert my autobiographical novel to a memoir, in keeping with the recommendations of three agents, at a time when I'd also come to recognize my fear and sense of inadequacy in relation to writing as conscious representations of my unconscious defiance of being the writer my parents wanted, I dreamed about me as a child being forced to say the "right thing" in a way that would kill me. I was strangling on those words while my parents stood over me, demanding that I say them perfectly even though they could see I was going to die from trying.

On waking from this symbolization of the conflict with my parents I realized that I was in the process of losing or giving up my fantasy of being *not* a writer. In September 1998, as I pursued regular and dedicated work on a new novel, the work went well despite being accompanied by aching sadness and depression. In the process I dreamed that my hands were so sore that I consulted a doctor. He said, "There's nothing wrong with your hands." "But they're red," I implored. Once awake, I realized, like a flash of lightning, that writing productively made me ache with sadness because I was losing myself as the crippled writer Father could love.

In 2002 after the publication of my memoir, my analyst saw me on a Friday and died suddenly before our next scheduled meeting on Monday. Again, the dream following this symbolized my feelings more powerfully than I could ever have stated: my right arm (the hand with which I write) had been cut off at the shoulder.

Not for the sake of science but certainly for the sake of creativity, I include one more informative dream. In 2004 after completing my newest novel, my first after 40 years of silence, and sending it to my agent, I dreamed: my beloved miniature dachshund Moonshine had driven off in my blue Volvo. I was terribly distressed—primarily about the loss of Moonshine. Then she came back and my worry shifted to what terrible destruction she might have caused with the car. So, even though I, as the underdog, was not lost, concerns about the destructiveness of my voice remained.

Another valuable lesson learned from returning to writing is the realization that the psychological conditions under which I wrote my first novel were ideal for me—not only then, but perhaps to be repeated now. Because I wrote *Caleb My Son* in my fifth year of mental hospital confinement and only in the early morning hours before taking the bus to my day job, I knew it would never see the light of day. Since no one would ever read it, I wrote it just to keep on writing for myself. Ideal safety for a person who feels her voice is destructive!

But for me, because of my two roles, this increased freedom to write has also, I believe, enhanced my capacity as a therapist: to appreciate the power in giving the patient the silent support needed to be him/her self. After all, I realized, as my dreaming to freedom advanced, it had not been my analyst's interpretations that created these dreams. It had been his capacity to listen in silence to *my* self-probing. And, as a result, my capacity to subjectively attend to and symbolize (in a way that assisted thought later) the emotional issues at hand had increased.

So, besides the dream screen's providing (in the context of analysis) potential space in which I could grow as a writer, this process showed me more clearly than ever before the significance of dream expression and the importance, as a therapist, of being able to accept a patient's communication in this form without violating his privacy. Or perhaps it would be more accurate to say that I later was also grateful to my own dream experience for making me more appropriately sensitive and unintrusive with a patient who could report very significantly symbolic dreams even though his capacity to relate was hugely limited by apprehension of being himself with others.

William

William's parents had consulted me about him in his junior year of high school, because they were concerned about his being so withdrawn and isolated. Though he was a straight A student and about to be an Eagle Scout, he had no friends and they feared he was seriously depressed. William was depressed but mostly about his isolation and his fears of leaving home as an adult. He very early related this to something his parents had told me about—his premature birth and complications from it early in life. William's strongest memory of the effects of all that was that in preschool if his mother was late picking him up he would *know* that he would stop existing if she didn't come.

In speaking about his current isolation William talked at length about how uncomfortable he felt with peers and about how he could not be himself with other people. He preferred being alone, because he did not think others could like the real him. In our twice-weekly work together, William also very early (and without any urging) began reporting dreams. He seemed to do this not so much to deal with problems as to just have something to report. Perhaps this was even an unconsciously defensive effort to risk/but not really risk being himself with me. Initially these dreams appeared long and rambling but relatively pointless. But then, of course, as the same rambling situations repeated, William began to talk about being "lost" in them. In time this led to dreaming about people or groups he was trying to get to and eventually to being with people he did not know. His parents were never in those dreams, though the places they might be located sometimes were.

One issue William did talk about was coming to avoid his parents a bit in life, because he felt (and he emphasized this was only a *feeling* of his) that they were too controlling and too caretaking. Perhaps, as a result of this, during his last three years of college and grad school, William supported himself, including his tuition and apartment rent, by working for computer companies. Since graduating, he has worked full time (in the same computer profession as his father) and has had dreams about not being able to find his father in his old office where William did visit as a child. Instead there was a high tower there from which the guard kept telling him that his father was still inside. William could think about these dreams as relating to his concerns about competing with his father in a field where he definitely has the educational advantage. Nowadays he has a couple of female (as well as male) friends, but has not mentioned (or dreamed about) dating.

In a couple of years this very isolated computer-whiz student managed, through reporting his dreams to receptive but unintrusive me, to recognize his own (amazingly brilliant) symbolizations of what held him back socially and to work effectively against it in life. In a sense, you could say, my capacity to let him be alone in my presence assisted his creativity in relation to himself. By the time he had completed two years of graduate school and was fully employed, he had some friends but was continuing to work very much on his own to be more himself with others. He has reported this work and its results to me but has rarely done the psychological work evident in his developing dreams and life in my presence. We might say that he has needed potential space to risk being himself with himself before attempting it with others.

WHAT MAKES SPACE "POTENTIAL?"

Since simple, but direct and suggestive statements like Winnicott's (1971) "it is in playing, and perhaps only in playing that the child or adult is free to be creative" can inspire discerning creative work in others, we might ask: Does potential space require such triggers? Or more to the point: What *is* potential space? Is it the same for everyone?

I would say, "no." Potential space, despite the universal conditions listed by Ogden (1993), is unique for each individual. And we can see examples of this uniqueness in the cases presented. Since neither of the child cases was in need of being "correct," both used the play room as they wished. I would not say that dreams always offer potential space. But for certain withdrawn individuals dreams may early on provide more creatively workable space than therapy sessions themselves. In the case of my writer's block, dreams (in the context of psychoanalysis) provided the information needed to restore the aloneness or autonomy I require to write.

One final point I would like to make is that playing and creating are alike in *not* being safe. Even or especially in the context of potential space which facilitates them. Because it is in just such a protected atmosphere that an individual is most likely to have the liberty (abandoned self-control) to create/express what he/she, for some reason, has considered unbearable or forbidden. And that can be traumatic even though once this unbearable material does come out; the ultimate result may be increased freedom. Provided that the player or creator (child or adult) has access to support (internally or externally) for assistance with facing and dealing with the trauma. Then, I would say, such play or creating can be valued even more for turning trauma into gold. And for evoking the courage to face and risk that extreme transition.

NOTES

1. Artists' Testimonial Film (in progress), Expressive Media, Inc. Pittsburgh.

2. The setting for these events was a family in which girls were worthless and where, because my father and grandfather were respected writers, I labored in school to gain worth through writing. However, at the unconscious level success made me guilty of receiving more than I deserved. In addition, even earlier, one summer afternoon when I was four, my eight-year-older half-sister came to the garden where I was confined alone and told me that my mother was pregnant. I told her that I already knew this. But then she told me (for the first time) that we were not sisters. Her mother had died having a baby (a boy who also died) that "broke her open coming out." She also told me that our father had put the baby in her with his penis. This led me to believe that my father was killing women by peeing inside them. And that made me *have* to confront him. So I did, saying "Did you love Babs (the name of my sister's mother)?" I expected him to get furious. But instead his eyes filled with tears as he softly answered, "I loved her very much." This secret was never spoken of again. And I only under-

stood in psychoanalysis fifty years later that I had always felt that my voice had destroyed our family as I knew it, because Father's response reflected much more love for Babs than he ever showed for my mother.

Chapter Ten

Play and Track II Diplomacy

Vamık D. Volkan

> "As citizens of the most powerful nation of the world and especially perhaps as psychoanalysts, it is our social responsibility to understand the complex nature of subjectivity as it is formed in relation to a socio-symbolic order." —Nancy Hollander, "Psychoanalysis and the Problem of the By-Stander in Times of Terror"

In their efforts to make agreements and resolve conflicts without resorting to force or international law, nation states employ modern official diplomacy governed by rules and regulations, some of which go back to the fifteenth century when permanent missions between large-group entities were established. Within the official protocol between nation-states, there are accepted and ritualized ways of carrying out diplomatic work, such as those that exist in religion and law. While on the surface it is difficult to imagine the concept of "play" and especially the concept of "playfulness" as having a role in rigid and serious bargaining protocols between nation-states, comparisons have been made between the diplomatic process and competitive sports. Changing times have forced us to reorganize our thinking about how large groups relate, nation-states as well as other large groups such as the unrecognized state of the Turkish Republic of Cyprus (recognized by Turkey only), and ethnic or religious large groups. Changing times also provide examples of how the representatives of opposing large groups, during periods of high tension in their relationships, may create symbolic toys and become involved in symbolic play in order to understand each others' identities and psychic realities, tame aggression, and find peaceful ways to coexist. This contribution explores the unconscious meaning of such play and gives an example of how enemy representatives, after years of dialogue, created mental toys and played with them.

DIPLOMACY

Nation-states came into being following the French and American Revolutions. Instead of being ruled by a monarch, people chose the notion of self-determination and the idea of nationalism. The "age of nationalism" was born at the end of the eighteenth century and crystallized in the nineteenth century. The model of nation-states was expanded to include other large groups that were liberated from the rule of "others" in what we came to know as colonialism. In the process, modern diplomacy was firmly established as a tool of protocol between nation-states. This protocol includes broad elements ranging from providing formal representation and serving as a listening post, to reducing friction in cases of conflict (when advisable), to managing change and creating, drafting and amending international rules (Barston, 1988).

Psychoanalyst Janine Chasseguet-Smirgel (1996) hypothesized that, although attachment to one's native soil is grounded in history, people are connected to each other by certain conscious feelings and beliefs, and when new nationalistic ideals appeared they replaced religious feelings and beliefs. While nationalism is linked to liberty and universal ideals, we all know it can also be used for racism, totalitarianism and destruction. Chasseguet-Smirgel hypothesizes that the more nationalism replaces religion and stands in for religious mystical feelings—in other words, the more it performs a function which religion no longer is able to fulfill—the more it has a tendency to become a lethal force. This happened in Germany when the National Socialist Party dominated. Since World War II there have been many developments forcing us to reconsider what diplomacy is, although it is beyond this brief paper to examine them in detail.

In 1983, Abba Eban, an orator and the Foreign Minister of Israel from1966 to 1974, noted a decline in the role of ambassadors and foreign-policy agencies. He referred to "the age of summitry" as emphasizing face-to-face meetings between leaders of opposing nations, thereby altering the function of such organs, such as departments of state, in foreign-policy determinations. In 1990, a former U.S. Assistant Secretary of State, Harold Saunders, stated that in the twentieth century, two world wars, and nuclear weapons made us question the legitimacy of nation-states using power unilaterally to pursue their own interests. He wrote:

> While most people do not yet see sovereign states fading away, a growing number observe that national sovereignties are increasingly limited in what they can accomplish by themselves and argue that genuine influence comes less and less from the use of raw power alone—that the nature of power and influence has changed. (p. 3)

In many locations in today's world a reversal of what Chasseguet-Smirgel (1996) described is occurring, in that shared religious feelings and beliefs that transcend the boundaries of nation states are replacing nationalistic feelings and beliefs. The existence of al-Qaeda is one example. This, of course, is influencing how modern diplomacy is practiced.

Today, several factors have reorganized our thinking about the nature of international relationships: the existence of religious conflicts alongside ethnic conflicts, worldwide terrorism (Volkan, 1988, 1997, 2004, 2006; Volkan and Kayatckin, 2006), as well as incredible developments in communications technology (Arnett, 2002), the ascendancy of an intrusive news media (Seib, 1996), a huge increase in international travel (Held, 1988), the influence of modern forms of "good" globalization that attempt to promote prosperity and well-being for societies (Çevik, 2003) and "bad" globalization that includes prejudice and racism (Liu and Mills, 2006; Morton, 2005; Kinnvall, 2004; Ratliff, 2004). Obviously, diplomacy still includes negotiations between sovereign nation-states, but it also includes talking to and dealing with religious, ethnic, or ideological leaders in official and unofficial ways. We can no longer reduce diplomacy to "correct" and ritualistic protocols. Many of today's international problems have created huge gaps in the physical and psychological borders of nation-states; they cannot be dealt with as issues confined only within the boundaries of opposing nation-states. Thousands of nongovernmental organizations (NGOs) associated or not associated with the United Nations and other major international institutions have emerged to establish one form of unofficial diplomacy or another alongside official diplomacy. These developments, in turn, have given us more opportunities to observe closely both violent interactions and attempts to find peaceful solutions to conflicts between sovereign nation states and other types of large groups. Sometimes, such observations also provide examples of representatives of national, ethnic, religious or political ideological large groups "playing" and even becoming "playful" when they get together to find solutions for their conflicts.

MY OBSERVATIONS

I have never been an official diplomat, with the exception of a few days when I was one of the representatives of the Turkish Republic of Northern Cyprus (attached to the mission from Turkey) at the November 1990 Paris Summit that focused on security and cooperation in Europe and was attended by world leaders ranging from George H. W. Bush to Margaret Thatcher to Michael Gorbachev to Turgut Özal. At this meeting, I ended up observing the rigid rituals of official diplomacy from a distance. However, during the last three decades I also had many opportunities to speak with political leaders from different countries, including Michael Gorbachev and Yasser Arafat, and closely observe some of them and their diplomats at work. Furthermore, I was a member of the Carter Center's International Negotiations Network (INN) under the leadership of former President Jimmy Carter during the late 1980s through the 1990s. This affiliation further exposed me to many world leaders and high-level diplomats and I learned about ways they were involved in diplomatic tasks. However, my ideas about relationships between nation-states (and other large groups) and the meaning of "play" and "playfulness" in negotiations primarily comes from my involvement, also during the last three decades, as a member and often the leader of an interdisciplinary facilitating team in years-long unofficial diplomatic negotiations between enemy groups such as Israelis and Arabs (Volkan, 1988, 2006). Through this work I have witnessed that "playing" and being "playful" in diplomacy helps to remove anxiety stemming from threats to one's large group's identity and open ways for emphatic understanding of the "other's" psychic reality. After perceived threats to one's large-group identity are removed, or at least tamed, more realistic and durable diplomatic exchanges can take place.

COMPETITIVE SPORTS AND DIPLOMACY

There are diplomats such as W. Nathaniel Howell, who was the U.S. Ambassador to Kuwait when Saddam Hussein's forces invaded that country, who are aware of the "playing" aspect of official diplomacy. Ambassador Howell (retired) is a tall man who played basketball in his youth. He compares good diplomatic negotiation to playing basketball. The opposing teams rush from one side of the basketball court to the other using rules and regulations and try to score points. In the end one team wins, but the other team also scores and achieves some degree of self-esteem for being a good competitor. According to Ambassador Howell (personal communication, 2000), involvement in a well-managed and fair diplomatic activity is as pleasurable as watching a well-played basketball game. The natural comparison between sports and diplomacy is not lost on the media where sports metaphors abound as well, and phrases such as, "Can Russia play hardball?"; "a dream team of negotiators"; or "They need a new game plan" are often used in reports on international conflicts and diplomatic efforts to resolve them. There are also board and computer games where participants play at diplomacy.

One well-known event linking diplomacy and competitive sports was Ping-pong Diplomacy. On April 6, 1971, the Chinese Communist government "unexpectedly" invited the United States' ping-pong team, which was then in Japan for the 31st World Tennis Championship, to come to China. Four days later, nine U.S. players, two spouses, and four officials crossed a bridge from Hong Kong, arrived in mainland China and spent eight days there. All expenses were paid by the Chinese. They were the first Americans to visit China since 1949. This historic visit, during which the U.S. team played exhibition ping-pong matches with the Chinese team, began a new chapter between the two enemy nation states. We now know that the United States and China had been quietly conducting back-channel talks beforehand, but nevertheless, the event symbolically illustrated that when enemies play they do not hurt one another and that successful diplomacy is like playing competitive games under rules and regulations. It paved the way for Richard Nixon's visit there the following year as the first U.S. president ever to visit China. During the thirtieth anniversary of Ping-pong Diplomacy, the former U.S. Secretary of State Henry A. Kissinger visited Beijing and played ping-pong with the Chinese Vice Premier, once more symbolically linking a competitive sport with the diplomatic process.

Most recently many NGOs attempting international conflict resolution seem to believe that in order to make peace between enemies—at least between their representatives who meet each other—they must "play" together. It is no wonder that some NGOs developed methodologies for conflict resolution that bring together youngsters from enemy groups to camps and playgrounds in neutral countries. These youngsters get to know each others by playing basketball, soccer, or other games. I suspect that such NGO authorities are not familiar with psychoanalytic findings on children at play and the therapeutic benefits of such activities (for a review see: Yanof, 2005); they are following their intuition, as well the example provided by Ping-pong Diplomacy.

On many occasions when tensions were high between Cypriot Greeks and Cypriot Turks high school students from each side were brought to some vacation spots in the United States. Under the supervision of American facilitators they had dialogues, became involved in competitive games and got to know each other. I know of another situation, this one involving adults, when high-level representatives, again from the two sides in Cyprus, were asked to play with small plastic pieces, Legos, like small children would do, to build houses or trucks. In these situations, unlike what happened during Ping-pong Diplomacy, a third party forced the games on the representatives of the enemy groups. Perhaps at times such games initiated by a neutral third party were useful in breaking the ice between the enemy representatives and helped them work on a problem together. Often however, they produce negative results. For example, at the time, the youngsters from the opposing sides on Cyprus could not continue to communicate with each other when they returned to the island because of the political division that included a concrete wall separating Cypriot Greeks and Turks. Furthermore, upon returning home, some of the youngsters were perceived by their own people as traitors for playing with the enemy, causing psychological difficulties for some of them. In the case of the LEGOs game, I recall speaking with a high-level official who had participated in the exercise with an enemy representative, and he told me how humiliated he felt by being forced to behave like a little child. We can generalize and say that forcing a game on the representatives of opposing groups is like a therapist suggesting or ordering a patient to go to Disneyland to recover from his depression.

CREATING AND PLAYING WITH SYMBOLIC TOYS

A different type of "play" may take place during an enemy representatives' negotiation process, especially when a tense and dangerous situation exists, but it is not of the kind that can be compared to competitive sports or that which is forced upon negotiators by outsiders. This kind of play appears spontaneously in the interactions of the enemy negotiators after they unconsciously create symbolic toys. This play helps the negotiators develop empathy for the opposing group, tame the "other's" realistic and fantasized sense of danger and strengthen each group's large-group identity. After such play more realistic and successful negotiations become possible.

Expanding Ambassador Howell's (2006) comparison of diplomacy to basketball, let us imagine that someone spills a large amount of oil on the basketball court. Now the basketball game becomes chaotic. The first thing required is to wipe off the oil spill and clean the floor. Creating symbolic toys and playing with them represents wiping off the spilled oil from the basketball floor. Then the routine basketball game can be played; a diplomatic process, under rules and regulations, can take place. Before giving an example of creating symbolic toys and playing with them, an examination of the concept of large-group identity is needed. As I will illustrate, symbolic toys represent large-group identities; they are effigies for the enemy groups in negotiations.

LARGE-GROUP IDENTITY

Over the past few decades, a growing number of borderline and narcissistic patients have visited our offices, carrying with them contradictory self- and object images. For example, George, a patient with a narcissistic personality organization, would look at the mirror every morning and say: "I am more handsome than any movie star!" Once, while walking on a beach in Greece, he felt that he was a Greek god and everyone on the beach was looking at him with adoration. Yet, this man kept a hundred cans of food in his kitchen cupboard so that he would never go hungry, and if his stock became even slightly depleted, he was anxious until he replenished it. He had friends who totally adored him, while he devalued those who did not perceive him as God's gift to earth. Because of our clinical experience with patients like George who divide themselves and their intimate external world into "good" and "bad" categories, clinicians frequently refer to the concept of identity when discussing these cases with colleagues. We say that people like George do not have an integrated and cohesive identity. Yet the concept of identity is relatively new in the psychoanalytic literature. Sigmund Freud seldom referred to identity, and when he did it was in a colloquial or unsophisticated sense. One of his well-known references to identity is found in a speech he delivered to B'nai B'rith (1926b), in which he wondered why he was bound to Jewry since, as a nonbeliever, he had never been instilled with ethnonational pride or religious faith. Nevertheless, Freud noted within himself "many obscure emotional forces, which were more powerful the less they could be expressed in words, as well as a clear consciousness of inner identity [as a Jew], the safe privacy of a common mental construction," (Freud, 1926b, p. 274). It is interesting that Freud's remarks linked his individual identity with his large-group identity.

Although there may be no clear description of identity in specific psychological terms, there is a consensus that it refers to a subjective experience. Unlike character and personality, which are observed and defined by others, identity refers to an individual's inner working model—this person, not an outsider, senses and experiences it. Erik Erikson, one psychoanalyst who focused on identity, first used the term "ego identity," and then dropped the word ego and used simply "identity." He described it as "a persistent sameness within oneself . . . [and] a persistent sharing of some kind of essential character with others" (Erikson, 1950, p. 57). In everyday life, an adult individual typically refers to his or her social or professional status as social or professional identities. If a person's career identity is threatened, the individual may or may not experience anxiety. Anxiety is more likely to occur if the threat is connected, mostly unconsciously, to an internal danger signal such as losing a loved one such as a mother (or her love), a body part (castration), or self-esteem. Imagine, for example, a man who habitually plays golf suffering a leg injury. He can no longer play golf and loses his "golfer identity." He may not experience much anxiety and may become a painter and develop a "painter identity." But if the leg injury unconsciously becomes connected with his castration anxiety, this man will feel anxious about losing his "golfer identity." My focus in this contribution is not on a person's surface identities; it is on the person's core identity, the subjective experience of his or her self-representation.

Salman Akhtar (1992, 1999) looked at the individual's core identity from different angles. He stated that the sustained feeling of inner sameness is accompanied by a temporal continuity in the self experience: the past, the present, and the future are integrated into a smooth continuum of remembered, felt, and expected existence for the individual. The individual core identity is connected with a realistic body image and a sense of inner solidarity and is associated with capacity for solitude and clarity of one's gender. Akhtar also connected the individual's core identity with his or her large-group identity, such as a national, ethnic or religious identity. Unlike losing one's professional or social identity, losing one's core identity is terrifying (Pao, 1979; Volkan, 1995). To understand "core identity," let us consider a young adult who decompensates and goes into schizophrenia. Such an individual's identity is fragmenting, and this person may have an inner sensation of a star exploding into a billion pieces (Glass, 1985). He or she will definitely experience severe anxiety; in fact, this anxiety is so extreme that it is unspeakably terrifying. In order to escape from this terror, as soon as the individual is capable, he or she will create a new sense of identity, albeit a false (psychotic) one. Losing one's core identity is intolerable; it is psychological death. I can add that a significant threat to one's large-group identity, which comes from the "other" with a different large-group identity, is also perceived as devastating and intolerable.

In the psychoanalytic literature the term "large group" often refers to 30 to 150 individuals who meet in order to deal with a given task. When this task is, by design, unstructured and vague, the large group regresses. At this time, observers notice increased anxiety, chaos, and panic among its members (Rice, 1965; Turquet, 1975). In order to escape the panicky atmosphere that envelopes them, a regressed large group exhibits narcissistic or paranoid characteristics and reorganizes itself by utilizing shared primitive mental mechanisms (Kernberg, 2003a, 2003b). My term "large group" refers to tens, hundreds of thousands, or millions of individuals—most of whom will never meet during their lifetimes—that belong to a large group from childhood on. Adapting Erik Erikson's (1950, 1956) description of individual identity, I define large-group identity—whether it refers to ethnicity, nationality, religion or political ideology—as the shared subjective experience of thousands or millions of people who are linked by a persistent sense of sameness, while also sharing some characteristics with others who belong to foreign large groups (Volkan, 1997): We are Arabs; we are French; we are Tamils; we are Communists. Dissenters in a large group are only important in changing the shared psychological processes within their large groups if they successfully start a major movement that attracts a substantial number of followers or are recognized and supported by foreign large groups.

The psychodynamics of ethnic, national or religious and some ideological large groups are different from the psychodynamics of small groups, "large

groups" composed of 30 or 150 individuals, or crowds (Volkan, 1988, 1997, 2004, and 2006). During their routine daily lives people are not keenly aware of their intense investment in large-group identities—the intertwining of their core individual identities with their large-group identities—just as they are not usually aware of their constant breathing. If they are in a burning building, they quickly notice each breath they take. Likewise, when facing enemies who are doing something to humiliate and destroy a large group, the members of the attacked or victimized group become preoccupied with its large-group identity and will do anything to stabilize, repair, protect and maintain it. They will be willing to tolerate extreme sadism or masochism if they think that what they are doing will help to protect and maintain their large-group identity.

Psychologically speaking, official and unofficial diplomacy refers to bringing together representatives of opposing groups and giving them tasks to be spokespersons and protectors of their respective large-group identities. Thus, negotiators in official or unofficial diplomatic processes are constantly aware of their large-group identities, especially during a tense and dangerous situation. While they talk about economic, legal and military issues, trades, cultural exchanges, and measurable gains and losses, all these real-world issues become contaminated with their psychological investment in large-group identity. Under tense and dangerous situations the negotiators, often without being aware of it, negotiate the repairing, protecting and maintaining of their respective large-group identities. They do so in order to prepare a foundation for a bargain by using intellectualization, power politics and persuasion under international rules and regulations. In other words, they attempt to keep the basketball floor clean and non-slippery. This process can be clearly observed if the negotiators come up with abstract "effigies" representing the enemy groups' identities and then play with them.

AN EXAMPLE OF PLAYING WITH EFFIGIES

In 1987, I founded the Center for the Study of Mind and Human Interaction (CSMHI) at the University of Virginia's School of Medicine and directed it until 2002. It was closed a few years later. It was an interdisciplinary center that practiced preventive medicine in its broadest sense by trying to reduce tensions in some troubled spots of the world. My colleagues and I at CSMHI evolved a version of "unofficial diplomacy" and called it the "Tree Model" (Volkan, 1999, 2006). The title of this methodology reflects the slow process of an unofficial diplomatic activity that grows like a tree and develops many branches. This methodology has three basic phases that are conducted under the auspices of a psychoanalytically informed interdisciplinary facilitating

team: (1) psychopolitical diagnosis of the situation between the enemy groups, (2) psychopolitical dialogues between influential delegates of the enemy groups, and (3) collaborative political/societal actions and governmental and societal institutions that grow out of the dialogue process.

The first phase includes the facilitating team's in-depth psychoanalytically informed interviews with a wide range of members of the large groups involved. This leads to an understanding of the main conscious and unconscious aspects that surround the situation that needs to be addressed. Sometimes, understanding unconscious shared processes in a large-group requires months or even years. During the psychopolitical dialogues between influential representatives of opposing large groups that take place in a series of four-day meetings over several years, resistances against changing large group's "pathological" ways of protecting large-group identity are brought to the surface, fantasized threats to large-group identity are interpreted and separated from realistic dangers, and the enemy group's psychic reality is understood. The facilitators do not offer advice or their own strategies for conflict resolution, but they utilize ideas stemming from psychoanalytic technique in conducting the psychopolitical dialogues. Eventually more realistic communications between the enemy groups take place. The second phase of the Tree Model is an unofficial diplomatic process during which the oil on the basketball court is wiped off. In order for the newly gained insights to have an impact on social and political policy, as well as on the populace at large, the final third phase of the Tree Model, which also lasts for some years, requires the collaborative development of concrete actions, programs, and institutions approved directly or indirectly by central governments and regional authorities.

This methodology allows several disciplines, including psychoanalysis, diplomacy and history, to work together to articulate and work through underlying psychological and historical aspects of existing tensions. Then what is learned is put into operation so that more peaceful coexistence between large groups can be achieved and threats (especially the fantasized ones) to large-group identity coming from the "other" can be tamed. As far as I am concerned, the Tree Model is the only psychoanalytically informed, interdisciplinary methodology for finding peaceful coexistence between enemy groups. It is beyond the scope of this chapter to describe this methodology further, but its most detailed description can be found in my book, *Killing in the Name of Identity* (Volkan, 2006).

The Tree Model does employ symbolic toys, effigies, and opportunities to play with them in the service of finding peaceful solutions for tense situations. One such opportunity arose in the newly independent nation-state of Estonia after the collapse of the Soviet Empire. Estonia has a total population of only one-and-a-half million people, but every third person is a Russian or Russian-speaker. When Estonia became a nation-state in 1991, this, along

with many other real-world issues such as border disputes, created large-looming dangerous problems between Estonians, Russians and Russian-speakers living in Estonia. The CSMHI facilitating team spent nearly seven years applying a Tree Model methodology to this situation (Volkan, 2006). During the second phase of this work, high-level representatives such as parliamentarians and well-known scholars from Estonia and Russia, along with the leaders of Russians and Russian-speakers living in Estonia, were involved in a series of unofficial diplomatic dialogues. At the beginning of this dialogue series some Estonian participants would literally turn purple with silent rage due to their perceptions of what the Russians had done to them, but they could not verbalize their thoughts. The facilitating team understood that living under the "other" for a long time had robbed them of the ability to be openly assertive in front of their common enemy. On the other hand, the facilitating team noted how Russians were humiliated by having lost their empire and having to now dialogue with their former subjects. As far as the representatives of the Russians and the Russian-speakers were concerned, most of them had ceased being the "bosses" and they had begun the shameful and difficult process of facing their new challenge of being accepted as citizens in a new country.

By using the Tree Model in Estonia, the facilitating team did help the negotiators from the opposing camps slowly listen and hear one another; during the latter part of this unofficial dialogue series, negotiators spontaneously created abstract toys and began playing with them. Their toys were an elephant and a rabbit. The game was spontaneously started by Arnold Rüütel, who was the last Chairman of the Supreme Soviet of the Republic of Estonia before Estonia became independent and who later would be elected President of Estonia. (Rüütel was president of Estonia from 2001 to 2006). One day at a meeting Rüütel turned to the leading Russian delegate Yuri Voyevoda, then a member of Russia's State Duma and said:

> You Russians are an elephant. You have a huge federation. We Estonians are a rabbit. We have a small country. If a rabbit becomes friendly with an elephant, it will not be careful around the elephant. It will face more danger because the elephant, even though it may not be aggressive, may step on it.

Then another Estonian noted that Russians living in Estonia were like elephant eggs in the rabbit's nest—at any moment they might hatch and squash the rabbit and its home. Referring to the Russians' perception that they had done much good for Estonia when Estonia was a part of the Soviet Empire, Voyevoda replied:

> All along I used to think that Estonians were ungrateful people. Now I understand that is not the case. You are telling me that Estonians are careful, not ungrateful. I

> can easily accept this. Let's see how an elephant and a rabbit can remain side by side without either of them getting hurt or humiliated.

Symbolic effigies of large-group identities were created. In a playful fashion negotiators played elephant and rabbit games for hours and even days. The facilitating team did not interfere. During this time, while I was observing the negotiators, I felt that I was watching children at play. Anxiety gave way to freer expressions of negative feelings. Estonians were angry since the elephant in the past had stepped on the rabbit. Now, should the elephant take care and watch out for the rabbit as it takes steps? Or, should the rabbit keep the necessary distance from the elephant in order to protect itself and also take responsibility for a peaceful coexistence?

While playing elephant and rabbit games Estonians and Russians experientially understood and felt what I call the "accordion phenomenon" (Volkan, 1988, 2006). The accordion phenomenon refers to the maintaining of two unalterable conditions in a relationship between enemy large groups, especially at times of conflict: (1) One large group cannot be the same as the second one; (2) there is a need for a psychological border between the two large groups. Imagine someone playing an accordion. The musical instrument is squeezed and then expanded. Enemy groups can get along peacefully when they do not stand far apart. But, if the enemy groups are forced to come too close and "love" one another, this also leads to a negative result, because too much closeness is perceived as mixing large-group identities, and this causes anxiety. Realistic discussions between the representatives of opposing groups cannot take place when the accordion is squeezed too much or is expanded too much. As the play with effigies between Estonians and Russians continued, laughter replaced anxious and angry feelings, and both parties understood that a rabbit does not need to love an elephant and be too close to it, and that they can be friendly with a necessary distance between them. Russians "re-humanized" Estonians as careful people rather than people seeking ways to humiliate their former rulers, and Estonians appreciated that people with past and present empires are simply proud and sensitive about being powerful and they do not need to use their power to smash others. Four months later when the participants came together for another four-day dialogue they continued, on and off, to play elephant-rabbit games. This development was a turning-point in Estonian-Russian relations. Soon they began to sign agreements.

Some years after watching Estonians and Russians play elephant-rabbit games, I was involved in an unofficial Turkish-Greek dialogue series between high-level Turks and Greeks. Interestingly enough they also came up with elephant (Turkey)–rabbit (Greece) symbols and attempted to play with these mental toys. These Turkish-Greek meetings were sporadic and came to an end two years prematurely because of a lack of funds to maintain them.

CONCLUDING REMARKS

If an international conflict becomes hot or chronic, and if there is high tension when the enemy representatives meet for negotiations, large-group identity issues contaminate all the real-world problems, such as economic and legal considerations. When large-group identity issues become inflamed and problematic, limiting international relations to typical routine, diplomatic rituals and protocols become very difficult and sometimes impossible. My observations suggest that if diplomatic efforts are to be successful, effigies standing for enemy representatives and their large-group identities need to be created and played with in order to avoid sliding into destructive and malignant international relations. From a psychological point of view, when representatives of opposing large groups consider themselves enemies and when the tensions in their relationship are very high, the deepest unconscious requirement for successful spontaneous play in diplomacy is for them to create, mostly unconsciously, effigies of themselves. The unconscious meaning and aim of playing with the effigies is to repair, protect and maintain their large-group identities. If diplomacy works when tensions are high, one large group can humiliate, beat on and kill the effigies of the opposing group, or they can come close to them in play in the name of morality and justice as the large group defines these concepts in selfish ways. This is far better than hurting and destroying real people who belong to the opposing group and their livelihoods in wars or war-like situations. If effigies representing large-group identities are not created to fill the space between the enemy negotiating teams in the form of play, diplomacy does not work, and nation states—and in today's world, other large groups—may resort to seemingly unending and unsuccessful angry negotiations or destructive and malignant ways of relating to each other.

I go back to Harold Saunder's (1990) call to rethink how nation-states and other large groups relate. This, of course, is a very difficult and perhaps impossible task. As Saunders reminded us, we cannot ignore the fact that nation states and other large groups around the world still use force and manipulation to achieve their goals and that there are malignant leaders as well as insensitive, ignorant and arrogant ones. Nevertheless, I am in favor of psychoanalysts who are willing to devote time to serious study and the application of psychoanalytically informed large-group psychology, speaking up for the rethinking of international relationships and diplomatic activities. Psychoanalysts who observe children in play and adults in the working-through processes of psychoanalytic treatment have much to offer, especially regarding the role creating mental toys and playing with them has in diplomatic activities—if we are to make a more peaceful world.

Part IV

Technical Implications

Chapter Eleven

Aggregression in Children: Origins, Manifestations, and Management through Play

Mali Mann

"The emphasis on facilitating the discovery of meaning rather than the uncovering of hidden meaning places the therapist in the play with the child. In this situation, we are no longer purveyors of knowledge or omniscient translators of psychic experience; rather, we are curious co-explorers." —Arietta Slade, "Making Meaning and Making Believe: Their Role in the Clinical Process"

How do we deal with aggressive behavior in children and adolescents? Does aggression in children turn into violence if not treated? How do we deal with therapeutic frame violation? What are the origins of these aggressive behaviors? How does the environment precipitate and encourage aggression? What is the role of media violent programming in aggression? How do sociopolitical factors influence these problems? These are important questions beyond the scope of our discussion in this chapter. What I want to do is to present a few cases and some intervention techniques in the therapeutic settings. Before my description of cases, I want to review some theoretical considerations about the origin of aggression in children.

AGGRESSION IN CHILDREN

We know that anger is a basic human emotion. It can be used adaptively in resolving conflict. It can be the cause of intense inner conflict, pain, and suffering. It can be used to manipulate others, and it can lead to aggressive, destructive, and violent behavior toward others. Freud (1930, 1933) was correct that violence is a part of the human condition. We see an increasing number of young children who perpetrate violent crimes, sometimes in places we thought were safe—in our schools or our homes. We wonder why children resort to violent behavior when they feel angry or slighted. What has gone wrong? Is violence among children connected to a chaotic environment, neglect, abandonment, and abuse in infancy and early childhood? Bowlby (1994) connected violence with abandonment. Absence of emotional ties to love objects is thought of as a cause for predatory violence. Greenacre (1941) thought anxiety was the root of violence. She wondered if severe trauma, pathological parent-child interactions, sexual over-stimulation, or unrelieved organismic distress during the first three years of life would compromise self-regulatory functions; and neuropsychological patterning might be affected. The child is left as a vulnerable, easily overwhelmed individual.

Greenacre's ideas are substantiated by psychoanalytic observation, attachment research and recent work in neuroscience. Stressful, unpredictable and violent home environments, disorganized attachment and early trauma compromise emotional regulatory systems. Early intervention and possible treatment models can help these children. Contemporary research substantiates many of these early hypotheses. Attachment disorder and pathological parent-child interactions, unpredictable environments, neglect, abuse, and out of home placement (as in unfriendly and hostile foster parent homes) are correlated with excessive anger and violent behavior. Twemlow, Fonagy, and Sacco (2005) have outlined a health policy attitude for a project that intervenes in multi-problem families. The proposal encourages mentalization and reduces coercive power dynamics. Such families who are considered as socially high risk often have multiple problems with school communities as well as social services and the criminal justice system. These are families who have several generations of individuals with borderline personality disorders, substance abuse, post-traumatic stress disorders, exposure to violence, and lack of family support.

A broad range of psychopathology has been seen as one or another form of specific mentalizing dysfunction. The mind is misperceiving or misinterpreting the status of its own contents and its own functions. PTSD may entail a collapse of mentalizing, and therapy aims at the restoration of normal mentalization. I believe the concepts of agency, self-regulation (including affect regulation), and mentalization are important. We need to describe these concepts before suggesting some ideas for intervention in the treatment situation. Providing developmental models of affect regulation can be an important therapeutic intervention. The importance of timely intervention in early childhood aggressive disturbance ought to be emphasized in day care centers and the home environment.

CLINICAL ILLUSTRATIONS

I will now offer several clinical illustrations and describe treatment models and strategies to help these children develop greater capacity for affective modulation and tolerance.

Aaron

Aaron, age four-and-a-half, is angry and upset because his foster mother does not give him his favorite stuffed animal to take with him every day to the early child center. He throws temper tantrums and hits and bites other children at the center. His foster mother thinks he is very demanding, and she gets infuriated with him. He was in several foster homes until Mrs. M, his recent foster mother took a liking to him; and has been thinking seriously about adopting him. She gets doubtful about adoption when Aaron acts out or demands that his bedroom has to remain unchanged. Objects have to be in the same spot as he left them. For example, if juice spills on his shirt, he demands to have a new shirt or a new pair of shoes if his old ones get dirty. He becomes easily angered and will scream and bite. Mrs. M's tolerance was running short, and she worried she might lose her temper and hurt him physically. Thus, she was referred to me for parent guidance treatment.

George

At age twelve, George was expelled from yet another in a series of schools because his teachers could not manage his angry outbursts and abusive behavior toward his classmates. His father would punish him whenever he disobeyed or wanted to get his own way. His mother would also over-interpret his tension during those incidents and become fearful for her own life. His stepfather challenged him once when he said he was not going to clean up after himself by saying in a testing tone of voice "let's see what you will do when I make you do it!" George lost his temper and then threw a glass full of orange juice he took from the counter at his step father. His mother then called the police, and they considered him a danger to others. He was admitted to the hospital for further evaluation. During the course of the treatment it became apparent that his mother, who had a history of being abused physically and sexually by her father, would regard any normal behavior as aggressive. She expected that her son would also get out of control and hurt his family members or cause other damages.

John

John, age four-and-a-half, was referred by his pediatrician to me because he was violent to his classmates in kindergarten and attacked his only friend from behind on a swing set. His mother was unable to control his angry attacks on her and his younger brother who was one-and-a-half years his junior. His mother would behave at his age level and get into a physical fight with him as if she were his sibling. She would be remorseful and was afraid of losing her control and hurting John. He would make farting (by putting his hand under his armpit or under his knee), shrieking or animal noises in the class, and say mean words to his teachers and class mates.

During the course of my psychoanalytic work with John and parental work with his mother, I was able to establish a dialogue in which experiences, thoughts and emotions could be labeled and integrated. During the first several sessions, he would come to the waiting room and crawl on the floor, would make animal sounds and refuse to come into the consultation room. I observed his behavior several times and paid attention to his mother, noticing she was being overwhelmed and desperately needed my help. At the same time, she communicated to me, "See how impossible he is! It can't be my fault if he is this way." I pointed out to him that "it made you feel stronger and better, sounding this way especially when you feel that you could not show your big, angry, fighting feelings. You wish it were not so hard for you to become the boss of your feelings." He abruptly stopped the animal sounds and sat on the floor after one or two promptings on my part. I said, "We would do better if you and I could play together inside the playroom and try to figure out a way to make you to become the boss of your big feelings." I also said, "You expect bad things could happen when you get mad at your mother; and also not knowing what I would do or feel if you get mad at me." He accepted to come inside the room and I showed what he could do there with the toys and the games. He showed interest in exploring the board games and the toys. During his playtime, I was able to respond to his affective tone and disregulation in a timely responsive manner. Our interactions continued to move in a more trusting and positive direction. He learned how I would take his feelings very seriously and respond empathetically to his distress, particularly when he had a bad day at school or a tough time with his mother. Our interaction over some period of time helped him feel safe and he was able gradually to organize his feelings and be less frightened by them.

Some of the time through story telling and narrative work, I helped him imagine how his feelings can be understood and labeled. I was able to label his feelings and actions in order to move and lift his behavioral problems to a level of mental representation and symbolization. He learned how his emotions could be modulated and mastered. Over the course of one year's intensive therapy, he was able to use the metaphor to elaborate emotional states through symbolic play. At this point, I continued working with him and seeing his mother in weekly parent's work to help her with her feelings when she becomes overwhelmed.

Anna

Anna, at age seven, was brought to see me because her teachers were at a loss about how to deal with her aggressive behavior: hitting her class mates and stealing food from their lunch boxes. Her mother also had a difficult time managing her at home. Her younger brother was born when she was seventeen months old, and her younger sister when she was five.

She wished that her brother would just drop dead, and she would be the happiest child in her school. Her family immigrated to the states when Anna was two years old. Her mother had a difficult time acculturating to the new environment: she was very critical of other mothers, and she felt inferior to them since they seemed to be more interested in the lives of their children. Anna was more of her pal than a daughter, and was confused about her mother's inconsistent rules at home.

Anna's play was disorganized and chaotic, involving destruction and murdering family dolls with sadistic pleasure. I helped Anna's mother to mourn the loss of her country of origin in order to become available to Anna's deprived inner world. She suffered from a deficient sense of agency and insecure attachment. The generational boundary between mother and daughter was blurred, and the rules and regulation at home were disregarded since there was confusion in parental authority. Her treatment involved my active parent work, especially with her mother, and analytical play therapy work with Anna. Helping parental superego to make Anna recognize herself as an active agent was part of my treatment strategy. Anna had to learn to differentiate between desire, emotion, and the consequence of impulsive actions.

DISCUSSION

The importance of partial presence or total absence of the sense of agency in self-regulation is quite evident in the above cases. William James first de scribed the "sense of agency." There are two components, "me" and "I." The "me" part was given considerable attention in psychoanalysis, and the "I" part, which refers to the self-concept, is one's sense of self as an active agent. The I-self is the intentional designer, creator, instigator, organizer, actor, regulator and manager of all activity. The I-self is the chief executive who brings about action; the instrument of that action and the self-action is what brings about change. Fonagy (2001) writes that a sense of agency requires a sense of the self as an intentional mental being. Actions are deliberate. Children come to realize that there are links between actions and feelings. The idea that agency must include a sense of the self as an intentional mental being builds on the work of Fonagy. He defines mentalization or "reflective function," a capacity to form and reflect on representations of mental states that is thoughts and feelings: (1) becoming aware that thoughts and feelings are lodged internally in the mind; (2) thinking about and reflecting on them; and (3) realizing that others also have thoughts and feelings.

Mentalization also involves perceiving that not only one's own behavior but also the behavior of others can be understood in terms of thoughts and feelings, beliefs and desires—that is, mental states. Understanding the feelings of others helps us to make sense of and to anticipate their actions. Once children recognize that they can have intentions or desires without acting on them, they are faced with the challenge of self-responsibility. In recognizing the "I" self as the master, the agent, the chief executive of all thoughts, feelings, desires and actions, this "I" self becomes accountable for those thoughts, feelings, desires and actions. Self-responsibility involves accountability for one's actions, but also for one's feelings, impulses, motives, and desires. It involves "owning up to one's needs and impulses as one's own" (Loewald, 1979, p. 392). This means acknowledging ownership of one's angry, hateful, envious, jealous, competitive, vengeful, destructive, greedy, and murderous feelings, admitting guilt, and not blaming others for their existence. This is a developmental challenge for any child, and we know there is a lag between the child's recognition of the feelings that follows actions, perceiving fault and admitting guilt (Anna Freud, 1936, p. 119). Yet a mature sense of agency requires this kind of self-responsibility. Self-responsibility also involves mastery. Angry feelings in their many forms are ubiquitous; they come with the human condition.

Related conflicts, whether interpersonal or intrapsychic, at whatever developmental level never become fully "resolved." This is because the emotional challenges that arouse these feelings are also part of the human condition. The developmental challenge influences the creation of a sense of mastery. It is taking ownership of them, and then finding the most adaptive way of gaining control over these feelings, desires, and impulses rather than feelings and desires being in control. Anna Freud (1965) once said that the task for the child in early childhood is to learn to be in control of the drives instead of the drives being in control of the child. In fact, it is the task of every human being regardless of age to learn to be in control of his or her emotions.

A competent sense of self also needs a sense of organization, cohesion and stability over time. Self-regulation requires the capacity for self-reflection, mastery over feelings, desires and impulses, as well as flexible response. Owning and developing mastery over one's feelings, desires, and impulses requires some competence in keeping these feelings, desires and impulses within manageable limits.

By keeping them within manageable limits, the feelings do not disorganize and overwhelm self-regulatory functions. Self-regulation relies on the capacity to utilize the signaling function of affect: First, the child must be able to identify, label and reflect on feelings as they begin to emerge. Second, the child must also have sufficient frustration tolerance to be able to delay automatic reflexive response, and instead, exercise control over emotional response systems. Third, through the process of imitation, introjections and identification with the caregiver, the maturation of affective regulation becomes solidified. The self-regulatory agent would have to attend to all aspects of the current situation, retrieve conscious and unconscious memories of similar past situations. This involves being able to fantasize the possible consequences of one action versus another. The ability to reflect on possible associated affective states, and integrate all of this relevant information in the mind, review and compare a number of possible plans, and decide which actions and emotional procedures would be most effective and adaptive. Finally, the mind would be able to execute an effective decision. This entire process takes place unconsciously and almost instantaneously. But the ability to process affects in this way equips the mind to avoid the disorganization and distress that results from intense and overwhelming emotional arousal.

The self can be experienced as a regulating agent. To develop a capacity to self regulate requires the caregiver to provide structure, consistency and safety, involving consistent rules, regulations and parental expectations. The child has to develop a capacity to tolerate frustration and adhere to the rules of society. Rules at home and school and in society are in conflict with the child's desire. As a result, feelings of intense anger, hate, protest and rage may erupt. Safety and predictability during such times of conflict are essential.

For caregivers, providing structure and consistency can be a challenge if they suffer from fragile psychic structure and consequently more vulnerable to their own affective storms. The caregiver must resist being drawn into the child's normal angry protests to rules and restrictions and should withstand provocation. The caregivers' role is to maintain safety and distinguish between their own emotions and those of the child. This allows them to be empathic to the feelings and needs of the child while providing a regulating balance to intervene before the child becomes overwhelmed. The caregiver must absorb the child's ambivalence and rage, contain and label the feelings, and at the same time remain firm and consistent with the child's demands and expectations.

If caregivers or therapists can "survive" the child's projection (Winnicott, 1969), they can help the child progressively differentiate the inner world of psychic reality and emotional reaction from the outside world of real experience. Symbolic play can be particularly helpful at this time. This genre of play is an important means by which a child repeats and masters traumatic experiences, which was one of Freud's early observations in child development (1920, p. 14). The research of Fonagy and his colleagues (2002, p. 257) indicates that children of three or four generally make little distinction between the inner world of psychic reality and outer world of real experience. Although cognitively they distinguish the two, they live in the inner world of emotions; their perceptions and the meanings they assign to them are not felt to be representations, but rather direct replicas of reality. Consequently it feels true to them.

However young children also use a pretend mode. In their pretend mode, ideas, wishes, and fantasies are representational. The idea and what it symbolizes can be distinguished and manipulated. Symbolizing, labeling and verbalizing thoughts and emotions through pretend play enables the child to elaborate the inner world of wishes, fears, feelings, and fantasies, and gain some control and mastery over their feelings (Katan, 1961). If the therapist can create what Winnicott called a "play space," the therapist can become a part of this process and help the child distinguish his inner world of angry feelings which lead to angry projections and views of mother or care giver as a frightening and punishing figure from the mother of real experience. The child can then use the therapist to reflect on the feelings, find flexible and adaptive ways of expressing and managing rage and other distressing feelings. Thus, finding the adaptive and flexible ways of compromise and conflict resolution helps the child to contain his or her feelings. In doing so, the child learns that intense affects such as anger and rage can be managed and regulated.

Rewards in the form of recognition and praise for their efforts as well as for success are essential to the child's developing capacity to tolerate frustration and capability to adhere to rules and expectations. A satisfaction and pride shared between the mother-child dyad can be fostered by following rules and parental guidance. Such sharing of positive emotions generates a sense of pride. It also fosters the development of moral emotions as the caregiver's rules and moral values gradually become those of the child through the process of "internalization." Not only are these self-regulatory functions supported and enhanced by the structure, consistency and safety provided by the caregiver; but this also helps the child become increasingly aware of the links between intentions, actions, consequences, and emotional states.

Ideally the child gradually begins to associate following the rules with shared pleasure. In addition, there is a realization that bereft and lonely feelings follow bouts of hateful rage or refusal to comply. Once a child recognizes choices between desires and actions, anticipates consequences and responds to anger and anxiety with verbalization instead of action or repression, we as clinicians see important evidence that the child is beginning to use the signal function of affects. Using affects as signals of danger enables the child to become increasingly competent in emotional regulation and a more effective self-agent.

Perry (1997) has found that young children who grow up within an environment of chronic stress, disturbed attachment and lack of the reciprocal verbal dialogues that foster effective skills often develop excessively active and reactive stress response apparatuses. These children are unable to integrate their own mental states and consequently become hypervigilant to the environmental cues, particularly nonverbal ones, and hypersensitive to physiological anxiety. They then develop maladaptive emotional procedures that predispose them to peremptory reflexive responses such as rage, anxiety and fear.

CONCLUSION

The children I presented have a disorganized, impoverished sense of self and inadequate sense of agency. They have not experienced sensitive mirroring, safety or comfort, nor have they experienced intersubjective dialogues with their caregivers. Therefore, the basic tools for thinking, labeling and reflecting on their emotions and intentions are missing. Although they may recognize themselves as the active agents of certain physical actions, they do not appear to understand the concept of choice, that their actions are intentional and deliberate, and that not all impulses and desires need to be acted upon. That is, they do not recognize themselves as intentional mental beings.

Unable to recognize their actions as deliberate results of their intentions and choices, they are unable to reflect on their actions, recognize links between their actions, consequences, and subsequent painful affective states. They are unable to take responsibility for their actions. Instead, their actions are reflexive, and are experienced as reactive impulses to environmental provocations.

These children also have little capacity for delay, self-control and self-regulation. Their inner world is a chaotic one. They lack a capacity to label and think about their emotions and recognize links between their actions, consequences, and feelings. They have little executive control over emotional response systems and lack the higher order of integrative processes that make self-reflection, self-regulation and flexible response possible. Their marked insecurity and narcissistic vulnerability leads them to focus their attention on controlling others. They are not able to regulate their affects, fear and panic. As a result, they end up with disrupted self-regulation.

Psychoanalytic intervention with very young children, due to their innate brain plasticity and the resiliency in their psychological functioning, presents a hopeful prospect for child analysts. The new direction in our work with such children ought to take into consideration two important principles. These important principles in treatment of such cases involve fostering a sense of safety and secure attachment, and a timely response to a child's distress, helping to create an optimal play space. Therefore, it is of outmost importance to set limits and provide a consistently predictable structure for the child. A parent-child dialogue is also necessary for the child to develop a capacity to use affects as signals.

Chapter Twelve

Play and Very Young Children in Object Relations Family Therapy

Jill Savege Scharff

> "The child who has a weak symbolizing function requires therapeutic strategies which help that function to mature, while the child who has a competent symbolizing function requires a strategy using play therapy, the working through of conflicts, and the interpretation of fantasy." —Charles Sarnoff, *Latency*

In family therapy, my task is to provide a helpful environment for the whole family, babies included. A recent study showed that marriage and family therapists are unwilling to include young children in their family therapy sessions, because they have not been trained to understand children (Sori and Sprenkle, 2000). Learning about development and the nature of communication in play, along with experience in individual play therapy or child analysis, are essential preparations for the family therapist. Using play as much as verbal interaction, I aim at providing a context in which every member of the family can express themselves and show the family's usual patterns of relating. These derive from the complex interaction of present relationships in the family, previous experiences with significant others in the family of origin, and experiences with the present family during earlier periods of development.

OBJECT RELATIONS THEORY AND FAMILY THERAPY

Object relations theory derives from study of the therapeutic relationship. It focuses on the nature of relationships between the self and others and between parts of the self and its objects in the internal world. Because of this focus, I find it is the analytic theory most easily applicable to therapeutic work with groups and families (Scharff and Scharff, 1987). The family is a small group with the job of supporting its members through the life cycle. As family therapists we step in when one of its members needs more than the family group can offer. At this point, the family is blocked in doing its work and our job is to help the family understand why. What are the defensive purposes served by their repeating patterns of interaction and inaction? What are the un-nameable anxieties that are being avoided? As we help the family to explore its defensive structures, basic assumptions, and underlying anxieties, we build skills for dealing with the current problem and for future developmental challenges.

OBJECT RELATIONS FAMILY THERAPY

Object relations family therapy uses nondirective analytic techniques invented by Freud (1912). Listening for the unconscious theme in word, silence and gesture is augmented by the value of watching and responding to the play. Following the affect is easy when play gives us a direct route to the child's feelings expressed in relation to the toys. Working with dreams and fantasies takes on a graphic dimension when we see them put into the form of the family doing something fun together in a painting. Repeating defensive patterns are detected in the repetition of play sequences and the family's typical reactions to the play. Throughout the session, we tune into the unconscious communication in the play and notice how it makes us feel. This helps us to detect how the parents feel about their children and how the whole family as a group feels about us, the therapist—the outsider to their family process. Playing with the children, or sitting quietly but engaging with the play in a playful attitude, we resonate with the unconscious themes. Play helps us reach deep inside our own experience, to make a connection with the family's pain, and to find a way to speak to them about it, either directly in words, or through our response to the play.

PLAY IN FAMILY THERAPY WITH VERY YOUNG CHILDREN

Freud recommended that the analyst's stance maintains a neutral position of equal distance from superego, ego and id. Similarly, the family therapist maintains a stance that gives equal weight to the contributions of various generations of the family. That means that we must be able to talk and play at the same time and to work with groups and not just individuals. We must also be willing to tolerate noise, mess and confusion.

Clinical Vignette

A family asked for help with their seven-year-old boy's tantrums. This boy and his five-year-old brother played well with rockets while their parents talked. The next session, they brought the baby. The five-year-old played as before, but the seven-year-old brought the skunk puppet and pretended that it was farting, pooping and spraying me. I linked this to angry feelings about Mommy having the baby on her lap and there being no room there for him. He responded by tying me to my chair with wool thread, taping my mouth shut with Scotch-tape, blocking my ears with tissue taped to my face, and he wound pipe-cleaners round my fingers. I pretended that Stinky the Skunk said to me that the boy had taped me up because he didn't want me to be able to see or hear what was happening in the family and certainly not to speak about it because it made him feel bad. He then spun me in my swivel chair. I again used Stinky to say how much he wanted to separate me from the family so I couldn't see or say anything about how people felt about the baby on Mom's lap. The baby got off Mom's lap. The father observed my situation with amusement and made the perfect comment to describe the role of the family therapist. He said, "I've just learned that to be a family therapist you have to be able to hit a moving target while tied down and spinning."

WHOLE FAMILY UNDERSTANDING

Why have the young children there? Unless you do, you cannot get whole family understanding (Zilbach, 1986). Having the children present gives a vivid picture of problems that have less impact when only spoken about. The youngest children make deeper problems more visible and therefore intervention can happen earlier.

Clinical Vignette

A mother complained that nine-year-old Eduardo was violent at home, tormenting his brother Guido and even punching his mother. In an individual session Eduardo was a delight to talk to about how he didn't mind his sister, Valentina, but that he couldn't stand Guido always interrupting him when he was trying to do his homework. He refused to play with me because he no longer liked Legos, and he didn't want to draw, because he only played games with balls now that he was nine. At school and at home he only played football, baseball, and street hockey. I offered to play indoor catch with the soft Nerf ball but he said that wouldn't be fun.

Later in a family meeting with the parents, Eduardo, Guido, and two-year-old Valentina, I noted how the family sat in total silence, their attention riveted adoringly on Valentina as she trotted around the room with no inhibition and engaged me with paper and crayons. Eventually, the boys began to color. Guido simply tested all the colors and made a color chart, while Eduardo drew a rattlesnake in the desert. No longer the focus of attention, Valentina got fussy and Mother offered her some crackers. Now the boys talked about fighting, the main problem. Guido said that Eduardo starts the punching to get Guido to leave him alone, but Eduardo said that Guido really starts the fights by bugging Eduardo to play with him. Eduardo's inability to enjoy play at his brother's level was the cause of the fights. Eduardo said that he only liked sports and he couldn't play with Guido because Guido couldn't throw straight or far enough. Guido tried to appeal to Eduardo by telling him that he had played football with older kids. Guido said, "I was playing with the 5th graders and the quarterback fumbled the ball, but I was right there and I caught it. So then I was playing quarterback and they all said it was a great play." Eduardo squashed him by explaining, "Yes, you could recover the fumble but, no, you couldn't suddenly become the quarterback. You're still playing defense. And no, you didn't get a touchdown, no, you didn't score, so it wasn't a great play at all."

I said, "Eduardo knows so much more about football than I do that if I try to argue the point, I'll end up getting defeated like Guido. What I do know is that Guido is trying hard to join Eduardo and appeal to his interests, but Eduardo doesn't want to be drawn into being friends with him because he alone wants to be the oldest and the best." "Yes," Eduardo agreed. "I'm in 4th grade now and I just don't care about toys any more."

By having the whole family present I could see how the mother focused attention on the baby and got the whole family to join her in doing that. This clued me in to how excluded her first-born, Eduardo, could have felt at the time of Guido's birth. Eduardo's need to distance himself from longing to be his Mom's baby meant that he had rejected his brother, put him down, and gave up the toys of childhood that might have let them bond together.

This play example is quite easy to understand. That is not always the case.

Clinical Vignette

A student was reporting a family session to me. I noticed that she was telling me information that the parents had told her, and was not giving me a sense of the session. I asked her to describe the children's play. She said that she hadn't seen any "good play" to report. I told her that there is no such thing as "good play." There is only play that we can understand and play whose message we don't yet receive. The important thing is to report what happened whether you understand it or not. Simply describing the play to yourself as it is happening and monitoring how it makes you feel can make the meaning clear. I then found out that she had not provided any toys.

We want to create an environment in which children will play so that they can feel comfortable and communicate their hopes, conflicts and fears. This does not require masses of toys, but some toys and art media are necessary to stimulate the play activity and to give the message that play is welcomed.

HOW PLAY WORKS

Children express their ideas and feelings both directly and symbolically in play. The inhibited child who is fearful of the family's disapproval sits quietly on the chair and may be too afraid to play at all. The aggressive child may attack the paper with such gusto that he breaks the pencil. The anxious child may flit around the room unable to settle to one play area. The attitude toward the toys and the art media offered to the family is as important as the message conveyed thematically. For instance, a child may fill the page with colorful hearts and rainbows. The hearts and rainbows may represent parents and siblings and the way that they are arranged in size and in order may tell a lot about the family dynamics. Equally important may be the child's wish to give an impression of happiness and normality, and the physical pleasure of painting with color rather than drawing with pencil. In another family, one brother may make a block building that expresses how concerned he is with big blocks and little blocks and which of the children has the most attention from the parents, whereas another brother may simply want to knock down the building. This could be simply about the sibling relationship or it might also reflect the mother's wish to discuss her feelings and the father's wish to get rid of tension. Sometimes the play follows the words and the family therapist realizes that the children and the adults share an understanding of the family problem. Sometimes it seems to be on a totally different track, leading the therapist to ask about matters that had been kept out of the discussion but which the child's play reveals as important.

Children need to play in the office as they do at home and at school. This gives them an environment that is child-centered; a familiar place where they can behave as usual, even while doing the difficult task of dealing with conflict and the mystery of family life. Very young children play with much movement and bodily contact. They use their bodies to relate to the toys, and in so doing they find physical release for pent-up energy and anxiety. Children of school age play in a less physical way than younger children. They conceptualize and execute a plan. Perhaps they write diaries, make paintings individually or in series, establish families of animals or dolls, create armies, re-create lesson plans in schoolroom scenes. Adolescents often pretend that they don't play, but they will fiddle with their hair, pull on their clothing, and try out different positions on the floor, the couch and so on. Babies play too.

They play at holding on and dropping their toys, waiting for a parent to fetch the lost object. They play hide and seek. They play with their mother's bodies.

The therapist must tune in to the type of play that the particular family brings to the session, sometimes commenting on it, and sometimes being content to let it unfold. Using tact and a good sense of timing, the therapist may enter into the play in order to make a point conveyed by one of the characters in the play or may use the play to illustrate what the family has been talking about. The play may then become an arena in which the family can find solutions to their problems.

PLAY IN THERAPY WITH A LATENCY CHILD AND A BABY

Ana and her husband Pedro complained about their six-year-old Maria's temper, her stubborn behavior and her failure to build a good relationship with Pedro, her stepfather, even though she was close to his seven-year-old daughter Arion, who didn't live with them. Ana and Pedro have a six-month-old, Pedro Junior, a large, blond, beautiful baby who is able to sit upright but who is not yet crawling. Propping Pedro up by the arms, Maria walked him into the session as if he were a one-year-old, teasing him about deciding where to sit, and telling him to sit forward on the couch. I said that she wanted him to grow up quickly, walk and play games with her. Mother explained that Maria had had a horrible tantrum on Saturday night. But, as soon as Pedro had said it was awful, Mother pointed out that Maria had gained control of it. During this disagreement between Mother and Pedro as to how awful the tantrum was, Maria pretended to be asleep.

I said, "If I were Maria, I'd be glad that Mom noticed I did better, but I wouldn't be able to see why Pedro and Mom saw it so differently. Maybe that's why Maria is closing her eyes." Mother said that she and Pedro often disagree and see behavior differently, depending on whether it is her daughter or his daughter whose behavior is at issue. Maria suddenly woke up and asked for lunch. It felt like a startling change of subject. Suddenly I got the idea that her request might be motivated by sensing that the baby was about to be fed. I asked if this was so, and the mother said yes, she was just getting ready to breastfeed Pedro Junior. Maria had a little bit of a tantrum, grabbed her mother's leg and began to mouth it.

I said, "Maria is showing us one of the things that leads her to feel like having a tantrum—that is when the baby is going to be breastfed and lie close to Mom. Then Maria feels hungry and feels like grabbing and biting on Mom, too. What was happening on Saturday night before Maria had her tantrum?" Mother remembered that the baby was being fed then, too. She explained, "Pedro Junior wakes up at 4 o'clock in the afternoon. He feeds a lot off and on, and especially from 8:30 to 9:30 pm. Maria goes to bed at 7:30 pm, so she gets jealous that he gets to stay up with us after she has gone to bed, when he is younger than she is." As Mom explained this and the baby nursed, Maria lay on Mom's foot. Then Mom took him off the breast momentarily and Maria put him back on. She then pulled off Mom's dangling earring. Mom checked her for interrupting when she was trying to talk to me.

I said, "No, Maria's playing is her way of talking to us. She's putting the baby on the breast and she's taking Mom's earring off. The earring comes off, and Maria can play with that, but the breast stays where it is. It doesn't come off and she can't take control of it, because it is only there for the baby." Maria then switched her attention to the other earring. This happened just before Mom was ready to put the baby on the other side. Suddenly Mom was soaked by Pedro Junior. The feeding had to be interrupted while the baby was changed. During this changing, Maria played with both of her mother's earrings. I asked her to come over and talk to me about them. She showed them to me, dangled them to make them move, and said, "There are two earrings, and each of them is a circle with another circle." I now saw the earrings clearly. Each one was a big hoop with a small circle inside it. The two of them looked like a pair of mobile breasts each with a nipple in the middle. She turned to place the earrings back on Mom's ears at the same moment that the baby went back on the breast. I was struck by how Mom was surrounded by children while Pedro, the father, was sitting by himself. I asked how he felt. He said, "Fine, not jealous. I'm just waiting until we can interact again." I said, "Pedro, you're a grownup and it's okay for you to wait. But for Maria, waiting is more difficult and that's what leads to tantrums."

In this example, the presence of the whole family provided a vivid illustration of the family dynamic around the new baby and its connection to the presenting symptom of the index patient.

WORKING WITH A LATENCY CHILD AND A PUBERTAL CHILD

Mrs. Silver is a widow, an ambitious professional and a devoted single mother of Ruth, her twelve-year-old girl, and Liz, her nine-year-old. Liz and Mother are often nasty to each other, because Liz is irritating, refuses to help, clings to her mother, and has trouble making friends. They asked for an early morning appointment but they were often late and one week they missed the session altogether. This week they came in sleepily as usual, but the girls got to work at the desk. They were angry that their mother was staying too late at work, but she explained that she had to get her work done so that she could get away to take them to a Bar Mitzvah in the South where she was from. Liz was upset because she felt excluded by the other cousins at the Bar Mitzvah anyway. Mrs. Silver talked about being excluded for being so aggressive and successful, which was not what had been expected of her as a Southern woman.

As she talked, the girls drew at the desk. Liz produced a painting of a witch with long, red, raggedy fingernails. Ruth noticed that Liz had mistakenly spelled it w-h-i-c-h. Thinking of her outspoken mother, and looking down at my own chipped red nail polish, I said, "W-h-i-c-h is the real title. Which witch is it?" In her Southern phrasing, pausing after "what," Mrs. Silver asked, "What—do you mean Dr. Scharff?" I said, "Yes, I do mean Dr. Scharff. My nails are like the witch's. I wonder if there are witchy things about me that are bothering you, Liz." Ruth said, "I made the red for the nails, so that can't be true." I connected the red nails to drops of blood and I said, "I remember Ruth had been angry at me for mentioning the fact of her getting her first period last week when she wanted it to be kept a secret from her sister who might blab. You thought that was mean of me, and perhaps you aren't the only one."

Mrs. Silver took the opening to confront me quite aggressively. She said at length how mean I was for charging them for that missed session some weeks earlier. When I said I knew that was hard for her especially as the only breadwinner, she smiled and said, "I'm glad I told you. I wasn't going to say anything, but Liz's drawing helped me to get to it." Liz beamed at her helpfulness being appreciated.

By recognizing and naming the witch transference I detoxified it so that Mrs. Silver could express her own witchiness toward me while confronting my witchiness, and this reduced the witchiness between mother and Liz. It was the girls' play that made this possible.

TESTING THE RESPONSE TO INTERPRETATION IN A FAMILY WITH ADOLESCENTS

In both family meetings sixteen-year-old Ashley sat in a chair in the corner, while the parents sat with thirteen-year-old Deirdre between them on the couch, Mother and Father alternately cuddling with her, although she seemed too old for that. I said that from their angry exchanges I had learned that the parents and children were disappointed in each other and had spoken as if there were nothing of the loving or positive sort going on. From Mother's and Father's cuddling with Deirdre, I could see that each parent was demonstrating a need for affection and closeness between them, while Deirdre was representing for herself and Ashley a wish to fill the emptiness. The parents agreed, and said that they had used Ashley that way, too. They were already disappointed in each other before she was conceived, and when she was born they turned to her with wonder and delight. I said that Ashley became a perfect, doted-on child who fulfilled their need for an ideal object until adolescence. Incidentally, in subsequent sessions, Deirdre took her own chair.

To find her own identity and to separate from her parents, Ashley had to rebel against this projection into her. When she did so, it was with the vehemence of the return of the more repressed projection she had also received, that of the disappointing, rejecting object that has been destroyed or made "shitty" by greed and rage. Following my interpretation, Ashley reached quietly for the paper and markers which she had been talked out of using earlier in the session when her parents made fun of drawing pictures. She drew a picture of an attractive young girl's face, which I took to be the need-exciting object on which my comments had focused. No sooner had I thought this than she "spoiled" the beauty of the drawing by writing "Aargh" coming from the mouth. In this way, I thought she had demonstrated and confirmed what I had just said to the family, that she had been a "beautiful" tantalizing object for her parents who had been spoiled by growth and the family situation. The interpretation in the session focused on the way that the rejecting and angry elements operated to secondarily repress unrequited mutual longing in this couple, pointing out that the reason the children were used was the intolerable pain coming from a sense of failed love in their relationship. The couple's capacity to accept this statement with little defensiveness, and to make use of it to spur further understanding, provided positive evidence of their ability to work therapeutically. As they did this, Ashley provided evidence not only of her unconscious agreement with my interpretation, but of the family's capacity to work productively and even creatively in the family therapy situation, when she drew a picture illustrating, and "fleshing out," what I had been saying.

In a couple's session that followed, I referred back to the family meeting and asked the couple about the emptiness in their relationship. They said that they had no sexual life recently, and very little since Ashley's birth. Mrs. Brown felt too angry to want it, and often caused a fight before bedtime. She was angry that this was important to Mr. Brown when other things like being more ambitious about earning money to provide for them were not. Mr. Brown was unhappy and felt frustrated, but he did not pursue his sexual aim assertively. The family came for treatment when Ashley, at sixteen, was no longer willing or able to substitute as their idealized exciting object, but instead was becoming tentatively interested in her own adolescent sexuality. This is often a point of stress for an empty couple's relationship, because it brings back longing and hope from earlier years and sometimes an unbearably envious response.

The Browns accepted a recommendation for family therapy in which the couple would meet once a week and the family once a week. Ashley, who had been the index patient, refused individual assessment or therapy because she felt that her parents' relationship needed so much work. Although she was resisting the emergence of her unconscious, she was nevertheless handing back to the parents their projection of the good-object-gone-bad.

CONCLUDING REMARKS

Children who may not do well in individual therapy can do well and learn about themselves in the family setting. If their attachments are insecure, proximity to family members may be helpful. Some children who deny that they have any difficulty can be confronted in the family and at the same time have the therapist's support. Children who cannot conceptualize their individual difficulties and have no insight into themselves can see the problem as a group problem and work on it in the group. Even so, therapy is an anxiety-provoking undertaking, and play helps them to release their tension in bodily displays of energy and to cope with anxiety by doing what is familiar. Play makes it fun, and that encourages the family to stay with the therapy task. Fun moves the learning forward.

Chapter Thirteen

Playfulness in the Adult Analytic Relationship

Melvin Bornstein

> "Be not afear'd; the isle is full of noises, Sounds and sweet airs, That give delight and hurt not." —Shakespeare, *The Tempest* (III.ii.144–52)

Playfulness is a state of mind of the patient and analyst immersed in analytic work. It is an adjunct in the development of the intimacy that is necessary for a successful analysis. The analyst and patient work toward improving the patient's ability to tell the parts of her story that she has been unable to tell because they have been fragmented and expressed in a repetition not included in her narrative or Self. Playfulness belongs in a space in which the patient and analyst experience themselves as whole people, Selves with authenticity, being alive, vital, communicating, and striving toward intimacy.

The task for the analyst is to promote inclusion of the patient's fragmented parts. The fragmented parts that are repeated are filled with trauma, suffering, humiliation and hopelessness of never being able to include them into her narrative and Self. Yet the repetition is only part of the patient's experience. The patient experiences herself also as a whole person, a human being who is an agency living in the present moment. She runs her life, but she is plagued by the repetition that feels real and interferes with her ability to function optimally with joy and creativity. The analyst promotes the patient's courage to include the repeated fragmented parts that seem so powerful and frightening, demonstrating that they can be transformed into greater awareness that one is more than the repetition with its illusive defeatism. The patient is encouraged to join in this quest for greater freedom and wholeness. So, the analyst must set a tone that is directed toward the space within the patient of being a whole person who is an agency, communicating to her analyst, principally through language, invested in doing something more with the fragmented repetitive parts that are the source of her suffering. It is in this space of wholeness where the patient knows her self better than the analyst. She has some awareness of whether the analyst understands and is empathic. It is in this space of wholeness where she is searching for indication of hope that the analytic relationship can help her be more inclusive of her fragmented experiences. Playfulness belongs in this space underscoring the humanness of the analytic relationship.

In placing playfulness in a psychoanalytic model, I am considering the whole of the patient and analyst striving to attain the goal of the analysis. The whole patient and analyst are people who strive to deal with their repetitive fragmented emotional parts inclusively which results in a greater solidity of Self, openness and intimacy that leads to the transformation of suffering into joy and creative living. Without a picture of the wholeness of the patient and analyst, I would be left with a picture of only the parts of the patient. I could not conceptualize how the whole becomes more than the individual parts.

Unfortunately most analytic literature and public discussions address only the parts and not the whole. The psychoanalytic lexicon is filled with theories and concepts about the parts of the person. We understand and talk about conflict, compromise formation, transference, unconscious fantasies, resistances, object and personal relations, but not the person who has to deal with these parts and strives to achieve transformation of their suffering by being intimate with her analyst.

Playfulness assists in conveying humanness and openness in the midst of the terrors, dangers and hopelessness that are actually reminiscences but feel so real (Freud, 1895) or the ghosts that are laid to rest by tasting the blood of the transference (Loewald, 1960). This can only occur if the analyst is able to show that she is aware of the terrors and ghosts in the patient that feel so real and that transformation will occur in the presence of warmth and love directed at the patient as a whole person.

The dilemma that has pervaded psychoanalytic thinking since Freud's initial discoveries is that although psychoanalytic models rests upon understanding what goes on in people, i.e., a whole living subjective human being, psychoanalytic models correspond more to the canons of empirical science which are devoted to the examination of the parts over the whole. The dilemma comes down to solving the riddle of how we can consider the objective with the subjective in the same situation, in other words, as seen psychoanalytically a patient is a subjective whole with objective parts. Once the parts contribute to the whole, the cloak of a Self embraces the objective parts. This dilemma has been extensively described (Berger, 1985). He describes how psycho-analytic conceptualizations are derived from a Cartesian approach in contrast to the wholeness of a subjective self. Recently there has been a trend in the philosophy of science that the traditional means to derive empirical evidence through the examination of the parts over the whole does not direct our understanding to facts. Rather, beginning with a whole that is continually evolving by the inclusion of more and more parts brings us closer to scientific facts. Similarly, in analysis we are closer to analytic facts by including an evolving Self that is inclusive of objective parts (Bohm, 1980).

The psychoanalytic literature on play and playfulness reflects a focus on the parts within an analytic process, but rarely gives attention to how play or playfulness contributes to the evolving whole person of the analyst and patient as they work toward including their fragmented parts. Freud (1914) described the work of an analysis as directed to the patient's repetition and turning it into a motive for remembering in the handling of the transference. He states, "We render the compulsion harmless, and indeed useful, by giving it the right to assert itself in a definite field. We admit it into the transference as a playground in which it is allowed to expand in almost complete freedom and in which it is expected to display to us everything in the way of pathogenic instincts that is hidden in the patient's mind" (p. 154)

Winnicott (1971) described play in psychoanalysis and in development occurring in a transitional space where reality and fantasy fuse. He states that it is in this transitional space that individuals are able to gain an appreciation of reality through the creativity of playing. In fact he believed that this was the only place that one acquires clarity in differentiating reality from fantasy.

Play has been described as a necessary regression in dealing with conflict (Huizinga, 1944; London, 1981). Play supplies the primary data for nonverbal communication (McLauglin, 1987). Enactments are a modification of an early action in the form of play (Loewald, 1975). Play is integral to role responsiveness (Sandler and Sandler, 1978). Play contributes to the working through of conflicts that are engaged in an analysis (Mahon, 2004). Playfulness in analysis is described as extremely useful when dealing with regressed and resistant patients by creating an atmosphere of hope (Ehrenberg, 1990; Coen, 2005).

The references that I have cited on play and playfulness have illuminated and extended the psychoanalytic understanding and technique, but as I have stated, they do not address play and playfulness in the analyst and patient as whole people, as agencies invested in a shared task of bringing coherence and inclusion to their communications with each other. I will set the stage for a discussion of playfulness by describing myself in the whole person space.

I feel vital, alive with appreciable self-esteem and self-regard. I am aware that I am an agency with an appreciation of my identity and my history. I am especially aware of the roles of my patient and myself as her analyst. As her analyst I have a specific agenda based upon my understanding of how I can help her in our analytic relationship. I am helping her transform her fragmented repetitive experiences into her narrative and identity so that she can attain a greater freedom to use her energy for joy and creativity. With my help, she needs to turn to the frightening repetitive experiences, and as a whole person reveal those to me which she associates with terrifying humiliation. In this repetition, she believes she is incapable of bringing coherence and inclusiveness to her repetitive experiences. In the analytic relationship the belief of failure and hopelessness is itself a repetition

My role as her analyst is to support the use of her courage and honesty to do today, with me, what she couldn't do at an earlier time when she was immature and living in a less-than-adequate environment. I am challenged to support her powerful desire to maintain her self-esteem and self-regard. To perform my role as her analyst, I must focus on my past inability to find sufficient strength and courage to bring coherence and inclusiveness to the sources of my pain and convey to her that I understand her early defeated experience, but it is not the same today for her and for me. My role as an analyst is immersed with values of honesty and courage about being open and able to live with myself without fragmentation. My experiences are no longer too much to live with as in the past. These sentiments were voiced by Freud (1923) many years ago in the *Ego and the Id* as he outlined his new structural theory. In it he described that the ego was made up of the id. The ego gets its power from the id and it has the capability to organize mental entities, use language, relate and adapt. The ego has more power and sophistication than the id could ever imagine. The ego is where the effective power resides in human life

Playfulness within the whole person space conveys hope. Playfulness communicates a message between analyst and patient. Although we are dealing with overwhelming experiences that appear to reflect the true state of affairs where one could only disengage from them, we are not in that situation as we are working together. The analyst conveys to the patient that we can bring coherence and inclusion and even a state of playfulness to experiences that, at one time, were hopeless. We can actually have a good time as we work together. This attitude in the analysis is in contrast to a long-standing view within the history of classical analysis where analysis is so painful and so difficult that only a small number of people can endure successfully.

I will illustrate my discussion with clinical examples.

CLINICAL VIGNETTE

A successful middle-aged man began analysis because of a lack of well-being and joy, and problems with an adult child who was chronically depressed and unproductive. His mother, a Holocaust survivor, traumatized him by being physically abusive during his early childhood. He grew up feeling numb to her with several somatic complaints, yet professionally and in most of his relationships, he has been reasonably successful. With me, he hoped to change the emptiness and lack of joy that diminishes his living. He had been in several psychotherapies in the past. With the people in whom he is most emotionally invested he feels numb and distant.

For months prior to the sessions that I will describe, we had focused on material related to how he protected himself against feeling alive and open with his mother after she was physically abusive. He felt neither pain nor humiliation nor need for her. Denying his value and turning away from his passion toward others was his solution expressed in his repetition. He could not include his traumatic experiences in his narrative because he had no one who was interested or capable of helping him. These ideas, in a variety of forms, were conveyed as he spoke about his unhappiness, lack of feelings, difficulties with his wife, son, and with me.

He began the session by stating that he could not sleep the previous night. He had been in a state of diffuse anxiety. He said that was new; he usually didn't experience so much anxiety. I smiled warmly and said, "Good," which reflected my enthusiasm, realizing that he was communicating to me that he had made some progress in the analysis. He smiled and said that he thought I would say that. I said, "You are right. The change from last week when you were not anxious, but just numb without interest in your wife may be the result of the weakening of your being so protective of your feelings and vitality, so that is great!" I then asked, "What comes to mind?"

After a lengthy silence he said playfully that he didn't have the slightest idea. He continued with his silence, but then said that he had a dream. He didn't know much about it, but he had had similar dreams recently. "There are things in this room that I am trying to organize, but it is impossible. I get more and more frustrated in the dream then I wake up." He said that it didn't mean anything to him. I took a deep breath. He laughingly asked, "What?" I responded with another "What?" After a lengthy silence, I said, "This last week, you spoke about your mother and your rage. You spoke about her enormous rage from her deprivation which was directed at you. You had no one who understood what you were going through. Maybe what troubles you is that you are beginning to make order out of your experiences, which allows you to feel and know more. At that time, to feel and know more was too much to handle without support. It became protective to feel confused and numb. Maybe that is expressed in the dream. You are beginning to feel and understand more, but it reminds you that to feel and understand was too much to endure, so you dream that you can't get it together."

With more animation than usual, he said, "That sounds reasonable, but it doesn't mean much to me." He then went on to talk about the warmth in his son's responses to him recently, which was unusual. I said, "You are saying that something is different. I think that you are not only talking about your son, you are talking about yourself." He responded laughingly by asking, "What do you mean?" I said, "That's just what I mean." He responded with "Well, it doesn't mean anything to me. I don't have those feelings."

I said, "After your mother beat you, you were filled with feelings of hurt, anger and humiliation. You felt that living with those feelings was more than you could handle. Insisting that it didn't mean anything to you and everything was in disorder enabled you to hide your vitality and feelings, like in the dream." He said, "My neck is beginning to hurt again." After he elaborated on his physical discomfort, I said, "You are saying to me that since you were hiding your feelings and experiences they went into your neck, which you are now living out with me."

He returned the next session and told me for the first time that throughout his adolescence, when he was eating with his parents, he would throw up. He would have to sit in another room. I said that at that time, he could not deal with the feelings and he had no one to help him. During this sequence, I understood that he was expressing derivatives of his early trauma with his mother that included overwhelming desire, rage, hurt, pain, humiliation, and more importantly, hopelessness that he could never find a way to be inclusive and coherent about the trauma. The derivatives of his early trauma with his mother were repetitions from the depth of his inner life that had influenced his character problems. My understanding was based on his communications since he began analysis three years earlier. He was reluctant to get involved in the treatment. He had temporarily reduced the frequency of his sessions. He stated that he hated his mother, but conveyed his frustrated longings for her. Although he manifestly denied all transference interpretation, there had been progressive movement in the analysis especially related to transference interpretations.

As he expressed his repetitive conviction that he did not have any capacity to deal with the trauma except by withdrawal with a variety of defenses, he lost sight of who we were in the analytic situation and what we are doing, i.e., helping him discover himself. Playfulness was an essential helpful technique. For me, as I listened to him I was aware of waves of anxiety, momentary emotional paralysis and vague areas within my mind of terror and trauma belonging to my narrative. Bringing coherence to my patient's communication helped him transform his experience into his personal narrative.

CLINICAL VIGNETTE

The patient, a middle-aged man, is in his third year of analysis. He came to me for help because he was considering marrying for the third time, and for the first time in his life he was intent on not repeating his past failures should he marry. He felt that he loved the woman he wanted to marry. She was deeply concerned about his reliability and ability to maintain a marital relationship. During the three years of analysis he married and was immersed in the analytic work of bringing more coherence and inclusion to his narrative and personality.

The analysis has been strongly characterized by playfulness. We laugh, joke and tease. He asks me why I start so early in the morning. I reply because I am eager to see him. He said his wife asked him to stay with her at a party where she knew no one. So, he went into the kitchen to get a piece of pizza, leaving her alone. My reply was "Oy!" He said, "I get a low grade on that." I said, "Oh—about a D minus. Let's try to understand what happened that you ignored your wife." He described wanting to ignore a son who was continually slighting and ignoring him; he hadn't even invited his father to his graduation. He decided to go and get things worked out. I said, "You'd get an A minus for that!"

Integral to the playfulness was an experience that we were friends who cared about each other. This was part of the analytic relationship and a recognition that we could move into the whole person space. It followed then, when he was having difficulty with his foot, I asked about his foot at the beginning of a session, which in the past, was technically "a forbidden technique." When my daughter was in a very serious auto accident that necessitated my cancelling several sessions, I told him about her and briefly discussed the details. I could not use playfulness without conveying caring and friendship that involved us as whole people. The atmosphere in the sessions reflects two playful friends with a common task. The analytic work of transformations took place in this setting.

In the third year of analysis, he missed a regular scheduled appointment without notifying me. He began the next session by reference to our talking about getting better and maybe finishing treatment soon. I said, "We can talk about it, but what does this have to do with your missing last hour?" He said that he completely forgot about it.

"Never did I think of it and before I left, I said I would see you tomorrow." Exaggerating the drama, I said, "I was sitting waiting for you. I was all alone. I had no one to talk to and it was already turning dark outside." I continued by saying, "I recall that last hour you were talking about an emotional moving experience. In a speech, your employee remarked how you were like the father he never had. You told me that you cried being so moved by his remarks. You also told me that this display of emotions was extremely rare." I said, "Maybe those feelings were also what you are experiencing about me and you felt that it was not possible to express them toward me, so you forgot about the appointment." Later in the session, he elaborated on the theme of his father by describing his disappointment and loneliness about not having a father who could help him grow up instead he continually observed his father being dominated by his mother. In the previous three years, he expressed in derivative form early trauma from a distant mother who was intolerant of the depth of his feelings. Over many sessions we worked with this theme. The overwhelming nature was expressed in his acting out with me, which resembled his provocative rejecting behavior with his wife. He gradually was able to bring greater coherence and inclusion into these experiences. Overall, he had gained added strength to handle his inner life.

New material related to his longing for his father began to directly appear with considerable affect which had been intolerable in the past. The work, together with our banter and playfulness helped us keep focus on our identities and purpose together in contrast to the repetitive experiences that were inundated with suffering and hopelessness.

CLINICAL VIGNETTE

After two years of analysis, a business man with a perversion of seeing transvestite prostitutes had opened up about some of the dynamics of his perversion and depression. Although there was a strong suggestion of sexual abuse in the family, the details of which were not clear, a fantasy was expressed repeatedly where he had the power of ruining his father. He has a history of being self-defeating. As he worked on more details of his early history with his parents when they promoted his defensive, self-defeating role in the family, he improved in his general functioning. He decided to reduce his weekly sessions to once a week. We understood that this was playing out a history of withdrawing from achievements. Pursuing prostitutes contained a component of this dynamic.

After several weeks on his abbreviated schedule, he called to cancel his next session. When he returned the following week, he said that he hadn't come the previous week because he wanted to relax and lay around all morning. I said that was like assuming the role he had had in his family as a child, the unreliable black sheep. "You felt you could not talk to me about what it meant to be a black sheep in the family so you avoided coming here. You were frightened that you would end up revealing too much of your hurt, anger, humiliation, and desire to damage yourself which you felt was impossible for you to endure and for me to help you."

He said, "You are right," and elaborated by describing how he has also left things undone especially when he begins to feel that he gets it. Playfully I asked, "So why the hell aren't you coming four times a week?" He said that he was afraid. He went on, remembering his father telling him that he brags too much. Several weeks later he returned to a four session a week schedule.

CLINICAL VIGNETTE

A forty-five-year-old man began psychoanalysis with me because of depression, low self-esteem, and difficulty in establishing a long term relationship with a woman. His depression was revealed to be related to a dominating mother who was not responsive to the patient's considerable intelligence and creativity. His father was emotionally abusive. During childhood he was withdrawn, depressed, and rebellious which peaked during his adolescence and young adulthood.

After entering psychotherapy he settled down, became CEO of a professional community-directed business. As the analysis began to deepen he developed ALS (Lou Gehrig's Disease). Within a year he was confined to a wheelchair. He had lost the use of his vocal muscles that eventually resulted in a complete loss of his voice. He could only communicate with an audio keyboard. During the next four years, his body musculature deteriorated. He lost control of his bowels and urine and could only take food by tubes inserted in his stomach. He could not operate an audio keyboard because his fingers could not bend. He had to learn to communicate with a visual GPS computer. By looking at a screen keyboard and blinking his eyes, the position of his eyes simulated pressing keys on a key board. Words would be formed and translated into an audio rendition.

In spite of the enormous physical hardship, since he developed ALS, he has continued to operate his business. He married and had a natural child. I continued to conduct the analysis with modification because of his physical limitations. I eventually began traveling to his home because of his difficulty in getting to my office. Regardless of his devastating physical deterioration, he progressed in his analysis. Many aspects of his infantile depression were brought into the present moment in a setting that included my emotional availability and my interpretations. We dealt with his childhood injuries, desires, humiliation and fear of feeling intimate. In the foreground was the ever-present progression of his illness and the enormous physical and emotional demands that were necessary for him to remain alive and functioning. To my surprise, the analysis was the dominant aspect of our relationship. His physical condition was not where our attention gravitated. Our relationship was devoted to helping him be inclusive, feel whole, vital alive and open, which enabled him to achieve a degree of pleasure and fulfillment in his living. The openness and ability to express and communicate his experience, consciously and unconsciously, contributed to his survival and successful adaptation. Although the illness progressed rapidly at first, progression over the last four years has been exceedingly slow.

We understood that without the state of mind of feeling open, whole, alive and vital, he was not going to survive for long and the analysis enabled him to overcome the obstacles that interfered with achieving that state of mind. In the analytic setting it was not difficult to trace his childhood depression and hopelessness in the context of his early life and reality where he felt that it was impossible to deal with the components of his depression, i.e., his rage, vulnerability, frustration and narcissistic injuries essentially in relationship to his intrusive and emotionally unavailable mother.

The enormous difficulties that he had to contend with because of the ALS were always very apparent. He was capable of dealing with the multiple problems related to the progressive ALS. They included his intense affects of rage, vulnerability, humiliation and fear. His strength in adaptation was intact. Episodes of emotional upset were followed by the use of his intelligence, adaptive emotional capacities and the fortunate resources of wife and family and a large nursing staff to take care of him. The problem that the patient and I were invested in reducing in the analysis was the repetition of his early traumas that interfered with his adaptive capabilities. Playfulness was a vital component of the therapy. It underlined for each of us the reality of the intimacy and joy of our work together which transformed his fragmented parts into a narrative with increase in energy and a more solid sense of self which then was used to deal with the horrible illness.

I will discuss sessions during the fifth year of his analysis. For several years as I was observing the deterioration of his body, whenever I would see him at the beginning of a session, I felt joy, eagerness and enthusiasm. The reactions were based upon the intimacy and the achievement that were developing as a result of the treatment. I could see the development of hope and optimism as he expressed the sources of his depression and the hopelessness that were connected to his present situation. As he expressed the fragmented parts of his story and found that I listened and interpreted their meaning, he had a new experience: he was with someone who he could reach out to and be intimate with, in contrast to the context of his past environment within the fragmented parts. He could be playful.

He began a session stating that this had been a terrible week, his hand muscles were like boards. His family was telling him to slow down. He was depressed. He spent the last two days in bed not doing much. His wife was yelling at him about not wanting to go to the family's Thanksgiving Day dinner. "She threatened to leave me." He said that he hates her. "It is all too much. I am depressed." This response has not been uncommon during his years in analysis. Considerable analysis has taken place exploring his early depression and hopelessness, anxiety, frustration and rage which illuminated how a school phobia evolved that contained similar components to his current communication.

I said, "You certainly don't sound like Stephen Hawking! You are never going to get a Nobel Prize that way. You couldn't get me to nominate you." Stephen Hawking was an ideal for the patient and we spent lengthy periods exploring the meaning of Stephen Hawking as someone who, the patient feels, has preserved his soul in spite of his infirmity. Stephen Hawking's courage reflects what he wished he could have mobilized as a child. He responded to my comment about not sounding like Stephen Hawking saying he had given up trying to ever be like Stephen Hawking. I said, "Oh my goodness that is the biggest bull— that I have heard in my life." He smiled. After a silence I said, "To be like Stephen Hawking, with his zeal and optimism, at one time was just too difficult. You felt to be open, vital, and committed to living made you too vulnerable and you could really get hurt. It was safer to withdraw in anger and depression. You are here with me and your family today with all your capacities. You can handle whatever happens without using your anger and withdrawing."

He smiled again. He said, "This damned thing is not going to get me down." "You are my model," I said, "And you are going to write a book about this experience and win the Pulitzer Prize." In fact, he has been planning to write a book about how he has survived his illness. He began crying. He said that his wife is waiting to hear about his MRI. I said, "Maybe the anger that your wife and you are expressing to each other is related to trying to protect yourselves from your feelings of vulnerability and no control which is related, for you, at least, to how hopeless your life seemed to be with your parents, at school and in your early life." There appeared to us that a transformation had occurred from distance to intimacy in this session. Playfulness helped make the progression in this session possible.

CONCLUDING REMARKS

Years ago I listened to Merton Gill discuss his psychoanalytic technique. He said that he only intervened with interpretations or comments that would lead to an interpretation. He said nothing else because his intent was to promote the patient's free associations; no hello! no goodbye! This took place during a period in the history of psychoanalysis when the ego psychologists were strongly influence by Eissler's (1953) admonition that interventions that were not interpretation or would lead to interpretations were not analytic. At that time, neophytes like me, when presenting their clinical material, felt that the most dreadful comment from a senior analyst would be that we were not being analytic. At a conference, an analyst described a comment from a patient who was terminating his analysis. The patient said, "When I see you I will turn around and show you the back of my head so you will know who I am." Had I presented the clinical material in this paper at that time, I probably would be told that I needed further analytic training. I should get more analysis or I did not have the talent to conduct an analysis. I belong to a generation of psychoanalysts that have been traumatized by being taught to ignore the qualities of the whole person of the patient and analyst because of the emphasis on the parts that contribute to dynamics. I imagine our teachers were even more traumatized. Gill, who continued to be inclusive in his analytic thinking, changed from his position and argued that metapsycholgy was an impediment in our psychoanalytic thinking and technique because the theory moves us away from the human elements of psychoanalysis. He then went further by promoting a two-person model to replace a one-person model in conceptualizing psychoanalysis.

As I described earlier in the paper, there are references to playfulness in the analytic literature. Yet, playfulness is exclusively devoted to descriptions of the therapist attempting to promote an alliance or dealing with resistances and defenses in the dynamics of the clinical situation. There is no reference in the literature to playfulness in the analytic work of the whole patient and analyst devoted to overcoming the effect of a repetition of the hopelessness of being intimate by exposing the parts of one's story that are humiliating and shameful and transforming the repetition into increased coherence and evolution of Self.

A male patient grew up with chronic trauma of sexual abuse and physical beatings. A defensive component of the chronic trauma was repeated in the analysis in the form of being emotionally invisible. He was very bright and with an abundance of analytic knowledge. He could take the experiences within the session and partially integrate them into his life and function reasonably well. But for years in the sessions I felt that he was hiding. As I connected some of the details of his chronic trauma with his current experiences, I would interpret that his hiding was a defense against revealing being overwhelmed by his chronic trauma. He would frequently complain that I was unable to find the correct language that would enable him to think about his experiences. For a long time, I thought this was simply his resistance, but with his help, I gradually understood that he was communicating as a whole person, wanting help to enable him to do more with the repetition which included having to feel invisible as a way of dealing with the shock and humiliation of being traumatized. He felt that he was incapable of being too open, alive and vital in telling me his story of his trauma. My role was to demonstrate that it was possible. Playfulness was an essential component in our relationship that enabled the psychoanalysis to progress. The creativity of our playfulness became a demonstration that the shock and humiliation of the trauma could be revealed today in spite of the shame and humiliation. This is different than the attempt to undo the entire situation by withdrawing from the immediacy of life and repeating the original event.

By discussing playfulness from the perspective of the analyst and patient as whole people, we are provided with a window that enables us to follow analyst and patient as agencies being immersed together in working at having the patient tell her story with openness and intimacy. Their work together result in the transformation of the repetition which contributes to the patient's suffering, into greater authenticity for the patient. The patient is able to communicate in the present moment what has happened to her while feeling vital and alive. Qualities of courage and honesty are necessary to achieve this goal. The experiences of the patient and analyst as they reach for this goal have their own dynamics. The analyst's role is the provider of hope that the transformation can occur even though the repetition has hopelessness within it. Playfulness in this setting is a vital element in conveying hope.

The perspective of a whole person in the clinical situation suggests concepts of an ego instinct (Freud, 1917), drive for mastery (Hendrick, 1942), and effectance (White, 1959; Greenberg, 1991). These concepts are part of the psychoanalytic lexicon, but never have found a comfortable place because they were antithetical to the instinctual drives and placed the drive as an energy source within the ego. I am arguing that it is impossible to understand clinical material without an understanding of the dynamics of the parts of the mind, but also how the mind deals with the parts that are present in the immediacy of the clinical moment. Playfulness is a technical asset for mastery and effectance. Symington (2007) addresses this issue. He states that psychoanalysts have approached clinical material the wrong way. They did not begin with integration and inclusion. Phillips (1995) uses the language of the whole person in his psychoanalytic writing. For example, in *Terrors and Experts* he describes the human characteristic that begins early in childhood of asking an infinite number of questions. One question always leads to another question because it is impossible to fully understand any aspect of life. People are always looking for experts who are wishfully seen as having the ability to understand and have the correct answer. In the analytic situation, the patient who is seeking an expert, makes the analyst the expert on what to feel, what to know and how to live. The analysis moves to the patient's recognition that the analyst does not have the answers that the patient hopes to be given. The patient slowly realizes that only she can deal with the hazards and joys of her life. The patient in the repetition feels that this is just too much to recognize. In the analysis she begins to realize that the pessimism is itself a repetition that is superseded by the reality of the analytic situation.

I grew up analytically being told that analysis is too difficult and too painful to explore one's powerful desires and traumas for most people. It is only for the strong at heart. Being with a loving, playful analyst as the hopelessness of the past is experienced and lived out is not so painful and difficult. It is a life changing, intimate, and joyous experience.

References

Ablon, S. L. (2001). The work of transformation: Changes in technique since Anna Freud's normality and pathology in childhood. *The Psychoanalytic Study of the Child* 56: 27–38.

Abrams, S. (1981). Insight: The Teiresian gift. *Psychoanalytic Study of the Child* 36: 251–70.

Adler, A. (1989). Transitional phenomena, projective identification, and the essential ambiguity of the psychoanalytic situation. *Psychoanalytic Quarterly* 58: 81–104.

Akhtar, S. (1988). Hypomanic personality disorder. *Integrative Psychiatry* 6: 37–52.

———. (1990). Paranoid personality disorder: A synthesis of developmental, dynamic, and descriptive features. *American Journal of Psychotherapy* 64: 5–25.

———. (1992). *Broken Structures: Severe Personality Disorders and Their Treatment.* Northvale, NJ: Jason Aronson.

———. (1999). *Immigration and Identity: Turmoil, Treatment and Transformation*. Northvale, NJ: Jason Aronson.

———. (2001). From mental pain through manic defense to mourning. Pp. 95–113 in *Three Faces of Mourning: Melancholia, Manic Defense and Moving On.* Edited by S. Akhtar. Northvale, NJ: Jason Aronson.

———. (2003). Things: Developmental, psychopathological, and technical aspects of inanimate objects. *Canadian Journal of Psychoanalysis* 11: 1–44.

———. (2007). Disruptions in the course of psychotherapy and psychoanalysis. Pp. 93–108 in *Severe Personality Disorders: Everyday Issues in Clinical Practice*. Edited by B. van Luyn, S. Akhtar, and W. J. Livesley. Cambridge: Cambridge University Press.

———. (2009). *The Comprehensive Dictionary of Psychoanalysis*. London: Karnac.

———, ed. (2010). *The Wound of Mortality: Fear, Denial and the Acceptance of Death*. Lanham, MD: Jason Aronson.

Alexander, F. (1958). A contribution to the theory of play. *Psychoanalytic Quarterly* 27: 175–93.

Altman, N. (1994). Relational perspectives on child psychoanalytic psychotherapy. Pp. 175–94 *Relational Perspectives in Psychoanalysis*. Edited by N. Skolnick and S. Warshaw. Hillsdale, NJ: Analytic Press.

———. (1994). A perspective on child psychoanalysis: Recognition of relational theory and technique in child treatment. *Psychoanalytic Psychology* 11: 383–95.

Appelbaum, S. A. (2000). *Evocativeness: Moving and Persuasive Interventions in Psychotherapy*. Northvale, NJ: Jason Aronson.

Arlow, J. A. (1961). Ego psychology and the study of mythology. *Journal of the American Psychoanalytic Association* 9: 371–93.

———. (1969). Unconscious fantasy and disturbances of conscious experience. *Psychoanalytic Quarterly* 38: 1–27.

———. (1987). Trauma, play, and perversion. *Psychoanalytic Study of the Child* 42: 31–44.
Arnett, J. J. (2002). The psychology of globalization. *American Psychologist* 37: 774–83.
Aronson, S., S. Scheidlinger, and F. Hajal, eds. (2002). *Group Treatment of Adolescents in Context: Outpatient, Inpatient and School*. Madison, CT: International Universities Press.
Aston, W. G. (1972). *Nihongi: Chronicles of Japan from the Earliest Times to A.D. 697*. Tokyo: Charles E. Tuttle.
Auerhahn, N., and D. Laub. (1987). Play and playfulness in Holocaust survivors. *Psychoanalytic Study of the Child* 42: 45–58.
Azima, F., and L. Richmond. (1989). *Adolescent Group Psychotherapy*. New York: International Universities Press.
Bachelard, G. (1969). *The Poetics of Space*. Boston, MA: Beacon Press.
Balint, M. (1959). *Thrills and Regressions*. London: Hogarth.
Barston, R. P. (1988). *Modern Diplomacy*. London: Longman.
Bauer, P. J., and S. S. Wewerka. (1995). One-to-two-year-olds' recall of event: The more expressed the more impressed. *Journal of Experimental Child Psychology* 59: 475–96.
Beebe, B., and Lachmann, F. (1988). The contribution of mother-infant mutual influence to the origins of self and object representations. *Psychoanalytic Psychology* 5: 305–37.
Berger, L. S. (1985). *Psychoanalytic Theory and Clinical Relevance: What Makes Theory Consequential in Clinical Practice?* Hillsdale, NJ: Analytic Press.
Bergman, A. (1978). From mother to the outside world: the use of space during the separation–individuation phase. Pp. 147–65 in *Between Reality and Fantasy*. Edited by S. Grolnick and L. Barkin. New York: Jason Aronson.
Bernfeld, S. (1938). Types of adolescence. *Psychoanalytic Quarterly* 7: 243–53.
Billow, R. (2004). The adolescent play: Averting the tragedy of Hamlet. *Contemporary Psychoanalysis* 40: 253–77.
Birch, M. (1997). In the land of counterpane: Travels in the realm of play. *Psychoanalytic Study of the Child* 52: 57–75.
Bittle, W. E. (1964). Unpublished field notes.
Blakemore, S. J. (2008). The social brain in adolescence. *Nature Views/Neuroscience* 9: 267–77.
Blos, P. (1962). *On Adolescence: A Psychoanalytic Interpretation*. New York: Free Press.
———. (1967). The second individuation process of adolescence. *Psychoanalytic Study of the Child* 22: 162–86.
———. (1968). Character formation in adolescence. *Psychoanalytic Study of the Child* 23: 245–63.
———. (1976). When and how does adolescence end? Pp. 5–17 in *Adolescent Psychiatry, Vol V*. Edited by S. C. Feinstein and P. L. Giovacchini. New York: Jason Aronson.
Blum, H. (2005). The language of affect. Pp. 1–18 in *The Language of Emotions*. Edited by S. Akhtar and H. Blum. New York: Jason Aronson.
Bohleber, W. (2007). Remembrance, trauma, and collective memory: The battle for memory in psychoanalyis. *International Journal of Psychoanalysis* 88: 329–52.
Bohn, D. (1980). *Wholeness and the Implicit Order*. London: Routhledge and Kegan Paul.
Bonovitz, C. (2009). Countertransference in child psychoanalytic psychotherapy: The emergence of the analyst's childhood. *Psychoanalytic Psychology* 26: 235–45.
Bornstein, B. (1945). Clinical notes on child analysis. *Psychoanalytic Study of the Child* 1: 151–66.
Bourgeois, L. (1999). *Vogue Magazine*, p. 412. November, 1999.
Bowlby, J. (1988). *A Secure Base*. New York: Basic Books.
———. (1994). *Attachment and Loss*. New York: Basic Books.
Brenner, I. (2004). *Psychic Trauma: Dynamics, Symptoms, and Treatment*. Lanham, MD: Jason Aronson.
———. (2009). *Injured Men: Trauma, Healing, and the Masculine Self*. Lanham, MD: Jason Aronson.
———. (2010). Is that all there is? Pp. 171–186 in *The Wound of Mortality*. Edited by S. Akhtar. Lanham, MD: Jason Aronson. [AQ: Article pg. #?]

Bretherton, I. (1984). Representing the social world in symbolic play: Reality and fantasy. Pp. 3–41 in *Symbolic Play: The Development of Understanding*. Edited by I. Bretherton. Orlando, FL: Academic Press.

Breuer, J., and S. Freud. (1893–1895). Studies on hysteria. *Standard Edition* 2: 1–17.

Bruner, J. S., and V. Sherwood. (1976). Peekaboo and the learning of rule structures. Pp. 277–85 in *Play: Its Role in Development and Evolution*. Edited by J. S. Bruner. New York: Basic Books.

Busch, F. (1993). In the neighborhood: Aspects of a good interpretation and a developmental lag in ego psychology. *Journal of the American Psychoanalytical Association* 41: 151–77

———. (2005). Conflict theory/trauma theory. *Psychoanalytic Quarterly* 74: 27–45.

Caputi, A. (1988). *Pirandello and the Crisis of Modern Consciousness*. Chicago: University of Illinois Press.

Caspary, A. (1993). Aspects of the therapeutic action in child analytic treatment. *Psychoanalytic Psychology* 10: 207–20.

Çevik, A. (2003). Globalization and identity. Pp. 91–98 in *Violence or Dialogue: Psychoanalytic Insights to Terror and Terrorism*. Edited by S. Varvin and V. D. Volkan. London: International Psychoanalysis Library.

Chasseguet-Smirgel, J. (1996). Blood and nation. *Mind and Human Interaction* 7: 31–36.

Coen, S. (2005). How to play with patients who would rather remain remote. *Journal of the American Psychoanalytic Association* 53: 811–34.

Cohen, R. M. and A. Solnit. (1993). Play and therapeutic action. *Psychoanalytic Study of the Child* 48: 49–63.

Corradi Fiumara, G. (2009). *Spontaneity: A Psychoanalytic Inquiry*. London: Routledge.

Czech, D. (1990). *Auschwitz Chronicle 1939–1945: From the Archives of the Auschwitz Memorial and the German Federal Archives*. New York: Henry Holt and Co.

Damasio, A. R. (1994). *Descartes' Error*. New York: Grosset Putnam.

Daniels, L. (1956). *Caleb My Son*. New York: J. B. Lippincott Co.

———. (1961). *High On a Hill*. New York: McGraw-Hill.

———. (2001). *With a Woman's Voice*. Lanham, MD: Madison Books.

———. (2005). *Dreaming Your Way to Creative Freedom*. New York: iUniverse.

———. (2005). *The Eyes of the Father*. New York: iUniverse.

Demos, V. (1992). The early organization of the psyche. Pp. 200–33 in *The Interface of Psychoanalysis and Psychology*. Edited by J. Barron and D. Wolitzky. Washington, DC: American Psychological Association Press.

Deri, S. K. (1984). *Symbolization and Creativity*. New York: International Universities Press.

Dobroszycki, L., ed. (1984). *The Chronicle of the Łódź Ghetto, 1941–1944*. New Haven, CT: Yale University Press.

Drucker, J. (1979). The affective context and psychodynamics of first symbolization. Pp. 21–41 in *Symbolic Functioning in Childhood*. Edited by N. R. Smith and M. B. Franklin. Hillsdale, NJ: Erlbaum.

Dwork, D. (1991). *Children With a Star—Jewish Youth in Nazi Europe*. New Haven, CT: Yale University Press

Eban, A. (1983). *The New Diplomacy: International Affairs in the Modern Age*. New York: Random House.

Ehrenberg, D. (1990). Playfulness in the psychoanalytic relationship. *Contemporary Psychoanalysis* 26: 74–95.

Eisen, G. (1988). *Children and Play in the Holocaust—Games Among the Shadows*. Amherst: University of Massachusetts Press.

Eisenberg, A., ed. (1981). *Witness to the Holocaust*. New York: Pilgrim Press.

Eissler, K. R. (1953). The effect of the structure of the ego in psychoanalytic technique. *Journal of the American Psychoanalytic Association* 1: 104–13.

Emde, R. (1980). Emotional availability: A reciprocal award system for infants and parents with implications for prevention of psychosocial disorders. Pp. 87–115 in *Parent-Infant Relationships*. Edited by P. Taylor. Orlando, FL: Grune and Stratton.

———. (1991). Positive emotions for psychoanalytic theory: Surprises from infancy research and new directions. *Journal of the American Psychoanalytic Association* 39S: 5–44.

Erikson, E. H. (1950). *Childhood and Society*. New York: W. W. Norton, 1963.
———. (1956). The problem of ego identity. *Journal of the American Psychoanalytic Association* 4: 56–121.
———. (1959). *Identity and the Life Cycle: Psychological Issues Monograph: I*. New York: International Universities Press.
Etezady, M. H. (1995). Narcissism: Primary-secondary, fundamental or obsolete? Pp. 3–9 in *The Vulnerable Child, Vol. 2*. Edited by T. Cohen, M. H. Etezady and B. Pacella. New York: International Universities Press.
Feiner, A. (1979). Countertransference and the anxiety of influence. Pp. 105–28 in *Countertransference*. Edited by L. Epstein and A. Feiner. New York: Jason Aronson.
———. (1990). Playfulness and the interpersonal ideology. *Contemporary Psychoanalysis* 26: 95–106.
———. (1992). Playfulness as a way. *Contemporary Psychoanalysis* 28: 407–10.
Ferenczi, S. (1932). Suggestion in (after) analysis. Pp. 269–70 in *Final Contributions to the Problems and Methods of Psycho-Analysis*. New York: Brunner/Mazel, 1980.
Fenichel, O. (1946). On acting. *Psychoanalytic Quarterly* 15: 144–60.
Fischer, R. M. S. (2004). Fathers, history, and psychoanalysis. Pp. 1–11 in *Real and Imaginary Fathers: Development, Transference, and Healing*. Edited by S. Akhtar and H. Parens. Lanham, MD: Jason Aronson.
Fonagy, P. (2001). *Attachment Theory and Psychoanalysis*. New York: Other Press.
Fonagy, P., G. Gergely, E. Jurist, and M. Target. (2002). *Affect Regulation, Mentalization, and the Development of the Self*. New York: Basic Books.
Fonagy, P., and G. S. Moran. (1991). Understanding psychic change in child psychoanalysis. *International Journal of Psychoanalysis* 72: 15–22.
Fonagy, P., G. S. Moran, R. Edgecumbe, H. Kennedy, and M. Target. (1993). The roles of mental representations and mental processes in therapeutic action. *Psychoanalytic Study of the Child* 48: 9–48.
Fonagy, P., and M. Target. (1996). Playing with reality: I. Theory of mind and the normal development of psychic reality. *International Journal of Psychoanalysis* 77: 217–33.
———. (1997). Attachment and reflective function: Their role in self-organization. *Development and Psychopathology* 9: 679–700.
Fraiberg, S. (1959). *The Magic Years*. New York: Charles Scribner's Sons.
Frank, A. (1969). The unrememberable and the unforgettable: Passive primal repression. *Psychoanalytic Study of the Child* 24: 48–77.
Frankel, J. (1998). The play's the thing: How the essential processes of therapy are seen most clearly in child therapy. *Psychoanalytic Dialogues* 8: 149–82.
Freeman, D. M. A. (1968). Adolescent crises of the Kiowa Apache Indian male. Pp. 157–204 in *Minority Group Adolescents in the United States*. Edited by E. B. Brody. Baltimore, MD: Williams and Wilkins.
———. (1977). Psychoanalysis, folklore and processes of socialization. *Journal of the American Psychoanalytic Association* 25: 235–52.
———. (1981). Mythological portrayal of developmental processes and major intrapsychic restructuralizations. Pp. 319–40 in *The Psychoanalytic Study of Society, Vol IX*. Edited by W. Muenster-berger, L. B. Boyer and S. Grolnick. New York: Psychohistory Press.
———. (1994). *Some Aspects of Japanese Female Development Reflected in the Female Story Line in Mythology and Folklore, Parts I and II*. Presented at The American Psychoanalytic Association Discussion Group and Interdisciplinary Colloquium, December 1994. Also presented at a conference on "Folklore as a Family Portrait," Jikei University, Tokyo, September 3, 1995.
———. (1997a). *Emotional Refueling in Development, Mythology, and Cosmology: The Japanese Separation-Individuation Experience*. Presented at the Twenty-eighth Annual (100th Anniversary) Margaret S. Mahler Symposium on Child Development, in Philadelphia, April 1997. Published in *The Colors of Childhood*, eds. S. Akhtar and S. Kramer, pp. 17–60. New York: Jason Aronson, 1998.
———. (1997b). *Japanese Developmental Experiences and Object Relations as Reflected in Mythology*. Presented at The Eighth Abram Kardiner Lecture on Psychoanalysis and Cul-

ture, The Columbia University Center for Psychoanalytic Training and Research, New York, June 1997.
———. (2005). Joint looking, shared experiencing, and verbalizing affects in the U.S. and Japan. Pp. 49–67 in *Language of Emotions: Development, Psychopathology, and Technique*. Edited by Salman Akhtar and Harold P. Blum. Lanham, MD: Jason Aronson.
Freeman, P. A. (1971). Kiowa-Apache concepts and attitudes regarding the child. *Papers in Anthropology* 12: 90–160.
Freeman, R. N. (1995). *"Other People's" Music: Improvisation, Interaction and Community Formation*. Master of Arts thesis, University of North Carolina at Chapel Hill.
Freud, A. (1926). Four Lectures on child analysis. Pp. 3–69 in *Anna Freud, Vol. I*. New York: International Universities Press, 1974.
———. (1927). *The Psychoanalytic Treatment of Children*. London: Imago, 1946.
———. (1928). The theory of child analysis. Pp. 162–75 in *Introduction to Psychoanalysis*. London: Hogarth Press, 1974.
———. (1929). On the theory of analysis of children. *International Journal of Psychoanalysis* 10: 29–38.
———. (1936). *The Ego and the Mechanisms of Defense*. New York: International Universities Press.
———. (1958). *The Writings of Anna Freud, Vol. 5*. New York: International Universities Press.
———. (1965). *Normality and Pathology in Childhood*. New York: International Universities Press.
———. (1966). *The Ego and the Mechanisms of Defense*. New York: International Universities Press.
———. (1981). Insight—its presence and absence as a factor in normal development. *Psychoanalytic Study of the Child* 36: 241–49.
Freud, A., and S. Dann. (1951). An experiment in group upbringing. *Psychoanalytic Study of the Child* 6: 127–68.
Freud, S. (1895). Project for a scientific psychology. *Standard Edition* 1:295–343.
———. (1900). Interpretation of dreams. *Standard Edition* 4–5: 1–626.
———. (1905). Jokes and their relation to the unconscious. *Standard Edition* 7: 1–122.
———. (1906). Psychopathic characters on the stage. *Standard Edition* 7: 305–10.
———. (1908). Creative writers and daydreaming. *Standard Edition* 9: 209–26.
———. (1911). Formulations on the two principles of mental functioning. *Standard Edition* 12: 213–16.
———. (1912a). Recommendations to physicians practising psycho-analysis. *Standard Edition* 12: 109–20.
———. (1912b). Totem and Taboo. *Standard Edition* 13: 1–161.
———. (1914a). Remembering, repeating and working through. *Standard Edition* 12: 147–56.
———. (1914b). On Narcissism: An introduction. *Standard Edition* 14: 67–102.
———. (1916). Some character types met with during psychoanalytic work. *Standard Edition* 14: 310 33.
———. (1917a). Mourning and melancholia. *Standard Edition* 14: 237–58.
———. (1917b). A difficulty in the path of psychoanalysis. *Standard Edition* 17: 135–44.
———. (1920). Beyond the pleasure principle. *Standard Edition* 18: 7–64.
———. (1923). The ego and the id. *Standard Edition* 19: 1–66.
———. (1926a). The question of lay analysis. *Standard Edition* 20: 179–258.
———. (1926b). Address to the B'nai B'rith. *Standard Edition* 20: 271–74.
———. (1933). New introductory lectures on psychoanalysis. *Standard Edition* 22: 1–182.
———. (1939). Moses and monotheism. *Standard Edition* 23: 7–137.
———. (1940). Splitting the ego in the process of defence. *Standard Edition* 23: 275–78.
———. (1961). *Civilization and its discontents*. New York: W. W. Norton, 1961.
Freud, S., and D. Oppenheim. (1911). From Sigmund Freud to D. E. Oppenheim. Pp. 13–14 in *Dreams in Folklore*. New York: International Universities Press, 1958.
Friedman, I. R., ed. (1982). *Escape or Die: True Stories of Young People Who Survived the Holocaust*. Reading, MA: Addison-Wesley.

Gaensbauer, T. J. (1995). Trauma in the preverbal period: Symptoms, memories, and developmental impact. *Psychoanalytic Study of the Child* 50: 122–49.
Galatzer-Levy, R. M. (2002). Emergence. *Psychoanalytic Inquiry* 22: 708–27.
Galatzer-Levy, R. M., and Cohler, B. (1993). *The Essential Other: A Developmental Psychology of the Self.* New York: Basic Books.
Garvey, C. (1977). *Play*. Boston: Harvard University Press.
Gay, P. (1988). *Freud: A Life for Our Time*. New York: Norton.
Geertz, C. (1972). Deep play: Notes on the Balinese cockfight. *Daedalus* 101: 1–37.
Ghent, E. (1992). Paradox and process. *Psychoanalytic Dialogues* 2: 135–60.
Glassner, M. I., and Krell, R., eds. (2006). *And Life is Changed Forever—Holocaust Childhoods Remembered.* Detroit, MI: Wayne State University Press.
Gilligan, C. (1982). *In A Different Voice: Psychological Theory and Women's Development.* Cambridge, MA: Harvard University Press.
———. (1983). *In Different Voice*. Cambridge, MA: Harvard University Press.
Gilmore, K. (2005). Play in the psychoanalytic setting: Ego capacity, ego state and vehicle for intersubjective exchange. *Psychoanalytic Study of the Child* 60: 213–38.
Giovacchini, P. (1986). *Developmental Disorders: The Transitional Space in Mental Breakdown and Creative Integration.* Northvale, NJ: Jason Aronson.
Glass, J. M. (1985). *Delusion: Internal Dimensions of Political Life*. Chicago: University of Chicago Press.
Glenn, J., ed. (1978). *Child Analysis and Therapy*. New York: Jason Aronson.
Glenn, J. and I. Bernstein. (1990). The fantasy world of the child as revealed in art, play, and dreams. Pp. 319–48 in *The Neurotic Child and Adolescent*. Edited by M. H. Etezady. New York: Jason Aronson.
Green, A. (2005). The illusion of common ground and mythical pluralism. *International Journal of Psychoanalysis* 86: 627–32.
Greenacre, P. (1941). The predisposition to anxiety. *Psychoanalytic Quarterly* 10: 66–94, 610–38.
———. (1954). The role of transference. *Journal of the American Psychoanalytic Association* 2: 671–84.
———. (1969). The fetish and the transitional object. *Psychoanalytic Study of the Child* 24: 144–64.
———. (1970). The transitional object and the fetish with special reference to the role of illusion. *International Journal of Psychoanalysis* 51: 447–56.
Greenberg, J. (1991). *Oedipus and Beyond*. Hillsdale, NJ: Analytic Press.
Greenson, R. (1965). The working alliance and the transference neurosis. *Psychoanalytic Quarterly* 34: 155–81.
Greig, D. (2001). *Dr. Korczak's Example*. Edinburgh, Scotland: Capercaillie.
Hare, R., L. McPherson, and A. Forth. (1988). Male psychopaths and their criminal careers. *Journal of Consulting and Clinical Psychology* 56: 710–14.
Harris, A. (2005). *Gender as Soft Assembly*. Hillside, NJ: Analytic Press.
Hartmann, H. (1939). *Ego Psychology and the Problem of Adaptation*. New York: International Universities Press, 1958.
Heaney, S. (1995). *A Redress for Poetry*. New York: Farrar, Strauss, and Giroux.
Held, D. (1988). Democratization and globalization. Pp. 11–27 in *Re-imagining Political Community*. Edited by A. Archibugi, D. Held, and M. Kohler. Palo Alto, CA: Stanford University Press.
Hendrick, I. (1942). Instinct and the ego during infancy. *Psychoanalytic Quarterly* 11: 33–58.
Herzog, J. (2005a). Los degradados: Out, down, dead: Transmitted and inflicted trauma as encountered in the analysis of a six year old girl. *International Journal of Psychoanalysis* 86: 291–310.
———. (2005b). Triadic reality and the capacity to love. *Psychoanalytic Quarterly* 74: 1029–52.
Holder, A. (2005). *Anna Freud, Melanie Klein, and the Psychoanalysis of Children and Adolescents*. London: Karnac Books.

Hollander, N. C. (2006). Psychoanalysis and the problem of the by-stander in times of terror. Pp. 154–65 in *Psychoanalysis, Class, and Politics: Encounters in the Clinical Setting*. Edited by L. Layton, N. C. Hollander and S. Gutwill. London: Routledge.

Hopkins, L. (2000). Masud Khan's application of Winnicott's "play" techniques to analytic consultation and treatment of adults. *Contemporary Psychoanalysis* 36: 639–63.

Hug-Helmuth, H. (1919). *A Study of the Mental Life of the Child*. Ithaca, NY: Cornell University Library Press, 2004.

Hughes, F. H. (2003). *Children, Play and Development*. Thousand Oaks, CA: Sage Publications.

Huizinga, J. (1955). *Homo Ludens; A Study of the Play-Element in Culture*. Boston: Beacon Press.

Inhelder, B., and J. Piaget. (1958). *The Growth of Logical Thinking from Childhood to Adolescence*. New York: Basic Books.

Innes, B. (2006). *Serial Killers: The Story of History's Most Evil Murderers*. London: Quercus Publishing.

Jacobs, T. (1986). On countertransference enactments. *Journal of the American Psychoanalytic Association* 34: 289–307.

Jaffe, C. (2000). Organizing adolescent(ce): A dynamic systems perspective on adolescence and adolescent psychotherapy. *Adolescent Psychiatry* 25: 17–43.

James, W. (1980). *The Principles of Psychology*. New York: Dover Publications.

James, W. (1902). *Varieties of Religious Experience*. New York: MacMillan, 1961.

Jones, E. (1922). *Anal Erotic Character Traits: Papers on Psychoanalysis*. 3rd edition. New York: William Wood.

Kaplan, L. (1984). *Adolescence: The Farewell to Childhood*. New York: Simon and Schuster.

Karski, J. (1944). *The Story of a Secret State*. Boston: Houghton Mifflin.

Kassow, S. D. (2007). *Who Will Write Our History: Rediscovering a Hidden Archive From the Warsaw Ghetto*. New York: Vintage Books.

Katan, A. (1961). Some thoughts about the role of verbalization in early childhood. *Psychoanalytic Study of the Child* 16: 184–88.

Katz, G. (1997). Where the action is: The enacted dimension of analytic process. *Journal of the American Psychoanalytic Association* 46: 1129–67.

Kernberg, O. (1970). A psychoanalytic classification of character pathology. *Journal of the American Psychoanalytic Association* 18: 800–22.

———. (1975). *Borderline Conditions and Pathological Narcissism*. New York: Jason Aronson.

———. (1991). Sadomasochism, sexual excitement, and perversion. *Journal of the American Psychoanalytic Association* 39: 333–62.

———. (2003a). Sanctioned social violence: A psychoanalytic view, part 1. *International Journal of Psycho-Analysis* 84: 683–98.

———. (2003b). Sanctioned social violence: A psychoanalytic view, part 2. *International Journal of Psycho-Analysis* 84: 953–68.

Kestenberg, J. S., and I. Brenner. (1988). Le narcissisme au service de la survie. *Revue Française de Psychoanalyse* 6: 1393–408.

———. (1996). *The Last Witness—The Child Survivor of the Holocaust*. Washington, DC: A.P.P.I.

Khan, M. (1963). The concept of cumulative trauma. *Psychoanalytic Study of the Child* 18: 286–306.

Kieffer, C. C. (2010a). Cyberspace, transitional space and adolescence. In *The Electrified Mind*. Edited by S. Akhtar. New York: Jason Aronson, forthcoming.

———. (2010b). Discussion: Psychoanalysis and cyberspace. *Psychoanalytic Inquiry*, forthcoming.

———. (2010c). The waiting room as boundary and bridge: Towards a dissociative model of the mind. Presented at the 2010 Winter Meeting of the American Psychoanalytic Association Convention. New York: January 2010.

———. (2009). A ship made of paper: Sailing the seas of the forward edge. Presented at the 2009 International Psychology of the Self Conference. Chicago: October 2009.

———. (2007). Emergence and the analytic third: Working at the edge of chaos. *Psychoanalytic Dialogues* 17: 683–704.

———. (2004). Self objects, oedipal objects, and mutual recognition: A self-psychological reappraisal of the female oedipal victor. *Annual of Psychoanalysis* 32: 69–80.

Killingmo, B. (1989). Conflict and deficit: Implications for technique. *International Journal of Psycho-Analysis* 70: 65–79.

Kinnvall, C. (2004). Globalization and religious nationalism: Self, identity, and the search for ontological security. *Political Psychology* 25: 741–67.

Kitayama, O. (1985). Pre-Oedipal "taboo" in Japanese folk tragedies. *International Review of Psychoanalysis* 12: 173–86.

———. (1991). The wounded caretaker and guilt. *Review of Psychoanalysis* 18: 229–40.

———. (2005). Cross-cultural varieties in experiencing affect. Pp. 33–48 in *Language of Emotions: Development, Psychopathology, and Technique*. Edited by Salman Akhtar and Harold P. Blum. Lanham, MD: Jason Aronson.

Kleeman, J. A. (1967). The peek-a-boo game. *Psychoanalytic Study of the Child* 22: 239–73.

Klein, M. (1921). The development of a child. Pp. 1–53 in *Love, Guilt, and Reparation*. London: Hogarth Press, 1981.

———. (1923). Early analysis. Pp. 77–105 in *Love, Guilt, and Reparation*. London: Hogarth Press, 1981.

———. (1923). Zur fruhanalyse. *Imago* 9: 222–59.

———. (1926). The psychological principles of early analysis. *International Journal of Psychoanalysis* 8: 25–37.

———. (1932). *The Psychoanalysis of Children*. London: Hogarth Press.

———. (1935). A contribution to the psychogenesis of manic depressive states. Pp. 262–89 in *Love, Guilt, and Reparation and Other Works—1921–1945*. New York: Free Press, 1975.

———. (1957). *Envy and Gratitude*. New York: Basic Books.

———. (1958). On the development of mental functioning. *International Journal of Psychoanalysis* 39: 84–90.

Kohut, H. H. (1978). The psychoanalytic treatment of narcissistic personality disorders: Outline of a systematic approach. Pp. 205–32 in *The Search for the Self*. Edited by P. Ornstein. New York: International Universities Press.

———. (1981). *How Does Analysis Cure?* Chicago: University of Chicago Press.

———. (1977). *The Restoration of the Self*. New York: International Universities Press.

Korczak, R. (1946). *Leharot-be-Efer*. Tel Aviv, Israel: Sifriyat Happalim.

Kretschner, E. (1925). *Physique and Character*. New York: Harcourt Brace.

Krimendahl, E. K. (1998). Metaphor in child psychoanalysis: Not simply a means to an end. *Contemporary Psychoanalysis* 34: 49–66.

Kris, E. (1956). The recovery of childhood memories in psychoanalysis. *Psychoanalytic Study of the Child* 11: 54–88.

Liu, J. H., and D. Mills. (2006). Modern racism and neo-liberal globalization: The discourses of plausible deniability and their multiple functions. *Journal of Community and Applied Social Psychology* 16: 83–99.

Loewald, H. (1960). On the therapeutic action of psychoanalysis. Pp. 221–56 in *Papers on Psychoanalysis*. New Haven, CT: Yale University Press, 1980.

———. (1975). Psychoanalysis as an art and the fantasy character of the psychoanalytic situation. *Journal of the American Psychoanalytic Association* 23: 277–99.

———. (1979). The waning of the Oedipus complex. Pp. 384–404 in *Papers on Psychoanalysis*. New Haven, CT: Yale University Press, 1980.

———. (1987). Therapeutic play in space and time. *Psychoanalytic Study of the Child* 42: 173–92.

London, N. (1981). The play element of regression in the psychoanalytic process. *Psychoanalytic Inquiry* 1: 7–27.

Louise Bourgeoisi. (1995). Coproduction Terra Luna Films, Centre George Pompidou. Produced by Anne Morieu.

Lyons-Ruth, K. (1999). Two person unconscious: Intersubjective dialogue, enactive relational representation, and the emergence of new forms of relational organization. *Psychoanalytic Inquiry* 19: 576–617.

McAllister, J. G. (1937). Kiowa Apache social organization. Pp. 99–169 in *Social Anthropology of North American Indian Tribes*. Edited by F. Eggan. Chicago: University of Chicago Press.

———. (1949). Kiowa-Apache tales. Pp. 1–141 in *The Sky is My Tipi*. Edited by J. Boatright. Dallas, TX: Southern Methodist University Press.

McDevitt, J. (1988). The origin of intrapsychic conflict during the separation-individuation process. Paper presented at the 19th Annual Margaret S. Mahler Symposium, Medical College of Pennsylvania. Philadelphia, May 5, 1988.

McLaughlin, J. T. (1987). The play of transference, some reflections on enactments in the psychoanalytic situation. *Journal of the American Psychoanalytic Association* 35: 557–82.

McLuhan, M. (1962). *The Guttenberg Galaxy: The Making of Typographic Man*. Toronto, Canada: University of Toronto Press.

Mahler, M. S. (1963). Thoughts about development and individuation. *Psychoanalytic Study of the Child* 18: 307–24.

Mahler, M., F. Pine, and A. Bergmann. (1975). *The Psychological Birth of a Human Infant*. New York: Basic Books.

Mahon, E. J. (2004). Playing and working through: A neglected analogy. *Psychoanalytic Quarterly* 73: 379–413.

Main, M., N. Kaplan, and J. Cassidy. (1985). Security in infancy, childhood, and adulthood: A move to the level of representation. *Monographs of the Society for Research in Child Development* 50: 66–104.

Markman, H. (1997). Play in the treatment of adolescents. *Psychoanalytic Quarterly* 66: 190–218.

Marks, J. (1993). *The Hidden Children: The Secret Survivors of the Holocaust*. New York: Fawcett Columbine.

Mayes, L. C., and D. J. Cohen. (1992). The development of an imaginative capacity in young children. *Psychoanalytic Study of the Child* 47: 23–47.

Mayes, L. C. , and D. J. Cohen. (1996). Children's developing theory of mind. *Journal of the American Psychoanalytic Association* 44: 117–42.

Meares, R. (1992). *The Metaphor of Play: The Self, The Secret and Borderline Experience by Hill of Content*. London: Routledge.

Meyer-Thoss, C. (1992). *Louise Bourgeois*. Zurich, Switzerland: Ammann Verlag AG.

Miller, D. (1978). Early adolescence: Its psychology, psychopathology and implications for therapy. *Adolescent Psychiatry* 6: 434–47.

Milner, M. (1955). The role of illusion in symbol formation. In *New Directions in Psychoanalysis: The Significance of Infant Conflict in the Pattern of Adult Behavior*. Edited by M. Klein, P. Heimann, and R. E. Money-Kyrle. London: Tavistock Publications.

———. (1957). *On Not Being Able to Paint*. New York: International Universities Press.

Mitchell, S. A., and L. Aron. (1999). *Relational Psychoanalysis: The Emergence of a Tradition*. Hillsdale, NJ: Analytic Press.

Moore, B. E., and B. D. Fine. (1990). *Psychoanalytic Terms and Concepts*. New Haven, CT: Yale University Press.

Moran, G. S. (1987). Some functions of play and playfulness—A developmental perspective. *Psychoanalytic Study of the Child* 42: 11–29.

Morton, T. L. (2005). Prejudice in an era of economic globalization and international interdependence. Pp. 135–60 in *The Psychology of Prejudice and Discrimination: Disability, Religion, Physique, and Other Traits, Vol. 4*. Edited by J. L. Chin. Westport, CT: Praeger.

Moskowitz, S. (1983). *Love Despite Hate: Child Survivors of the Holocaust and Their Adult Lives*. New York: Schacken Books.

Nelson, K., and J. Gruendel. (1981). Generalized event representation: Basic building blocks of cognitive development. Pp. 131–58 in *Advances in Development and Psychology, Vol. 1*. Edited by A. Brown and M. Lamb. Hillsdale, NJ: Erlbaum.

Neubauer, P. (1987). The many meanings of play. *Psychoanalytic Study of the Child* 42: 3–9.

Nir, Y. (1989). *The Lost Childhood: A Memoir*. New York: Berkeley Books.

Ogden, T. (1993). On potential space. Pp. 223–39 in *In One's Bones: The Clinical Genius of Winnicott*. Edited by D. Goldman. Northvale, NJ: Jason Aronson.

Ornstein, A. (1984). The function of play in the process of child psychotherapy: A contemporary perspective. *Annual of Psychoanalysis* 12: 349–66.

Ostow, M. (1987). Play and reality. *Psychoanalytic Study of the Child* 42: 193–203.

Panksepp, J. (1998). *Affective Neuroscience*. New York: Oxford University Press.

Pao, P-N. (1979). *Schizophrenic Disorders: Theory and Treatment from a Psychodynamic Point of View*. New York: International Universities Press.

Parens, H. (2004). *Renewal of Life: Healing from the Holocaust*. Rockville, MD: Schreiber Publishing.

———. (2008). *Renewal of Life: Healing From the Holocaust*. Rockville, MD: Schreiber Publishing.

Peller, L. E. (1954). Libidinal phases, ego development, and play. *Psychoanalytic Study of the Child* 9: 178–98.

Perry. B. (1997). Incubated in terror: Neurodevelopmental factors in the "cycle of violence." Pp. 124–49 in *Children in a Violent Society*. Edited by J. Osofsky. New York: Guilford.

Phillips, A. (1995). *Terror and Experts*. Cambridge: Harvard University Press.

Philippi, D. L. (1968). *Kojiki (Record of Ancient Things)*. Tokyo, Japan: University of Tokyo Press.

Piaget, J. (1932). *The Moral Judgment of the Child*. New York: Free Press.

———. (1962). *Play, Dreams and Imitation in Childhood*. New York: W. W. Norton.

———. (1963). *The Child's Conception of the World*. Paterson, NJ: Littlefield, Adams.

———. (1981 [1954]). *Intelligence and Affectivity: Their Relationship during Child Development*. Palo Alto, CA: Annual Review, Inc.

Piaget, J., and B. Inhelder. (1955/1958). *The Growth of Logical Thinking from Childhood to Adolescence: An Essay on the Construction of Formal Operational Structures*. Trans. by A. Parsons and S. Milgram. New York: Basic Books.

Pine, F. (1985). *Developmental Theory and Clinical Process*. New Haven, CT: Yale University Press.

Pirandello, L. (1956–1957). Novelle per un Anno. In *Opere di Luigi Pirandello, Vol. 1 and 2*. Edited by Corrado Alvard. Milan, Italy: Classic Contemporanei Itallani.

Pizer, S. A. (1996). Negotiating potential space: Illusion, play, metaphor and the subjunctive. *Psychoanalytic Dialogues* 6: 689–712.

Plaschkes, L. (2005). Affects in development and clinical work: Discussion of Blum's chapter "The language of affects." Pp. 19–32 in *The Language of Emotions*. Edited by S. Akhtar and H. Blum. New York: Jason Aronson.

Pretorius, I. (2007). Repeating and recalling preverbal memories through play. *Psychoanalytic Study of the Child* 62: 239–62.

Radin, P. (1956). *The Trickster: A Study in American Indian Mythology*. New York: Greenwood Press.

Ratliff, J. M. (2004). The persistence of national differences in a globalizing world: The Japanese struggle for competitiveness in advanced information technologies. *Journal of Socio-Economics* 33: 71–88.

Rice, A. K. (1965). *Learning for Leadership: Interpersonal and Intergroup Relations*. London: Tavistock Publications.

Ritvo, S. (1993). Play and illusion. Pp. 234–51 in *The Many Meanings of Play: A Psychoanalytic Perspective*. Edited by Solnit et al. New Haven, CT: Yale University Press.

Robinson, J. (1965). *And The Crooked Shall Be Made Straight*. New York: MacMillan.

Roland, A. (1996). *Cultural Pluralism and Psychoanalysis*. London: Routledge.

Roopnarine, J. L., J. E. Johnson, and F. H. Hooper. (1994). *Children's Play in Diverse Cultures*. Albany: State University of New York Press.

Rothenberg, A. (1990). *Creativity and Madness*. Baltimore, MD: Johns Hopkins University Press.

Sadker, M., and D. Sadker. (1995). *Failing at Fairness: How Our Schools Cheat Girls*. New York: Scribner.

Sandler, J., and A. Sandler. (1978). On the development of object relationships and affects. *International Journal of Psychoanalysis* 59: 285–96.

Sarnoff, C. (1976). *Latency*. New York: Jason Aronson.

Saunders, H. (1990). An historic challenge to rethink how nation states relate. Pp. 1–30 in *The Psychodynamics of International Relationships, Vol. I: Concepts and Theories*. Edited by V. D. Volkan, D. A. Julius, and J. V. Montville. Lexington, MA: Lexington Books.

Scaer, R. (2005). *The Trauma Spectrum: Hidden Wounds and Human Resiliency*. New York: W. W. Norton.

Scharff, D. E., and J. S. Scharff. (1987). *Object Relations Family Therapy*. New York: Jason Aronson.

Schwartzman, H. B. (1978). *Transformations: The Anthropology of Children's Play*. New York: Plenum Press.

———. (2001). *Children and Anthropology: Perspectives for the 21st Century*. Westport, CT: Bergen and Garvey.

Segal, H. (1989). *Klein*. London: Karnac.

Seib, P. M. (1996). *Headline Diplomacy: How News Coverage Affects Foreign Policy*. Westport, CT: Praeger.

Seligman, S. (2005). Complexity and sensibility: non-linear dynamic systems theory as a meta-framework for psychoanalysis. Presented at the Division 39 Spring Conference, New York.

Sender, R. M. (1986). *The Cage*. New York: MacMillan.

Settlage, C. F. (1989). The interplay of therapeutic and developmental process in the treatment of children: An application of contemporary object relations theory. *Psychoanalytic Inquiry* 9: 375–96.

Shapiro, W. (1987). One went right: Woes from Wall Street to the Gulf: But a happy ending in Texas. *Time* 130: 30.

Shengold, L. (1988). Some notes on play and playfulness. *Bulletin of the Anna Freud Centre* 11: 146–51.

Shopper, M. (1978). The role of audition in early psychic development with special reference to the use of the pull toy in the separation-individuation phase. *Journal of the American Psychoanalytic Association* 26: 283–310.

Slade, A. (1986). Symbolic play and separation-individuation. *Bulletin of the Menninger Clinic* 50: 541–63.

———. (1987a). A longitudinal study of maternal involvement and symbolic play during the toddler period. *Child Development* 58: 367–75.

———. (1987b). Quality of attachment and early symbolic play. *Developmental Psychology* 23: 78–85.

———. (1994). Making meaning and making believe: their role in the clinical process. Pp. 81–107 in *Children of Play: Clinical and Developmental Approaches to Meaning and Representation*. Edited by A. Slade and D. P. Wolf. New York: Oxford University Press.

Slavson, S. R. (1962). *Analytic Group Psychotherapy with Children, Adolescents and Adults*. New York: Columbia University Press.

Solnit, A. (1987). A psychoanalytic view of play. *Psychoanalytic Study of the Child* 42: 205–19.

———. (1998). Beyond play and playfulness. *Psychoanalytic Study of the Child* 53: 102–10.

Solnit, A. J., D. J. Cohen, and P. B. Neubauer. (1993). *The Many Meanings of Play: A Psychoanalytic Perspective*. New Haven, CT: Yale University Press.

Sori, C. E., and D. H. Sprenkle. (2000). *Training Family Therapists to Work with Children and Families: A Delphi Study*. PhD thesis, Purdue University, West Lafayette, Indiana.

Spitz, R. (1963). Life and the dialogue. Pp. 154–76 in *Counterpoint: Libidinal Object and Subject*. Edited by H. Gaskill. New York: International Universities Press.

———. (1965). *The First Year of Life*. New York: International Universities Press.

Sroufe, L. A. (1979). The coherence of individual development: Early care, attachment, and subsequent development issues. *American Psychologist* 34: 834–41.

Stein, M. (1985). Irony in psychoanalysis. *Journal of the American Psychoanalytic Association* 33: 35–58.

Steinberg, L., and A. S. Morris. (2001). Adolescent development. *Annual Review of Psychology* 52: 83–110.

Stern, D. (1977). *The First Relationship: Mother and Infant*. Cambridge: Harvard University Press.

———. (1985). *The Interpersonal World of the Infant: A View from Psychoanalysis and Developmental Psychology*. New York: Basic Books.

———. (1992). Pre-narrative envelope: An alternative view of "unconscious fantasy" in infancy. *Bulletin of the Anna Freud Centre* 15: 291-298.

Stoller, R. (1973). *Perversion: The Erotic Form of Hatred*. New York: Pantheon Books.

Stone, M. H. (2001). Serial sexual homicide: Biological, psychological, and sociological aspects. *Journal of Personality Disorders* 15: 1–18.

Sugarman, A. (2003). A new model for conceptualizing insightfulness in the psychoanalysis of young children. *Psychoanalytic Quarterly* 72: 325–55.

———. (2003). Dimensions of the child analyst's role as a developmental object: Affect regulation and limit setting. *Psychoanalytic Study of the Child* 58: 189–213.

———. (2008). The use of play to promote insightfulness in the analysis of children suffering from cumulative trauma. *Psychoanalytic Quarterly* 77: 799–833.

Summers, F. L. (1999). *Transforming the Self: an Object Relations Model of Psychoanalytic Therapy*. Hillsdale, NJ: Analytic Press.

———. (2005). *Self Creation: Psychoanalytic Therapy and the Art of the Possible*. Hillsdale, NJ: Analytic Press.

Szwajger, A. B. (1990). *I Remember Nothing More: The Warsaw Children's Hospital and the Jewish Resistance*. New York: Pantheon.

Terr, L. C. (1979). Children of Chowchilla: A study of psychic trauma. *Psychoanalytic Study of the Child* 34: 547–623.

———. (1988). What happens to early memories of trauma: A study of twenty children under age five at the time of documented traumatic events. *Journal of the American Academy of Child and Adolescent Psychiatry* 27: 96–104.

———. (1990). *Too Scared to Cry: Psychic Trauma in Childhood*. New York: Basic Books.

Tomkins, S. S. (1962). *Affect, Imagery, Consciousness*. New York: Springer.

Turquet, P. (1975). Threats to identity in the large group. Pp. 87–144 in *The Large Group: Dynamics and Therapy*. Edited by L. Kreeger. London: Constable.

Tustin, F. (1980). Autistic objects. *International Review of Psychoanalysis* 7: 27–39.

Twemlow, S. W., P. Fonagy, and F. C. Sacco. (2005). A developmental approach to mentalizing communities: I. A model for change. *Bulletin of the Menninger Clinic* 69: 265–81.

Van der Kolk, B. A., A. C. McFarlane, and L. Weisaeth, eds. (1996). *Traumatic Stress: The Effects of Overwhelming Experience on Mind, Body and Society*. New York: Guilford.

Volavkova, H. (1978). *I Never Saw Another Butterfly: Children's Drawings and Poems from the Terezin Concentration Camp 1942–1944*. New York: Schocken Books.

Volkan, V. D. (1981). *Linking Objects and Linking Phenomena: A Study of the Forms, Symptoms, Metapsychology and Therapy of Complicated Mourning*. New York: International Universities Press.

———. (1988). *The Need to Have Enemies and Allies: From Clinical Practice to International Relationships*. Northvale, NJ: Jason Aronson.

———. (1995). *The Infantile Psychotic Self and its Fates: Understanding and Treating Schizophrenic and Other Difficult Patients*. Northvale, NJ: Jason Aronson.

———. (1997). *Bloodlines: From Ethnic Pride to Ethnic Terrorism*. New York: Farrar, Straus and Giroux.

———. (1999). The Tree Model: A comprehensive psychological approach to unofficial diplomacy and the reduction of ethnic tension. *Mind and Human Interaction* 9: 130–81.

———. (2004). *Blind Trust: Large Groups and Their Leaders in Times of Crises and Terror*. Charlottesville, VA: Pitchstone Publishing.

———. (2006). *Killing in the Name of Identity: A Study of Bloody Conflicts*. Charlottesville, VA: Pitchstone Publishing.

Volkan, V. D., and S. Kayatekin. (2006). Extreme religious fundamentalism and violence: Some psychoanalytic and psychopolitical thoughts. *Psyche and Geloof* 17: 71–91.

Von Bertalanffy. (1968). *General Systems Theory: Foundations, Development, Application.* New York: George Braziller.

Waelder, R. (1933). The psychoanalytic theory of play. *Psychoanalytic Quarterly* 2: 208–24.

Wallace, A. (1956). Mazeway resynthesis: A bio-cultural theory of religious inspiration. *Transactions of the New York Academy of Sciences* 18: 628–38.

———. (1961). *Culture and Personality.* New York: Random House.

Webster's Collegiate Dictionary. (1998). Springfield, MA: Merriam Webster.

White, R. W. (1959). Motivation reconsidered: the concept of competence. *Psychoanalytic Review* 88: 297–333.

Winnicott, C., R. Shepherd, and M. Davis. (1989). *Psychoanalytic Explorations: D. W. Winnicott.* Cambridge: Harvard University Press.

Winnicott, D. W. (1935). The manic defense. Pp. 129–44 in *Collected Papers: Through Paediatrics to Psychoanalysis.* New York: Basic Books, 1958.

———. (1942). Why children play. Pp. 149–52 in *The Child and Outside World: Studies in Developing Relationships.* London: Tavistock.

———. (1953). Transitional objects and transitional phenomena. *International Journal of Psycho-Analysis* 34: 89–97.

———. (1958). The capacity to be alone. *International Journal of Psychoanalysis* 39: 416–20.

———. (1960). Ego distortion in terms of true and false self. Pp. 140–52 in *Maturational Processes and the Facilitating Environment.* New York: International Universities Press, 1965.

———. (1965). *The Maturational Process and the Facilitating Environment.* New York: International Universities Press.

———. (1967). Playing: a theoretical statement. Pp. 32–41 in *Playing and Reality.* London: Tavistock Publications, 1971.

———. (1968). Playing: It's theoretical status in the clinical situation. *International Journal of Psychoanalysis* 49: 591–99.

———. (1969). The use of an object and relating through identifications. *International Journal of Psychoanalysis* 50: 711–16.

———. (1971). *Playing and Reality.* London: Penguin Books.

———. (1971). Playing: A theoretical statement. Pp. 51–70 in *Playing and Reality.* New York: Routledge, 2005.

———. (1971). Playing: Creative activity and the search for the self. Pp. 71–86 in *Playing and Reality.* New York: Routledge, 2005.

———. (1989). Notes on play. Pp. 59–63 in *Psychoanalytic Explorations.* Edited by C. Winnicott, R. Shepherd, and M. Davis. Cambridge: Harvard University Press.

Wolf, E. S. (1988). *Treating the Self.* New York: Guilford.

Yanof, J. A. (2005). Technique in child analysis. In *Textbook of Psychoanalysis.* Edited by E. S. Person, A. M. Cooper, and G. O. Gabbard. Washington, DC: American Psychiatric Publishing.

Young-Bruehl, E. (1988). *Anna Freud: a Biography.* New York: Summit Books.

Zilbach, J. J. (1986). *Young Children in Family Therapy.* New York: Brunner/Mazel

Index

About the Contributors

Monisha C. Akhtar, PhD, faculty member, Psychoanalytic Center of Philadelphia, Philadelphia, PA; Private Practice, Ardmore, Pennsylvania.

Salman Akhtar, MD, professor of psychiatry, Jefferson Medical College; training and supervising analyst, Psychoanalytic Center of Philadelphia.

Anni Bergman, PhD, associate professor, New York University Post-Doctoral Program in Psychology; training and supervising analyst, New York Freudian Society, New York City.

Melvin Bornstein, MD, associate clinical professor of psychiatry, Wayne State University School of Medicine; editor, *Psychoanalytic Inquiry*; training and supervising analyst, Michigan Psychoanalytic Institute, Farmington Hills, Michigan.

Ira Brenner, MD, clinical professor of psychiatry, Jefferson Medical College; training and supervising analyst, Psychoanalytic Center of Philadelphia.

Lucy Daniels, PhD, founder and executive director, Lucy Daniels Foundation, Raleigh, North Carolina.

M. Hossein Etezady, MD, clinical director of psychiatric services, Paoli Memorial Hospital; faculty member, Psychoanalytic Center of Philadelphia.

Daniel M. A. Freeman, MD, clinical associate professor of psychiatry, Drexel University School of Medicine; faculty member, Psychoanalytic Center of Philadelphia.

James Herzog, MD, assistant professor of psychiatry, Harvard Medical School; training and supervising analyst, Boston Psychoanalytic Institute, Boston.

Christine Kieffer, PhD, faculty member, Chicago Institute for Psychoanalysis, Chicago.

Ilene Sackler Lefcourt, PhD, faculty member, Columbia University Center for Psychoanalytic Training and Research; founding director of The Sackler Lefcourt Child Development Center.

Mali Mann, MD, clinical associate professor of psychiatry, Stanford University Medical School; training and supervising analyst, San Francisco Psychoanalytic Institute.

Jill Savege Scharff, PhD, senior faculty member of the Washington School of Psychiatry; associate clinical professor of psychiatry, Georgetown University School of Medicine; teaching analyst at the Washington Psychoanalytic Institute, Washington, D.C; co-director of the International Psychotherapy Institute, Chevy Chase, Maryland.

Vamik Volkan, MD, professor emeritus of psychiatry, University of Virginia School of Medicine, Charlottesville, Virginia. Training and supervising analyst, Washington Psychoanalytic Institute, Washington, D.C.

Breinigsville, PA USA
17 January 2011
253410BV00004B/2/P

9 780765 707604